Orwell to the Present

transitions

General Editor: Julian Wolfreys

---

transitions Series
Series Standing Order ISBN 0–333–73684–6
(*outside North America only*)

You can receive future titles in this series as they are published by placing a standing order. Please contact your bookseller or, in case of difficulty, write to us at the address below with your name and address, the title of the series and the ISBN quoted above.

Customer Services Department, Macmillan Distribution Ltd
Houndmills, Basingstoke, Hampshire RG21 6XS, England

---

transitions

Orwell to the Present:

Literature in England, 1945–2000

John Brannigan

First published 2003 by
PALGRAVE MACMILLAN
Houndmills, Basingstoke, Hampshire RG21 6XS and
175 Fifth Avenue, New York, N.Y. 10010
Companies and representatives throughout the world

PALGRAVE MACMILLAN is the global academic imprint of the Palgrave Macmillan division of St. Martin's Press, LLC and of Palgrave Macmillan Ltd Macmillan® is a registered trademark in the United States, United Kingdom and other countries. Palgrave is a registered trademark in the European Union and other countries.

ISBN 0–333–69616–6 hardback
ISBN 0–333–69617–4 paperback

This book is printed on paper suitable for recycling and made from fully managed and sustained forest sources.

A catalogue record for this book is available from the British Library.

Library of Congress Cataloging-in-Publication Data
Brannigan, John.
    Orwell to the present : literature in England, 1945–2000 /
John Brannigan.
        p. cm. — (Transitions)
    Includes bibliographical references (p.) and index.
    ISBN 0-333–69616–6 (cloth) — ISBN 0–333–69617–4 (paper)
        1. English literature — 20th century — History and criticism.
    2. Orwell, George, 1903–1950 — Criticism and interpretation.
    3. England — Intellectual life — 20th century. 4. England —
    Civilization — 1945– I. Title. II. Transitions (Palgrave (Firm))
    PR471 .B68 2002
    820.9'00914—dc21   2002026765

10 9 8 7 6 5 4 3 2 1
12 11 10 09 08 07 06 04 04 03

Printed in China

Contents

General Editor's Preface

Transitions: *transition–em*, n. of action. 1. A passing or passage from one condition, action or (rarely) place, to another. 2. Passage in thought, speech, or writing, from one subject to another. 3. **a.** The passing from one note to another **b.** The passing from one key to another, modulation. 4. The passage from an earlier to a later stage of development or formation ... change from an earlier style to a later; a style of intermediate or mixed character ... the historical passage of language from one well-defined stage to another.

The aim of *transitions* is to explore passages and movements in language, literature and culture from Chaucer to the present day. The series also seeks to examine the ways in which the very idea of transition affects the reader's sense of period so as to address anew questions of literary history and periodisation. The writers in this series unfold the cultural and historical mediations of literature during what are commonly recognized as crucial moments in the development of English literature, addressing, as the OED puts it, the 'historical passage of language from one well-defined stage to another'.

Recognising the need to contextualise literary study, the authors offer close readings of canonical and now marginalised or overlooked literary texts from all genres, bringing to this study the rigour of historical knowledge and the sophistication of theoretically informed evaluations of writers and movements from the last 700 years. At the same time as each writer, whether Chaucer or Shakespeare, Milton or Pope, Byron, Dickens, George Eliot, Virginia Woolf or Salman Rushdie, is shown to produce his or her texts within a discernible historical, cultural, ideological and philosophical milieu, the text is read from the vantage point of recent theoretical interests and concerns. The purpose in bringing theoretical knowledge to the reading of a wide range of works is to demonstrate how the literature is always open to transition, whether in the instant of its production or in succeeding moments of its critical reception.

The series desires to enable the reader to transform her/his own reading and writing transactions by comprehending past developments. Each book in the second tranche of the series offers a pedagogical guide to the poetics and politics of particular eras, as well as to the subsequent critical comprehension of periods and periodisation. As well as transforming the cultural and literary past by interpreting its transition from the perspective of the critical and theoretical present, each study enacts transitional readings of a number of literary texts, all of which are themselves conceivable as having effected transition at the moments of their first appearance. The readings offered in these books seek, through close critical reading, historical contextualisation and theoretical engagement, to demonstrate certain possibilities in reading to the student reader.

It is hoped that the student will find this series liberating because the series seeks to move beyond rigid definitions of period. What is important is the sense of passage, of motion. Rather than providing a definitive model of literature's past, *transitions* aims to place you in an active dialogue with the writing and culture of other eras, so as to comprehend not only how the present reads the past, but how the past can read the present.

Julian Wolfreys

Acknowledgements

A book such as this which pretends to knowledge of a period in literary history spanning fifty-odd years cannot hide its many intellectual debts, and acknowledgements to those debts are best placed where they belong, in the text and bibliography of this book. My understandings of this period, as expressed in the arguments advanced in the book, have also profited hugely from the advice, encouragement and criticism of several friends and former colleagues: Adrian Page, Mark Clapson, Julian Cowley, Ruth Robbins, and Julian Wolfreys. I am still trying to catch up on their many helpful suggestions for reading, and I hope they recognise the value of their advice and friendship in these pages.

I have tested some of the arguments of this book elsewhere. I am grateful to Philip Tew for giving me the opportunity to rehearse the arguments of Chapter 3 at a conference in Jesus College, Cambridge, on contemporary British fiction in January 2000. My thanks also to Ken Womack and the journal *Interdisciplinary Literary Studies* for publishing a draft version of this chapter in the Fall 2000 issue. The ideas on trauma and contemporary drama were tried out in a course at the University of Luton between 1996 and 1999. I can at least hope that this wasn't a traumatic experience. The chapter on feminist fictions was also tested and clarified in a course on twentieth-century women novelists at Trinity College, Dublin in 2001.

This book has required a lot of faith from some people. I am grateful to Margaret Bartley at Palgrave Macmillan for commissioning me to write it, and to Anna Sandeman for her patience in waiting for its delivery. Julian Wolfreys, the series editor, has always given the most reliable, astute advice, and never fails to spot the weak points and gaps in my arguments. The remaining faults are all mine. My closest reader, and most trusted critic, is my partner, Moyra, who has constantly supported, encouraged and shaped this book into existence. My thanks and love to Moyra, then, not just for helping me to write the book, but also for helping me to get away from it. The author and publishers wish to thank the following for permission to use copyright material:

John Fuller, for the poem 'During a Bombardment by V-Weapons' from *Collected Poems: 1936–1961* by Roy Fuller. Reproduced by permission of John Fuller.

John Murray (Publishers) Ltd, for the extract from 'A Subaltern's Love-Song' from *Collected Poems* by John Betjeman. Reproduced by permission of John Murray (Publishers) Ltd.

Methuen Publishing Ltd, for the extracts from *Blasted* from *Blasted & Phaedra's Love* by Sarah Kane, and *Shopping and Fucking* by Mark Ravenhill. Reproduced by permission of Methuen Publishing Ltd.

Every effort has been made to trace all the copyright-holders, but if any have been inadvertently overlooked the publishers will be pleased to make the necessary arrangement at the first opportunity.

Introduction

For whom, it suddenly occurred to him to wonder, was he writing this diary? For the future, for the unborn … . For the first time the magnitude of what he had undertaken came home to him. How could you communicate with the future? It was of its nature impossible. Either the future would resemble the present, in which case it would not listen to him: or it would be different from it, and his predicament would be meaningless.

George Orwell, *Nineteen Eighty-Four* (9)

Beginning with Orwell

Why begin with Orwell? Perhaps because, more clearly than any of his contemporaries, Orwell was concerned in the 1940s with writing about the future, and with asking the question which preoccupies Winston in the epigraph: 'How could you communicate with the future?' Like many left-wing intellectuals of the period, Orwell was convinced that the end of the war had to bring substantial social change to England, and recognised that the war had made necessary new visions of England and Englishness. In the course of the war, Orwell wrote two essays explicitly concerned with defining the English: 'England Your England' (1941) and *The English People* (1944). Although he was circumspect about their literary value – describing *The English People*, for example, as 'a piece of propaganda for the British Council' (Orwell 1998b, 189), and ordering that neither essay be reprinted – he was also attempting to give expression to an England of 'the common people', which is to say an England markedly different from the England of the thirties. 'No more stagnation punctuated by wars, no more Rolls-Royces gliding past dole queues' (Orwell 1998a, 227). The year 1945 might have represented for Orwell, then, the beginning of a new time, a year zero in the imagination of a new England.

There is no vision of future England projected in Orwell's essays, other than the insistence that 'there should be no lost opportunities, no recurrence of the past' (Orwell 1998a, 227). Yet, Orwell's England is not new, and this forms a paradox in both essays. The England which Orwell brings to the fore, the new England of 'ordinary people', is also the deep England which he argues is continuous, stretching into the past and into the future. Orwell's England is imagined as a series of images of quiet, cosy havens of modesty, privacy and decency. 'It is somehow bound up with solid breakfasts and gloomy Sundays, smoky towns and winding roads, green fields and red pillar-boxes' (Orwell 1957, 64). It is this England which Orwell privileges over the well-worn stereotypes of 'an aristocrat with a monocle, a sinister capitalist in a top hat, or a spinster in a Burberry', which he argues have so far dominated images of England (Orwell 1998a, 200). These stereotypical images of Englishness base themselves, Orwell argues, 'on the property-owning class and ignore the other forty-five million'. To focus on those forty-five million, Orwell suggests, is to encounter the 'truly native' cultural habits, 'which even when they are communal are not official – the pub, the football match, the back garden, the fireside and the "nice cup of tea"' (Orwell 1957, 66). This is Orwell's England, not the England associated with empire, war, class snobbery, and capitalism. It is an imagined community which he fashions by rigidly distinguishing between classes; the property class which engineers and commands a vast, 'unEnglish' empire, and the 'common people', who are quiet in their patriotism and seem to behave as if the empire does not exist. This is, in a sense, the little England of Orwell's imagination, the quiet, stay-at-home England, which is deeply rooted in a popular libertarian tradition of individualism and political conservatism.

The English People was almost refused publication because of its apparently radical view of class divisions and popular culture in England, but in many ways it expresses a conservative notion of English national identity. This is perhaps understandable in the contexts in which Orwell was writing. Orwell begins 'England Your England' with the apparently serene observation that he is in the midst of immediate and terrifying war: 'As I write, highly civilized human beings are flying overhead, trying to kill me' (Orwell 1957, 63). Orwell's first sentence alerts us to the highly specific contexts in which he is attempting to assess the meanings of England and Englishness, and to argue for a view of the English as a conservative, modest, fiercely anti-authoritarian, and individualist people. It is a view which seems startlingly left-wing in its emphasis on an England of the 'common people', and yet startlingly conservative in its insistence on individualism and its evasion of the historical constitution of empire loyalism and militant xenophobia. There are justifiable reasons why Orwell argues that English people detest militarism and would never tolerate dictatorship. He wishes to protest that Hitler could never have risen to power in England, that the English 'character' would never countenance a society which builds death camps and cheers rallies of jackbooted soldiers. These are comforting, perhaps even necessary arguments at times when England was threatened with invasion (1941), and was by no means sure of its place in the postwar political order (1944), but they are by no means secure assumptions in Orwell's writings.

Animal Farm (1945) and *Nineteen Eighty-Four* (1949) are frequently read as satirical depictions of the Stalinist and Nazi regimes of the forties, but these readings ignore the salient point that Orwell chose to set both novels in England. They are political allegories, partly of situations and tendencies in English society and politics which already exist, partly of disturbing possibilities for the future. If Orwell seems in the essays on England to be complacent about the anti-authoritarian moral character of English people, in these novels and in some of his other writings he is deeply anxious about the future directions of English society. These anxieties are already apparent in his essays on England, however. He holds in tension in those essays the paradoxical ideas that England is continuous, and is imminently in danger of disappearing. Orwell's writings straddle the political time of his immediate social and cultural contexts and the prophetic time of a future unknown, yet dangerously close. *Animal Farm* and *Nineteen Eighty-Four* function by combining what is unfamiliar and distant with what is lurking ominously, uncannily in the present. Orwell's essays on England are likewise situated ambivalently on the cusp of a continuous, innate England ('it is *your* civilization, it is *you*' (Orwell 1957, 64)), and an England which needs to be constantly, anxiously represented, and reminded of its existence.

Orwell represents a beginning, the hope of a new society, a new nation, which is also the same, continuous England. In announcing Orwell as the beginning of a period, however, we need to be cautious of the extent to which Orwell is constructed as the founding figure, or progenitor, of specific lines of literary and political descent. The Movement poets and the Angry Young Men of the 1950s, for example, were largely understood to have 'inherited' Orwell's scepticism, his celebration of a masculine rationality and directness, his delineation of conservative notions of 'common sense' and 'decency', and his rejection of the effete, decadent strains of literary modernism in preference for the frank, masculine vigour of a purified, transparent language.[1] If we begin with Orwell, are we not constructing a master narrative of postwar literary history which privileges these masculine values above others?

Orwell closes doors as well as opens them. *Animal Farm* and *Nineteen Eighty-Four* can be read ultimately as bleak, nihilistic allegories of the futility of political resistance, for example. His suspicion of language which deviates from the nebulous ideals of common sense and frankness, his avowal that 'the worst thing one can do with words is to surrender to them' (Orwell 1998c, 429), are attempts to police language within coded political and ideological boundaries. In literary contexts, such statements seem to insist upon a particularly patriarchal curtailment and foreclosure of literary writing.

To begin with Orwell, then, is to begin not with the explanatory key to the literary history of the postwar period, but with a profoundly ambivalent, difficult, and contradictory figure, who is liberal and humanist in his grasp of the marginalised subjectivities of the colonised and the working classes, but who might also be seen to produce remarkably conservative, patriarchal and prohibitive legacies for subsequent writers. A literary history that begins with Orwell, therefore, would necessitate the stories of those writers who defy, exceed, resist or subvert Orwell's injunctions, as well as those who have strived to express similar values and sympathies. But we begin not just with Orwell, but with 'Orwell's England'.

Orwell tries in 'England Your England' to fix England into a narrative of succession, borrowing a horticultural metaphor – 'a turnip seed never grows into a parsnip' – to argue that England will develop according to the highly selective notion of English tradition and character which he elaborates in his essay (Orwell 1957, 65). In a revealing metaphor, however, Orwell describes England as 'a rather stuffy Victorian family, with not many black sheep in it but with all its cupboards bursting with skeletons' (Orwell 1957, 78). The new beginning in Orwell's vision is constantly threatened by these hidden skeletons, the repressed secrets and insidious silences of Englands past. In the literature written in England since 1945, both of these tendencies coexist, intersect, and frequently converse with one another. Orwell's writings might be located at the beginning of some of the narratives in this book (by no means all), not as a prophet, but as exemplary of the liminal, ambivalent construction of postwar English society and culture as inhabiting the time of the new, and the time of haunting, of the return of the past.

Orwell to the Present

This book, then, is about England. It is about the imagination and revision of ideas of England and Englishness in literature written since 1945. As an extension of that project, it is also about the revision of ideas of literature and literariness since 1945, and seeks to reflect some of the dynamic ways in which literature engages with the changing patterns of communication, social connection and cultural identity in contemporary England. It is my argument in this book that literature written in England since 1945 has been especially concerned with revisiting and re-mapping the imaginative geography of England. In some cases, this has been an exercise in cultural nostalgia. In others, the emergent politics of social, gender, racial, sexual and cultural differences have compelled writers to reconfigure the notions of home, community and belonging altogether.

The book is organised into two parts. The first, entitled 'England Revisited', contains three chapters which focus on the relationship between literature and history. Chapter 1 examines some of the works written and published in England in 1945, taking that 'year zero' of the period as a more specialised historical focus in order to analyse the speculative and arbitrary relationship between a text and its time of production. The texts discussed in that first chapter do exhibit habitual concerns and themes, and might begin to suggest some of the prevailing trends of postwar writing, but they also serve to defamiliarise the period, to reveal 1945 for what it is, neither a beginning nor an ending, but just a year. Chapter 2 examines the theme of history and memory in postwar writing, arguing that literature in England since 1945 has been centrally preoccupied with the past as a construct, and with the diverse, complex ways in which time is experienced and perceived. It begins by considering Orwell's *Nineteen Eighty-Four* as a modern fable about memory and history, and proceeds to discuss the writings of Evelyn Waugh, Pat Barker, Alan Sillitoe, Tony Harrison, Simon Armitage and Peter Ackroyd. Chapter 3 addresses another aspect of the preoccupation with the past in contemporary English writing. It responds to Ian Jack's suggestion in 1996 that contemporary literature in England could be characterised as 'a literature of farewell', by considering issues of nostalgia, conservatism, memory and anamnesis in texts by Martin Amis, John King, Kazuo Ishiguro, Graham Swift, Angela Carter, Pat Barker, and Ian McEwan.

The second part of the book, 'Making New Maps', contains three chapters which are concerned with the relationship between literature and society. Chapter 4 focuses on the 'feminist fictions' of the postwar period, arguing that contemporary women novelists have played a key role in critiquing the politics of consensus and identity in postwar English society. The chapter considers the ways in which women writers such as Lynne Reid Banks, Margaret Drabble, Doris Lessing, Jean Rhys, Ruth Prawer Jhabvala, Fay Weldon, Angela Carter, and Jeanette Winterson have experimented with fictional forms to articulate and imagine contemporary feminist politics of difference. Chapter 5 focuses on dramatic writing, underrepresented in other chapters in the book, but here made the focus of an enquiry into the relationship between trauma and social representation. This chapter analyses the significance of devices of shock, or experiences of trauma, in postwar drama, examining in detail plays by John Osborne, Ann Jellicoe, Edward Bond, Sarah Kane, and Mark Ravenhill. Finally, Chapter 6 takes as its subject the ways in which literary texts have attempted to re-imagine and reconfigure the cultural geographies of England. This includes consideration of the pastoral and counter-pastoral fictions of H.E. Bates and Angus Wilson, the topographical poetry of Basil Bunting and Geoffrey Hill, and the imagination of urban geography in the writings of Sam Selvon, Iain Sinclair, and Salman Rushdie. This last chapter attempts to make sense of those metaphors of cartography and landscape which pervade contemporary discussions of the relationship between literature and place, and to formulate some of the most significant ways in which literary texts since Orwell have sought to understand and imagine England as a place, as a landscape. The 'green fields and red pillar boxes' of Orwell's England are still there, but they don't mean quite the same things, nor do they reflect much sense of the continuous, deep England of Orwell's imagination.

The literary Englands explored and debated in this book are obviously selective. There are many omissions, and many roads untravelled, but my hope is that the book offers some new maps of literature in England since the war, new ways of reconceiving the relationships between texts and contexts in that period. If it succeeds, it does so mainly as a result of the great deal I have learned from other critical studies and histories of the period. The most thorough and lucid studies of writing in England since 1945 are as follows: Alan Sinfield, *Society and Literature* (ed., 1983), *Literature, Politics and Culture in Postwar Britain* (1989; Revised Edition 1997), and *British Culture of the Postwar* (ed. with Alastair Davies, 2000), Brian Appleyard, *The Pleasures of Peace: Art and Imagination in Postwar Britain* (1989), Robert Hewison, *Under Siege* (1977), *In Anger* (1981), *Too Much* (1986), and *Culture and Consensus* (1995), Steven Connor, *The English Novel in History, 1950–1995* (1996), Maroula Joannou, *Contemporary women's writing* (2000), Patricia Waugh, *Feminine Fictions* (1989), and *Harvest of the Sixties* (1995), Neil Nehring, *Flowers in the Dustbin: Culture, Anarchy and Postwar England* (1993), Neil Corcoran, *English Poetry since 1940* (1993), Flora Alexander, *Contemporary women novelists* (1989), D.J. Taylor, *After the War* (1994), Peter Middleton and Tim Woods, *Literatures of Memory: History, time and space in postwar writing* (2000). Of these, I believe Alan Sinfield should be credited in particular with constructing new, critical narratives of postwar literature, which compel us to recognise the inseparability of literature and politics, and to think through the cultural politics of our own recent histories. There are many excellent studies with a more specific period focus, such as Blake Morrison, *The Movement* (1980), Jerry Bradley, *The Movement* (1993), Harry Ritchie, *Success Stories: Literature and the Media in England, 1950–1959* (1988), Niamh Baker, *Happily Ever After? Women's Fiction in Postwar Britain, 1945–1960* (1989), Stephen Lacey, *British Realist Theatre: The New Wave in its Context, 1956–1965* (1995), Stuart Laing, *Representations of Working-Class Life, 1957–1964* (1986), and Deborah Philips and Ian Haywood, *Brave New Causes: Women in Postwar British Fictions* (1998). This book, along with my earlier study, *Literature, Culture and Society in England, 1945–1965* (2002), owes much to the work presented in these studies, in particular to the insistence in all of them on the necessity of situating literary texts in their social, cultural and political contexts.

I conclude this book with a chapter called 'English Journeys', but in a way each of the chapters is an 'English Journey'. The title of the book itself implies a journey, from Orwell to the present. It implies a trajectory, from Orwell writing in 1945, to writing in the present; or the trajectory *of* Orwell to the present, which is to say Orwell's projection to future readers, to those reading Orwell in the present; or the retrospective trajectory of looking back on Orwell for his relevance to the present. Journeys construct narratives from the places we visit. They imply connections, and perhaps make sense of the radical heterogeneity of postwar England in partial, speculative ways. Journeys enable, by their nature, ephemeral, transient views of the places which we pass through. They do not permit us to settle into authoritative narratives, and for this reason I like to think of the chapters in this book as migrant narratives, narratives which attempt to articulate the liminalities of English cultural identity, which question the cultural geographies and historical temporalities of postwar England. Among those narratives, there lies also the restless, rootless suspicion that terms such as 'postwar' and 'England' are convenient narrative constructs, which conceal more arbitrary, heterogeneous and anachronistic experiences of time and place. For this reason, it is important that we conceptualise from the beginning the dominant notions of historical periodicity which govern the historicist methodologies of this book.

Periodicity

'Periodization is not a frame of lived experience', writes Timothy Reiss. 'It is one aspect of one culture's frame of historical understanding, belonging to a particular moment of Western modernity no less than to a particular concept of Western identity' (Reiss 2001, 451). The period of literary history studied in this book, like any period in literary history, is a convenient fiction, which bears little resemblance to the actual set of relations between literary texts. The year 1945 represented no new beginning for literature in England, other than the fact that paper for publishing was becoming slightly more available than it had been in previous years. We might read into the texts produced in that year some lingering virtual conversations with previous literary periods and writers, or some prescient signals of future trends in postwar literature, but this would have been possible with any chosen year before and after 1945. In short, there is nothing significant about 1945, from the point of view of establishing a literary chronology, other than the fact that the Second World War ended. One could equally problematise the idea that the end of the war marked anything significant: 1945 marks the end of the war formally, but, as perhaps some of the writings discussed in the first chapter of this book attest, the war had already been won mentally sometime in 1942 or 1943. Thereafter, for example, we can read Orwell pondering what social changes will need to be planned for the end of the war. The very material circumstances of printing and publishing mean that in any case the texts produced in 1945 are necessarily belated. They cannot reflect the time of their production, if they 'reflect' any time at all.

It is a commonplace assumption that 1945 marks the beginning of a new literary period, or that the term 'postwar literature' carries some meaning beyond mere chronology. The period proposed in the scope of this book, 1945–2000, might suggest that there is a particular character or spirit to this age, that we might begin to define the period by its typical concerns, styles and qualities. This is a bearable (although by now extensively criticised) fiction in relation to older periods, such as the 'Augustan age', or the 'Romantic period', or the 'modernist era'. In the case of postwar, or contemporary, literature, it is an obvious fallacy, as the period since 1945 is too recent to see anything but its diversity and complexity, and is too diverse and complex to enable us to construct one coherent, meaningful narrative of its literary, cultural or historical events. Likewise, the year 2000 is too obviously rounded and convenient to be anything but a matter of arbitrary closure. Once we begin to interrogate the meanings of the process of periodisation, therefore, it is clearly meaningless. Am I really suggesting, for example, that Nancy Mitford's *The Pursuit of Love* (1945) shares more in common with Zadie Smith's *White Teeth* (2000) than it does with Mitford's earlier novel, *Pigeon Pie* (1940)? Clearly not, and yet this is an implication of the period boundaries erected in this study.

The problem with periodicity, with certain received ideas of literary history, is an overdependency upon an uncritical narrative structure which posits a recognisable origin or turning point, followed by a teleological progression of literary events, leading inevitably to our situation in the present. Thus, the literary productions of previous decades are understood to have made possible the available arts of literary writing in our own time, much as nineteenth-century historicists understood their time as the inevitable, cumulative product of centuries of gradual progress. In this conception, books appear to be events which emerge as developments of previous books, literary movements appear to be superseded by new, better literary movements (modernism by postmodernism, for example). The concept of periodicity which governs the writing of this book attempts to evade the teleological implications of such narratives of progress.[2] The book implies instead a more fluid, diverse exchange between texts, and between text and world, which is not mimetic but, in Deleuze and Guattari's terms, 'rhizomatic':

> In contrast to centred (even polycentric) systems with hierarchical modes of communication and pre-established paths, the rhizome is an acentred, non-hierarchical, nonsignifying system without a General and without an organizing memory or central automaton, defined solely by a circulation of states (Deleuze and Guattari 1987, 22).

The rhizome implies interconnection, a vast field of definite and specific interrelations, without a commanding narrative, without beginning or end. The chapters in this book attempt to trace discernible fields of interrelations between texts, in the sense that each chapter follows a set of connected themes, styles, tropes or contexts. In some cases, the narratives pursued in those chapters take a roughly chronological order, but they do not then adopt the developmental logic of such an order. There is no linear progression from the texts produced in 1945 to those published in 2000. Instead, the texts considered in this volume relate to each other as mobile nodes in a labyrinthine network of intertextuality. The chapters in this book are forays into the diverse spaces and times of postwar England – they are topographical and chrono-graphical journeys – which treat the literary text as an assemblage, not a unity, and which refuse to separate the literary text from the history which it produces and in which it is produced. The texts considered in this volume, then, are understood to be always already intertextual, and are situated in histories which are always already interhistorical.

Literature and History

What might we learn from such explorations of the relationship between postwar literature and its diverse historical contexts, however? If we move away from the mimetic, chronological model of literary-historical relations, how then do we begin to conceive of the effective relationship between literary texts and historical contexts? I argue in this book that these questions are not just asked by the critic and the historian, but are also a central theme and concern in postwar English writing. How has literature in England since 1945 addressed its time and place in 'history', its relationship to the past, its responsibilities towards the present and future? Orwell, for example perceived the relationship between literary intellectuals and the pressing concerns of English society to be perilously weak. 'English intellectuals', he wrote in 1944, 'especially the younger ones, are markedly hostile to their own country' (Orwell 1998a, 226). Orwell is addressing here specific allegiances among young English intellectuals in the forties to the socialist experiments in Russia, or to the increasing prestige and apparent freshness of the cultures of the United States of America. If the ideological divisions in the early twenty-first century are not quite the same as in Orwell's time, the sense that Englishness is trapped in the past, that it is bound up with conservative images of class snobbery and imperialism, remains a pervasive facet of contemporary English writing. Chapter 3 of the book addresses this question about the cultural politics of contemporary literary representations of Englishness. Orwell's observation that English writers are hostile to their own country implies the issues explored in that chapter, but it implies something more: that writers have become detached from the prevailing currents of English politics and society. This is to suggest that the role and place of writers in English society have changed, from serving as national poets, or 'unacknowledged legislators', to a more displaced, but more critical role. Orwell argues that in the particular kind of advanced capitalist society evident in twentieth-century England, intellectuals have 'security without much responsibility' (Orwell 1998a, 226). This is a debatable point. Intellectuals of a certain kind have security – academics, 'celebrity' authors, the poet laureate, perhaps – but there are also numerous examples in postwar English literature of writers who live on the margins of society, as migrants, dissidents, disenfranchised or oppressed women and men. Arguably, too, in a society in which the potential for cultural and political hegemony is greatly enhanced by the proliferation of mass media technologies, literary writers have a greater not lesser responsibility to make literature available as a cultural technology for representing diversity, dissidence, critical perspectives on our present conditions, and on the meanings of our varied, ambiguous histories.

This is the role of contemporary English literature envisioned in this book, one in which literature engages critically and dialogically with the culture it inhabits, with the society from which it is inseparable. Literature in my view is never a passive reflection of historical conditions, but an active participant in the construction and imagination of our social and cultural reality. We live in the places and times which literary texts help us to inhabit imaginatively and enable us to understand. The role of the literary critic, however, is not passive either. In reading literary texts, we do not receive their narratives, stories and representations uncritically. I tell my own stories here of how literature engages with recent history, and those stories are ultimately provisional, critical, and imaginary understandings of the literary productions of postwar England. This is to say that, in this book, I endeavour to show not just the interactive relationship between literary texts and history, but also that literature continues to exercise its capacity for imagining our times and places differently, its power to haunt and question our images and understandings of history, beyond the closed narratives of periodisation.

Notes

1. See Alastair Davies and Peter Saunders, 'Literature, Politics and Society', *Society and Literature: 1945–1970*, ed. Alan Sinfield (London: Methuen, 1983), 24; 26–7. Davies and Saunders argue that this 'inheritance' is based on a reductive misunderstanding of Orwell on the part of the Movement and the Angry Young Men, however.

2. The critique of conventional notions of literary history here shares many of the criticisms of Brian Richardson in 'Remapping the Present: The Master Narrative of Modern Literary History and the Lost Forms of Twentieth-Century Fiction', *Twentieth Century Literature*, 43: 3 (Fall 1997), 291–309. I differ from Richardson where he elaborates in place of these notions a model of modern literary history as a 'battleground where several continuous, competing poetics struggle for supremacy' (299).

Part I

England Revisited

1 'Small Disturbances': England in 1945

'War shook up the geography of England, unsettling people and their objects, transforming landscapes, moving things to where they weren't before.'

David Matless, *Landscape and Englishness* (173)

On Wednesday 9 May 1945, after an absence of almost six years, the weather returned to England. Or, to be more precise, it was once again possible to read or hear the weather forecast. The Air Ministry issued the first forecast to the public since September 1939: 'A large depression between Ireland and the Azores is almost stationary and small disturbances are moving northward over the British Isles. Weather will continue warm and thundery, with bright intervals in most districts'.[1] The weather, that curious register of the mutability and continuity of English life, had remained a national secret for six years, but with the official declaration of the end of hostilities in Europe, the 'small disturbances' could once again enter public discourse. As Homi Bhabha argues, the weather is central to the 'imaginative geography' of 'deep', conservative England: 'It encourages memories of the "deep" nation crafted in chalk and limestone; the quilted downs; the moors menaced by the wind; the quiet cathedral towns; that corner of a foreign field that is forever England' (Bhabha 1994, 169). War temporarily interrupted the ritual vision of the weather splashing its dappled hues across the English landscape, which perhaps explains the peculiar absence of meteorological images from Orwell's vision of 'deep' England in 'England Your England' (1941). When they resumed in May 1945, then, the weather forecasts symbolised the end of 'wartime' England, and seemed to fulfil Orwell's prophecy that when the traumas and disruptions of war were over, 'England will still be England' (Orwell 1957, 90).

In the immediate aftermath of the war, the notion of a deep, continuous England, unbroken and even re-enervated by war, became an important constituent in representing the nation to itself. It appeared in the familiar form of representations of the landscape or weather, to suggest at once the permanence and unknowable essence of this England. As Robert Hewison records, the imagery and iconography of the uninterrupted nation even found its way into the budget statement of the Labour Chancellor of the Exchequer, Hugh Dalton, in April 1946:

> There is still a wonderful, incomparable beauty in Britain, in the sunshine on the hills, the mists adrift the moors, the wind on the downs, the deep peace of the woodlands, the wash of the waves against the white unconquerable cliffs which Hitler never scaled. There is beauty and history in all these places. (Hewison 1995, 22)

Dalton was announcing a scheme to purchase sites of 'national' interest, of beauty or of history, so that they would be preserved as the heritage shrines of the nation, at once protecting and defining the topographical icons of Englishness. The war itself had served to enshrine the landscape as the imaginative site on which the struggle for English ways of life was being fought. This was epitomised, of course, in Churchill's wartime evocations of pastoral scenes threatened by invasion, but such conservative visions of national community were by no means confined to the right. The politics of the immediate postwar years may have shifted to the left in terms of social and economic policy, but they registered and helped to shape a conservative conception of English national community, crystallised in sentimental celebrations of communal resilience in the blitz as well as the familiar marshalling of English pastoral. The literary representations of the end of the war, I will argue in this chapter, returned to these symbolic and imaginative landscapes, and constructed England primarily through scenic and topographical modes of depiction. This chapter takes as its subject the literary depictions of England produced in 1945. It is in part a minor exercise in annualised literary history (of which the best recent examples are James Chandler, *England in 1819* (1998) and Michael North, *Reading 1922* (1999)), which seeks to question the notion of literary period through a close analysis of the 'starting point' of the period covered in this volume.[2] In examining the literary and historical meanings of 1945 as a point of cultural reference, the chapter will argue that literary texts are inevitably caught up in a liminal space between immediate relevance to historical contexts (in this case the end of the war), and a more durable dialogic relationship with literary and cultural traditions. The particular thematic focus here is the significance of landscape in the literary productions of 1945. The chapter argues that English landscape and its accompanying weather conditions exercised a powerful hold in the literary imagination of the mid-1940s, and served to reinforce popular conceptions of national community.

The poetry of John Betjeman perhaps best exemplifies the scenic mode in English literature of the mid-1940s. Betjeman was not yet as popular as he became in the 1950s, when his *Collected Poems* (1958) became a best selling book, but he had become known, as Jessica Maynard argues, for 'a poetry which celebrated a particular English geography' (Maynard 1997, 31), and not least for his poetic celebrations of suburban England, or 'metroland'. Not surprisingly, his wartime poetry continued to evoke English places and scenes. The collection he produced at the end of the war, *New Bats in Old Belfries* (1945), included poems on Henley-on-Thames, Bristol, Margate, Lincolnshire, Oxford, Bath, Cornwall, East Anglia, Swindon, and South London. As the title of the collection implies, Betjeman's poems drew new topics or places into old forms of poetic expression. The conservatism of his poetic forms, and the provincial landscapes he depicts, in part explain his mass appeal, although Betjeman's suburban pastorals also appear to invite ironic readings.

'Margate, 1940', for example, suggests in its last verse that the 'fairy-lit sights' of Margate, a Kentish seaside resort, are what 'we are fighting for, foremost of all' (Betjeman 1979, 100–1). War, the poem suggests, perhaps incredibly, is raging across Europe for the cause of such sights as a 'putting-course', 'a *thé dansant*', 'Harold Road', 'Norfolk Road', and a shabby, provincial hotel, 'the Queen's Highcliffe', with its 'tables for two laid as tables for four'. It is possible, maybe even desirable, to read this suggestion as ironic, particularly as the poem proceeds to offer a lightly comic portrait of the holiday-makers who return from the beach to 'wash the ozone from their skins / The sand from their legs and the rock from their chins, / To prepare for an evening of dancing and cards'. How is it possible that such mundane scenes and provincial pleasures are the cause of war?

The poem recalls happy memories of holidays spent in 'the salt-scented town', 'putting' on the course, hearing 'the strains of a band',

and walking 'by the Queen's Promenade'. It begins with these personal recollections:

> From out the Queen's Highcliffe for weeks at a stretch
> I watched how the mower evaded the vetch,
> So that over the putting-course rashes were seen
> Of pink and of yellow among the burnt green. (Betjeman 1979)

The scenes remembered in the poem are associated distinctly with a specific place – the streets and hotel names register that this is Margate – but at the same time, Margate is represented as a site of symbolic significance for England in general. Similarly, the sights the poem describes are the particular memories of the poet, and yet at the same time are what *we* are apparently fighting for. The poem moves, in fact, from the personal memories of the first verse, to the metaphorical significance of these memories for the imaginative community of England as a whole:

> Beside the Queen's Highcliffe now rank grows the vetch,
> Now dark is the terrace, a storm-battered stretch;
> And I think, as the fairy-lit sights I recall,
> It is those we are fighting for, foremost of all. (Betjeman 1979)

As a coastal resort, facing occupied Europe across the English channel, Margate symbolises the 'storm-battered stretch' of English coastline threatened by enemy invasion. The poem uses meteorological and topographical metaphors to suggest the effects of war and the danger of imminent invasion. Already, the vetch has grown rank, the terrace has darkened, in ominous anticipation of the destruction of Margate and its familiar sights and customs. Margate symbolised, then, a way of life, a distinctly English way of life, of holidays spent pleasurably in run-down hotels with their 'bottles of sauce and Kia-Ora and squash', and the children looking down to 'the sea / As it washed in the shingle the scraps of their tea'. Betjeman's poem elevates what appear to be the marginal, the obscure, the provincial aspects of English life to represent its very foundations.

Philip Larkin memorably celebrated Betjeman's representations of England as 'what I should want to remember ... if I were a soldier leaving England' (Larkin 1983, 214), a remark which seems particularly relevant to 'Margate, 1940'. Larkin produced his first collection of poems, *The North Ship*, in 1945, but had not yet found the poetic voice and style for which he became renowned in the 1950s and 60s. *The North Ship* imitated too closely the style and rhythm of Yeats. According to Larkin, in his own retrospective preface to *The North Ship*, it wasn't until he discovered Hardy's poetry after 1946 that he cast off his infatuation with Yeats, and thereafter began to write the poems which would appear in *The Less Deceived* (1955) (Larkin 1966, 9–10).[3] More than any other contemporary English poet, Larkin came to share many of Betjeman's preoccupations, particularly his poetic representations of quotidian suburban and provincial England. But there is little evidence of this in *The North Ship*, which abounds in abstruse Yeatsian symbolism.

Betjeman's England presented itself in ways which seemed too frank and translucent to require the complexities of modernist aesthetics. This is why Betjeman's poems sometimes appear to be self-parodically simple. A poem such as 'A Subaltern's Love-song', for example, uses a highly audible, repetitive rhyming scheme in the quatrain form (which was widely used in the nineteenth-century Anglican hymns which Betjeman admired) to give the poem a light-hearted, jaunty tone:

> Miss J. Hunter Dunn, Miss J. Hunter Dunn,
> Furnish'd and burnish'd by Aldershot sun,
> What strenuous singles we played after tea,
> We in the tournament – you against me! (Betjeman 1979, 87–8)

The 'love-song' recounts the subaltern's gleeful infatuation with Miss Joan Hunter Dunn, as they play tennis singles, then take 'lime-juice and gin' on the verandah, and then drive to a dance. The poem concludes with a fairy-tale happy ending: 'We sat in the car park till twenty to one/ And now I'm engaged to Miss Joan Hunter Dunn'. With its traditional quatrain form, its light-hearted treatment of love, and its romantic, happy conclusion, 'A Subaltern's Love-song' is, in some respects, a peculiarly anti-modern, historically naïve poem. When Betjeman wrote it, the world had been swept into mass carnage for the second time in his life, and the skills and intelligence of human beings were attuned to inventing new and more brutal methods of destruction. Modernist art and literature had attempted to wrestle with the grave difficulty of representing such a world in artistic form. But Betjeman's poetry seems an oasis of faith in traditional and

familiar forms, of continuity with the self-confidence and enlightenment beliefs of the Victorians. 'In a century that has restlessly destabi-
lized the formal poetic line', writes Dennis Brown, 'Betjeman's work
has consistently held to traditional boundaries, as if these constituted
the essence of poetic Englishness' (Brown 1999, 5). This seems to
render Betjeman somehow anachronistic, outside of his own time,
and constitutes something of a problem for the attempt to situate him
within a neat period chronology. Does Betjeman's collection belong
to the historical moment of 1945? Or are they more properly situated
anachronistically in relation to Victorian and Edwardian poetic
forms?

Larkin presented this traditionalist, nostalgic aspect of Betjeman's
work as a kind of studied myopia: 'For him there has been no symbolism, no objective correlative, no T.S. Eliot or Ezra Pound' (Larkin
1959). To put it another way, Betjeman's poetry seems to declare itself
as the progenic heir of specific lines of English poetry, which are
formally conventional and resistant both to foreign and modernist
influences. 'A Subaltern's Love-song' does this in its quatrain form,
but also in its imagery and allusions. The poem refers to tennis, tea,
'the six-o'clock news', 'lime-juice and gin', 'the Golf club', 'blazer and
shorts', to 'the Hillman' car, as well as 'Rovers and Austins'. These
images and allusions describe a social world which is quite specific to
the English upper middle class. This makes it all the more significant
that the poem is written from the perspective of a 'subaltern', which
we might assume to mean a junior officer in the military, but which
also carries with it the implication of lower social status. From this
perspective the poem's fetishistic representations of the detail of
upper-middle-class life is a revealing indication of social and cultural
differences between the subaltern and 'Miss Joan Hunter Dunn'. We
learn much from the poem about what Joan Hunter Dunn drinks and
wears, what kind of house she lives in and car she drives, how and
where she spends her days and evenings:

> The Hillman is waiting, the light's in the hall,
> The pictures of Egypt are bright on the wall,
> My sweet, I am standing beside the oak stair
> And there on the landing's the light on your hair. (Betjeman 1979)

The objects in Joan Hunter Dunn's possession, or which surround
her, appear to be of greater interest to the 'subaltern' than she herself.

The closest the subaltern comes to describing her, near the end of the poem, avoids any form of sentimental or romantic depiction: 'here on my right is the girl of my choice, / With the tilt of her nose and the chime of her voice'. These are hardly flattering terms of description, and perhaps suggest an attempt at precision rather than romantic evocation. The subaltern is precise about her name, about the time and place – twenty to one, Camberley, in Surrey – about the smells and sounds and sights, and also the feelings, which surround he and Joan Hunter Dunn on the night of their engagement. Even when he lapses into romantic declarations – 'I am weak from your loveliness' – there is the attempt to be precise about the quality and texture of romantic feeling.

'A Subaltern's Love-song' is, then, in this reading, an anti-romantic treatment of love. It attempts to describe a romantic relationship with careful precision, gently relieved by a jaunty rhyming scheme, and in contrast to the abstraction and vague sentimentality associated with neo-romantic poets such as Dylan Thomas and W.R. Rodgers. Betjeman's gravitation towards 'objective' description in this poem, towards localised, empirical detail, set the agenda for the 'Movement' poets of the 1950s, which included Philip Larkin, Kingsley Amis, Donald Davie and D.J. Enright. Larkin described the influence of Yeats, and of the neo-romanticists of the 1940s, as a kind of 'Celtic fever', from which he was cured only when he turned to the English lines of Hardy (Larkin 1966, 10). This conception of English forms of poetic representation as the antithesis of foreign experimental or romantic modes typifies one important strand of English writing at the end of the war, one that persists throughout the postwar period. England in its insularity, as an embodiment of intrinsic values and forms, became the subject of intense literary and cultural interest.

The reaction against modernism, and the intensification of interest in describing and representing Englishness in isolation, was not simply brought about by the experience of world war. It was present in the work of Evelyn Waugh, J.B. Priestley, W.H. Auden, Ivy Compton-Burnett, and indeed John Betjeman, among many others, before the war. But the end of the war also gave a particular significance to this trend, partly because of the experiences of combatants returning to England from the war, and partly also because of the introspective questions raised by the war itself. Both of these elements are addressed in Richard Goodman's poem, 'Return to England', which was published in John Lehmann's *Penguin New*

Writing in 1945. Lehmann sought literary contributions from new writers fresh from the experiences of war, to give a kind of urgency and contemporary relevance to writing. Goodman had served with the navy in North Africa, Sicily and Normandy, and his poem ranges across these experiences in considering the meanings of Englishness to the returning serviceman.

The images of England depicted in the poem are hardly original – England is imagined as a tree, 'that singing sap which powers our million lives', and as a landscape, a valley pictured in 'ascending peace' (Goodman 1945, 172–73). England's attractions are made all the more alluring in the poem by contrasting them with the unhomely, cruel landscapes of the European and North African battlefields. The poem imagines England in its tranquility and modesty after three verses which describe the harsh scenes elsewhere – 'the sour dust of Sicilian roads', 'the leprous stone of Malta's caves', 'Algiers where the sirocco crawls / To paralyse the will and the brain reels', 'the orange whirlwind blown from Ras el Ma / To silt the gates of Fez'. The landscapes of North Africa and Sicily are sickening, unaccommodating in contrast to England, to which the poem turns in eulogy in the fifth verse:

> to see from the easy train the first slim wood
> misted by autumn sun and the hedged road,
>   to watch quietly
> the harrow pattern with care the Devon field
> and the sheep crowd silent in the safe fold;
>
> to hear again the rooks chatter at evening,
> etching with lines of flight the day's ending,
>   and the last wind mourn
> the departed swallows, while a skylark strings
> its bubbled music through the curlews' songs.
>
> (Richard Goodman 1945)

This is a vision of the English landscape in which all is in order – even the sheep are in their 'safe fold'. The fields are 'patterned' by human agriculture, the roads are 'hedged', and time is marked by the rooks and swallows. It is a modern vision, one seen from a train, which enabled a way of seeing or discovering England quite distinct from other modes of transport, and which John Lucas argues became a recurrent perspective in twentieth-century English poetry (Lucas 1997, 37–55).

The images of England which Goodman depicts in his poem have echoes in some of the poets Lucas considers – Thomas Hardy, Edward Thomas, Louis MacNeice – especially, perhaps, in Thomas's search for the 'heart' of England. But this is what is most intriguing about Goodman's poem, for Thomas's view from a train – 'Adlestrop' is the obvious poem here – represented this deep, pastoral England as a place remembered only, lost in time, corroded and changed irrevocably by war. In Goodman's poem, the combatants return to rediscover this England, to pledge their renewed faith in an idyllic, continuous England:

> We who were born of England, who are bound forever,
> being of her strange earth, to be her lover;
>   whose precious dead
> walk, still erect, in her flowers and speak to us
> in her rivers' murmur and her rains' kiss –
>
> it is not for those who defile her, the slum captains,
> the headline bankers, the spinners of captions,
>   the millionaires –
> it is not for these that we fight, but, rather,
> to save from these our mother, our father,
> her earth, our dead, her past, our future,
>   who are her heirs. (Richard Goodman 1945)

'Return to England' concludes with this pledge, this explanation of the war as the defence of a particular notion of Englishness, one that must be wrested free from the rich and powerful, from the tycoons and the press barons. In fact, Goodman's poem must resort to images of the landscape and the weather in order to find the common ground on which England might be defined and defended. England is imagined not as a people, but as a 'strange earth', to which 'we are bound forever'. The penultimate verse of the poem gives expression to the notion that England's landscape is the palimpsest on which its dead generations have written, and through which its people now can hear the voices of those 'precious dead' in 'her rivers' murmur and her rains' kiss'. This suggests the comforting idea that 'England' is greater and more durable than the troubling events from which combatants like Goodman have returned, but also that those men and women killed in the war have now taken their place among the dead, speaking through the rivers and fields of England. 'Return', then, is a significant trope in the poem, in the renewal of faith which the poem pledges in the 'heart of England', in the figuration of England's history as cyclical recurrence and continuity, in the more polemical plea to struggle free of the trappings of power and wealth and to rediscover 'England'.

Goodman's poem constructs England as the homely antithesis to the estranging experiences of war and travel. It is the safe haven, the private space, in which the returning soldier can become himself again. But it is also a distinctive idea of home, which must be protected from 'the slum captains', and various other powerful influences. Goodman's poem suggests indeed that there is an England yet to be fought over, perhaps suggesting the imminent changes in the political sphere which gave rise to the consensus politics of the postwar decades. Towards the end of the war, literature increasingly became preoccupied with the England which might emerge after victory was achieved. The enormous toll of the war effort on civilians, and the widespread devastation of housing in London and many other British cities made it especially apparent that the nation would need to be re-imagined and reconstructed after the war. Not surprisingly, then, as the war slugged its way to an end, writers began to turn their attentions towards 'home'. Perhaps the clearest expression of this tendency is Roy Fuller's poem, 'During a Bombardment by V-Weapons':

> The little noises of the house;
> Drippings between the slates and ceiling;
> From the electric fire's cooling,
> Tickings; the dry feet of a mouse;
>
> These at the ending of a war
> Have power to alarm me more
> Than the ridiculous detonations
> Outside the gently coughing curtains. (Fuller 1962, 99)

The V-weapons of the poem's title – known to Londoners as 'doodle-bugs' – are 'ridiculous' in contrast to the intimate, even alarming, domesticity of 'home'. The curtains cough 'gently', as if embarrassed about the noise of detonations outside. There is, as R.P. Draper notes, something of a 'serio-comic' tone to Fuller's depiction of the house under bombardment (Draper 1999, 95). The poem treats as more disturbing the sounds of dripping, ticking, and the 'dry feet of a mouse', than the explosions of the rocket bombs outside. But the contrasting scenes of the house and the explosions outside are intimately connected. The V1 and V2 bombs differed considerably in their effect on London than the bombing raids of the blitz. V-weapons were rocket-propelled to the point above their targets, whereupon their engines were stalled and the weapons fell silently and then with a low whistle to detonate on impact with the ground. This method of bombing proved an eerie contrast to the intensity of noise and activity which greeted a Luftwaffe bombing raid. There was little warning to a V-weapon detonation, especially as the popular belief among Londoners was that the victims of a rocket attack were the only ones who did not hear the whistle of the incoming bomb. Arguably, Fuller's poem takes account of this experience of rocket bombardment in the way in which the speaker is alert to 'little noises', and is clearly kept awake listening. The fear of V-weapon bombardment heightens the sense of aural anticipation, and opens the mind to a rare consciousness of the sonic activities of the house at night.

Fuller's poem might then reflect the sensory experiences of a V-weapon bombardment, but it also considers the encroaching realities of post-war life. Herbert Read wrote in May 1941, during the blitz on London, that 'the only realities are tanks and aeroplanes, ships and food, productive labour of all kinds' (Read 1941, 310). But 'at the ending of a war', Fuller depicts the weapons as ridiculous, and somewhat unbelievable. The realities for the poem's speaker are closer to home:

> And, love, I see your pallor bears
> A far more pointed threat than steel.
> Now all the permanent and real
> Furies are settling in upstairs. (Fuller 1962, 99)

The nature of the 'threat' at home is suggested vaguely and ambiguously in the final stanza of the poem, reflected in the lover's 'pallor'. This might indicate illness or shock, or perhaps, since the speaker considers it a 'pointed' threat, it is anger towards the speaker. Whatever the cause of domestic discord, and whatever is meant by 'the Furies' settling in upstairs, it is considered more 'permanent and real' than the war, which, by implication, is now hard to take seriously. The war is considered here as a suspension of the real, a theatrical interruption, which as it ends leaves untouched the fabric of domestic life in England. This was by no means an uncommon representation, especially as the depression prior to the war, and the austere economic conditions after it, meant that in economic and social terms the character of life for most people in England did not change substantially between the 1930s and 1950s. When the threat of invasion and massive bomb damage waned, and the war looked increasingly likely to end, it became more important to imagine the realities and conditions which might apply in the aftermath of what Evelyn Waugh called 'the preposterous years of the Second World War' (Waugh 1977, 31).

Ancestral Homes

Waugh satirised the war in his *Sword of Honour* trilogy, published between 1952 and 1961, in which his hero, Guy Crouchback, witnesses every attempt at glory turn into ridiculous farce. In *Brideshead Revisited*, which Waugh wrote in early 1944, the war seems to serve merely as the context in which the narrator, Charles Ryder, comes to recall his association with 'Brideshead', the country mansion of the Marchmain family. Waugh's most famous novel attempts to fix the image and legend of an English aristocratic mansion as an icon of what is at once most deeply rooted in English history and most threatened in the late years of the Second World War. The house is no mere location, but instead the focus of imaginative attention and the symbolic heart of the traditions and ways of life for which Ryder (and Waugh) are fiercely nostalgic.

Brideshead Revisited opens and concludes with a scene in which Captain Ryder's company have been billeted at Brideshead, which enables Waugh to contrast the egalitarian pretensions of military life with the aristocratic values symbolised in Brideshead itself. Ryder's unit arrives in darkness, and it is not until morning that he discovers that he has returned to the house which he came to love in his youthful acquaintance with the Marchmain family. Between the prologue and the epilogue, Ryder's memoirs describe the effect of this house, and the values embodied in it, upon him as an undergraduate friend of the family. The family lead turbulent emotional lives, with which

Ryder finds it difficult to keep up, but the house is the model of serenity and sanctuary, and Ryder's impression of it, in his youth and on reflection during the war, is depicted in arcadian terms. In the 'Prologue', Waugh establishes a contrast between the haphazard, utilitarian inventions of the military camp, and the edenic landscape sculpted around Brideshead:

> A cart-track, once metalled, then overgrown, now rutted and churned to mud, followed the contour of the hillside and dipped out of sight below a knoll, and on either side of it lay the haphazard litter of corrugated iron, from which rose the rattle and chatter and whistling and catcalls, all the zoo-noises of the battalion beginning a new day. Beyond and about us, more familiar still, lay an exquisite man-made landscape. It was a sequestered place, enclosed and embraced in a single, winding valley. Our camp lay along one gentle slope; opposite us the ground led, still unravished, to the neighbourly horizon, and between us flowed a stream – it was named the Bride and rose not two miles away at a farm called Bridesprings, where we used sometimes to walk to tea; it became a considerable river lower down before it joined the Avon – which had been dammed here to form three lakes, one no more than a wet slate among the reeds, but the others more spacious, reflecting the clouds and the mighty beeches at their margin. The woods were all of oak and beech, the oak grey and bare, the beech faintly dusted with green by the breaking buds; they made a simple, carefully designed pattern with the green glades and the wide green spaces – Did the fallow deer graze here still? – and, lest the eye wander aimlessly, a Doric temple stood by the water's edge, and an ivy-grown arch spanned the lowest of the connecting weirs. All this had been planned and planted a century and a half ago so that, at about this date, it might be seen in its maturity. From where I stood the house was hidden by a green spur, but I knew well how and where it lay, couched among the lime trees like a hind in the bracken. (Waugh 1945, 18–19)

In his preface to the revised edition of the novel, published in 1960, Waugh confessed that he believed that the aristocratic houses of England were in a state of imminent extinction in 1944, and his novel was a desperate attempt to celebrate and monumentalise the values and traditions embodied in the architecture and landscapes of such houses (Waugh 1960, 7–8). In a revealing metaphor, Waugh compares the fate of the country house in 1944 with that of the monasteries in the sixteenth century. Waugh's veneration of the architecture and landscape of Brideshead in the novel is never far from his devotion to the rituals and symbolic traditions of Catholicism. *Brideshead Revisited* is not simply a 'Catholic' novel, as it has often been considered, however, for Catholicism is made to bear symbolic weight in an ideological struggle between tradition and modernity, between conservatism and utilitarianism. Waugh celebrates Catholicism in *Brideshead* where it signifies the restoration or continuation of some sense of aesthetic or cultural tradition. Likewise, the lavish descriptions of the arcadian qualities of landscape and architecture are not simply indications of the postwar trend for admiring and visiting country mansions, the 'heritage' craze which Waugh confessed not to have anticipated. Rather, Waugh's novel is interested in the seemingly divine effects of such beauty and artistic achievement on the spiritual and moral life of the individual. Ryder remains in awe of Brideshead not merely as a building, but for the values which it inspires and fosters in him.

For Waugh in 1960, *Brideshead Revisited* was something of an embarrassment, particularly in what he described as its resemblance to 'a panegyric preached over an empty grave' (Waugh 1960, 8). The postwar world was not nearly so 'egalitarian' nor philistine as he presumed it would be, nor the lifestyles and values of the English aristocracy so much a thing of the past. As a result, Waugh could only offer his novel, when he revised it, as a museum piece, 'a souvenir of the Second War', which articulated his anxieties about the onslaught of modern, democratic forms of life in postwar England. *Brideshead* was his desperate thrust at the democratic ideologies he opposed, as Adam Piette argues:

> Waugh's defence of Brideshead has three facets, then: defence of fine architecture against wholesale suburban planning and military utilitarianism; defence of conservative, private realms of Christian learning and aristocratic values against the incursion of a levelling egalitarianism; defence of the novelist's nineteenth-century spiritual, moral, stylistic and aesthetic allegiances against the Basic English of left-wing ideological prose. By the time he was writing *Brideshead Revisited*, Waugh had identified the British army, the People's Army, as his enemy, as the main force of the egalitarian, utilitarian, 'Basic' age of the common man. (Piette 1995, 97)

Waugh offered the conservative nostalgia of *Brideshead* as a counter to the modernising, democratic rhetoric of the national coalition in wartime England, as a parting shot at the ideologies he blamed for the demise of his 'traditional', ordered England. It is the landscape, specifically the 'exquisite man-made landscape' of the country mansion, that is made to bear the weight of argument in Waugh's novel, and that is shown to determine the action of the novel. *Brideshead* implicitly binds the topographical environment to those who move, act and speak within it, so that it becomes what Hillis Miller describes as 'a complex form of metonymy whereby environment may be a figure for what it environs' (Miller 1995, 20). Thus, the Brideshead estate in its arcadian beauty symbolises the aesthetic sensibility and spiritual grace of its founders and inhabitants, not just in its material reflections of their wealth and status, but in its quasi-mystical effect on Ryder and the various Marchmain family members.

The house in Waugh's hands, is no mere sum of its bricks and mortar, but is instead the vessel for what the author describes as the theme of his novel – 'the operation of divine grace' (Waugh 1960, 7). By extension, and in common with Betjeman, there is a sense in *Brideshead Revisited* that Waugh is suggesting the equation of a nation's values and virtues with the aesthetic appearance and symbolic function of its architecture and landscape. Brideshead, in this scheme of things, is the England which Waugh sees being gradually, irrevocably, superseded. Ryder suggests this in *Brideshead* when he describes the popularity of his work as an architectural writer in the 1930s:

> I loved buildings that grew silently with the centuries, catching and keeping the best of each generation, while time curbed the artist's pride and the Philistine's vulgarity, and repaired the clumsiness of the dull workman. In such buildings England abounded, and, in the last decade of their grandeur, Englishmen seemed for the first time to become conscious of what before was taken for granted, and to salute their achievement at the moment of extinction. (Waugh 1945, 197)

Waugh takes delight in this notion that the architecture of aristocratic England was never more splendid and venerable than in its last lease of life, a notion which pervades the epilogue to the novel in which Ryder sees a magical, ghostly connection between the military swarming across the grounds of Brideshead and the 'old knights' who were its founders. What connects the soldiers across the centuries, Ryder discovers cheerfully, is the 'small red flame' spluttering in the chapel adjoining the house: 'the flame which the old knights saw from their tombs, which they saw put out; that flame burns again for other soldiers, far from home, farther, in heart, than Acre or Jerusalem' (Waugh 1945, 304). The war, by implication, resonates historically with the military spirit of the crusades, even if it is 'farther in heart', by which Waugh presumably means that it is weaker in conviction and faith than the crusades. The concluding passages of the epilogue, then, might appear optimistic in evoking the image of an ancient flame rekindled 'among the old stones' of Brideshead, but it cheers Ryder only to the degree that it causes him to remember the great traditions and foundations of the house. The soldiers are ignoble in contrast to the venerated 'old knights' of Brideshead legend, and in 'the age of Hooper', the character whom Ryder despises as the epitome of the modern, egalitarian world, Ryder is left with nothing but memories of nobility, grandeur and order.

'My theme is memory, that winged host', Ryder declares (Waugh 1945, 197), and so, too, Waugh's concluding representation of the Brideshead landscape suggests that memory is all we will have of England's greatness and splendour. For Waugh 1945 seems to represent a definitive break from the past, from the very character of England as he sees it expressed in its landscape and history. The novel appears to announce the beginning of a new mournful time, the postwar time of loss, a new England which is, in a sense, post-English. *Brideshead Revisited* represented a new departure for Waugh, from the social satires of *Decline and Fall, Vile Bodies, Scoop*, and the more sombre satire, *A Handful of Dust*, to the pessimistic elegy for England of *Brideshead*. Waugh signalled, more than any other writer, the cynical elegiac note which would pervade literature in England after 1945. Ironically, it was a Labour government chancellor, Hugh Dalton, who would announce the scheme which would preserve intact many of the ancestral mansions for which Waugh showed such attachment. That Dalton celebrated the same vision of the heritage society through edenic depictions of the landscape indicates perhaps that the political rift on questions of national identity and culture was never so wide nor as irreparable as Waugh had imagined.

Landscapes and architecture can be designed deliberately to reflect the ambitions and self-image of a political community, of course, and literary representations participate in the construction of myths of national identity through depictions of topographical and architectural beauty. *Brideshead Revisited*, especially when it appeared as a television series in 1981, contributed to the popular veneration of English country mansions and estates, the sheer scale of which in the postwar period took Waugh by surprise. The roots of the postwar fascination with visiting and celebrating 'heritage' sites, as a means of rediscovering an England perceived to be vanishing, pre-dated *Brideshead*, however. It flourished as a genre in the inter-war period. Betjeman promoted this notion of an old, hidden England to be rediscovered in his *Shell Guides* in the 1930s. J.V. Morton's *In Search of England* (1927), A.G. MacDonell's *England Their England* (1933), and J.B. Priestley's *English Journey* (1934) are perhaps the best known examples of the genre, which compound the mythical association of landscape and national identity. As a genre, these writings reproduce the paradoxical impression that England is both essentially continuous and imminently threatened with extinction, and that England is both indubitably real and yet strangely intangible and unknowable.

Brideshead Revisited, along with other literary representations of the end of the war, was an attempt to fix, or give literary form to, an image of England, even as it was thought to be disappearing. In the same year as Waugh published Brideshead, he read and gave advice on another novel which fixed Englishness to the image and legend of an ancestral mansion, *The Pursuit of Love*, the fifth novel of his friend, Nancy Mitford. Waugh found the novel 'full of exquisite detail of Mitford family life' – it was fictionalised autobiography, for the most part – 'but planless and flat and hasty in patches' (Waugh 1976, 633). Mitford's novel describes the eventful and eccentric lives of the Radlett family, told from the perspective of their cousin, Fanny, through whose eyes the experiences of the Radletts are even more enchanting and colourful. The novel revolves around the ancestral home of the Radlett's, Alconleigh House, which, as in Waugh's novel, seems to define and give meaning to family life and identity. Alconleigh is no arcadian haven, however. In fact, Fanny and her cousins contrast its coldness, lack of cultural or artistic merit, and general disorder, with the more attractive merits of its neighbouring country-house, Merlinford. Merlinford, we are told, 'was a house to live in', in contrast to Alconleigh which is characterised as a house 'to rush out from all day to kill enemies and animals' (Mitford 1949, 39).

The Pursuit of Love invests little of the same spiritual significance in Alconleigh as Waugh brings to Brideshead, but Alconleigh does bear the same symbolic weight, if not more so, when it comes to national identity. It does so, however, only in time of national crises, during the war, when the gruff and unrefined character of the house seems to suit the spirit of gritty determination with which Mitford imbues her characters. Before the war, Alconleigh seems to be grotesquely at odds with the cultured tastes of its neighbours and occasional visitors, in bearing the appearance of a museum of war and death:

> Alconleigh was a large, ugly, north-facing, Georgian house ... . There was no attempt at decoration, at softening the lines, no apology for a façade, it was all as grim and as bare as a barracks, stuck upon the high hillside. Within, the keynote, the theme, was death. Not death of maidens, not death romantically accoutred with urns and weeping willows, cypresses and valedictory odes, but the death of warriors and of animals, stark, real. On the walls halberds and pikes and ancient muskets were arranged in crude patterns with the heads of beasts slaughtered in many lands, with the flags and uniforms of bygone Radletts. Glass-topped cases contained, not miniatures of ladies, but miniatures of the medals of their lords, badges, penholders made of tiger's teeth, the hoof of a favourite horse, telegrams announcing casualties in battle, and commissions written out on parchment scrolls, all lying together in a timeless jumble. (Mitford 1949, 39)

Here, Alconleigh is described in terms of its grim obsession with death, and is contrasted with the aesthetic virtues of Merlinford. When the war breaks out in 1939, however, Alconleigh symbolises the patriotic association of land and blood, and serves as a noble contrast to the rootlessness and selfish interests of the Radletts' in-laws, the Kroesigs. The Kroesigs reveal at the onset of war that their priorities lie with preserving their own wealth and status, regardless of community or national identity, and immediately make preparations to escape from England. The German sound of the name, which is a cause of immediate suspicion for Fanny's eccentric and xenophobic Uncle Matthew, serves to contrast the 'landed', patriotic ancestry of the Radletts with the rootless capitalism of the *nouveau riches*.

While Alconleigh symbolises what is presented as the simplicity and honesty of Englishness, the aesthetically crafted landscapes and architecture of the Kroesigs' country house, Planes, becomes the epitome of falsity and pretence:

Planes was a horrible house ... . The garden which lay around it would be a lady water-colourists heaven, herbaceous borders, rockeries, and water-gardens were carried to a perfection of vulgarity, and flaunted a riot of huge and hideous flowers, each individual bloom appearing twice as large, three times as brilliant as it ought to have been and if possible of a different colour from that which nature intended. It would be hard to say whether it was more frightful, more like glorious Technicolour, in spring, in summer, or in autumn. Only in the depth of winter, covered by the kindly snow, did it melt into the landscape and become tolerable. (Mitford 1949, 91)

For Linda Radlett, who marries Tony Kroesig, heir to the Kroesig banking fortune, Planes is an affectation of an English country house, its landscape gaudy, its architecture tasteless, and its owner, Sir Leicester, merely performing the role of English country squire. Nothing is real about Planes, a point which Linda presses to the Kroesigs when she declares that the forced, over-bright blooms of the garden, 'all this pointless pink stuff', will produce 'a riot of sterility' (91). Linda's distaste for the appearance of Planes signifies more substantial differences of class and culture. The Kroesigs have too eagerly crafted a hyperreal version of the stereotyped image of an English garden, an affectation which is shown to be false when war is declared and they abandon any allegiance to England or Englishness. The Radletts, by comparison, emblematise the patriotic spirit, led by Uncle Matthew with his grotesque 'entrenching tool', with which he had 'whacked to death eight Germans' in 1915, a leitmotif in the novel for the authenticity of the Radletts' commitment to English patriotism.

Mitford's novel implicitly suggests a blood and soil version of English nationalism, while caricaturing the urban middle class as rootless capitalists and the intellectual middle class as loveless communists. Uncle Matthew denotes, albeit too in caricatured form, the virtues of the landed aristocracy, who may offend bohemian and urban sensibilities in peacetime, but who are stalwart patriots in wartime: 'His land was to him something sacred, and, sacred above that, was England' (78). Matthew Radlett is essentially a comic figure, even in wartime, when he advises his family to burn their food stores in the event of invasion, so as to become a nuisance to the advancing Germans. But he is ultimately the figure to whom the family return loyalty and warmth, and turn to for their values and identity. His daughters and niece measure potential suitors for their imagined capacity to wield the deadly entrenching tool, while their various love affairs and marriages to non-English or non-patriotic men prove disastrous. The novel closes with the optimism of spring months in Alconleigh, 'with a brilliance of colouring, a richness of life, that one had forgotten to expect during the cold grey winter months' (191). The pursuit of love has been unsuccessful for Fanny and the Radlett girls, but Alconleigh remains the haven to which they return in times of need. In all the emotional turbulence of the novel, it is the country house, the ancestral mooring of blood and land ties, that remains the symbol of resilience and continuity, depicted almost clumsily at the end of the novel with Fanny, Linda and Louisa pregnant and dragging themselves around the house 'like great figures of fertility' (191). The metaphors of springtime and pregnancy, in contrast to Waugh's suggestions of demise and decay, indicate a more optimistic outlook on the war and its aftermath, as if the war has re-energised Alconleigh and brought new life to what it symbolises. Like Brideshead, it seems also to preside over misfortune and ruin – Linda dies in childbirth at the end of the novel – but it remains the defining symbol of English national identity in the novel. As such, Mitford's novel shares with *Brideshead* a common preoccupation with the role of landscape and country-house architecture in giving definition to conservative notions of Englishness and English tradition at the end of the war. As Simon Schama argues in *Landscape and Memory*, national identity requires 'the mystique of a particular landscape tradition: its topography mapped, elaborated, and enriched as a homeland' (Schama 1995, 15). At the end of the war, Waugh and Mitford contributed to the fetishisation of the ancestral mansion and its landscape as the symbolic home of Englishness, and attempted to identify the country house as an icon of national continuity and survival.[4]

Home and Nation

The currency of the imagery and iconography of English landscape and architecture in 1945 is perhaps explicable in relation to the war, although, as already indicated above, such representations were prevalent throughout the thirties too. The war served to intensify experiences of 'home', both for the returning forces and for those who endured the hardships of life in Britain. Waugh and Mitford attempted to fix the image of the English home, albeit of a peculiarly aristocratic, ancestral variety, as the symbolic centre of the war and its meanings for Englishness. Like Betjeman at Margate, there is a sense in both novels that the home encapsulates what 'we are fighting for, most of all'. 'Home' signified continuity, tradition and stability, and yet, the war served of course to destabilise radically the meanings and experiences of home. This is demonstrated amply in both novels. *Brideshead* becomes a military encampment, Alconleigh a Home Guard base, while both Linda and Fanny's Aunt Emily are bombed out of their homes in *The Pursuit of Love*. The war broke up families, temporarily and permanently, made people homeless, evacuated them to strange places, deprived homes of comfort, and redefined the function and ideology of home life. Rationing and utility measures converted homes from havens of individual and family identity into effective units of a war economy. Thus, 'home' functioned in wartime ideology as an ambiguous and paradoxical formation, on one level the symbolic line of defence of the nation – 'the home front', 'the Home Guard', and so on – while on another level the home was co-opted unsentimentally as a cog in the economic and productive machinery of the state. As Rosemary Marangoly George argues, '"home" becomes contested ground in times of political tumult either on the level of power struggles at a national communal stage or at the inter-personal familial level' (George 1999, 18). The war thus threatened as much as it re-energised discourses of homeliness, in both the private and public spheres, prompting interrogations of the meanings of 'home', of family, community and nation.

The impact of the war on notions of domesticity and homeliness is explored in Elizabeth Taylor's first novel, *At Mrs Lippincote's*. Taylor's novel tells the story of Julia Davenant, wife to an RAF officer, who attempts to set up home for her family in the house of an austere landlady, Mrs Lippincote. The house never quite manages to become a home, despite having 'every comfort', and Julia never succeeds in personalising or even familiarising the interior space of the house (Taylor 1995, 6). The house is adorned with Mrs Lippincote's photographs, curtains, shades and furniture, and Julia feels that the house is too full of the ghosts of other people, ghosts who 'haunted, [but] did not help or encourage' (9). Her husband, Roddy, remains aloof and detached from her and their son, Oliver, all the time waiting to be posted on to another station. The Davenants' living arrange-ments are thus always transient and unsettled, and Taylor's novel suggests an implicit connection between this rootlessness, or unhomeliness, and the friction and anxieties which come to disturb family life. Julia considers having an affair, Roddy actually does have an affair, and Oliver grows increasingly estranged and cold from his parents, particularly his father. When Julia discovers that they are to be moved on again, she gives expression to her sense of powerlessness: 'I am a parasite. I follow my man around like a piece of luggage or part of a travelling harem. He is under contract to provide for me, but where he does so is for him to decide' (199). Roddy objects, of course, since it is the RAF that decides his fate, but Julia is suggesting his culpability or compliance in such decisions and her own estrangement from them.

The experience of unhomeliness gives Julia an unusually cynical perspective on marriage and social relations, not surprisingly since the failure of Mrs Lippincote's house to become a home is itself a sign that all is not well between Julia and Roddy. 'There's no love in this house', Roddy's cousin, Eleanor, declares towards the end of the novel, which, read in one way, assigns blame for the strained marital relations to the building itself (211). Taylor's novel thematises this connection between 'home' and love, between the symbolic meanings of 'home' and the desire for security, warmth, family. Biddy Martin and Chandra Mohanty argue that there are political connotations to these experiences of home and the unhomely:

> "Being home" refers to the place where one lives within familiar, safe, protected boundaries; "not being home" is a matter of realizing that home was an illusion of coherence and safety based on the exclusion of specific histories of oppression and resistance, the repression of differences even within oneself. (Martin and Mohanty 1986, 191)

Julia's experience of the unhomely in *At Mrs Lippincote's* enables her to construct an oppositional perspective on the practices of oppression and exclusion which revolve around notions of 'home'. It is not an effective strategy of resistance, since she does not overcome or transgress the limitations of her status as housewife, as Roddy's 'piece of luggage', nor indeed is she empowered to move beyond the mores and values of her class. But it allows her to articulate a critical perspective on gender relations, and to identify 'home' as 'an illusion of coherence and safety'.

At Mrs Lippincote's endorses conservative notions of femininity and social relations in many respects, and it is far from certain that Julia is vindicated from the narrator's perspective in her outlook on home, marriage and gender. But Taylor's novel signals a dystopian view of the ideologies of 'home', which runs counter to the conservative constructions of Englishness of the time. The construction of national identity through the imagery and iconography of landscape, architecture and 'home' caught the literary imagination at the end of the war, and made it peculiarly resistant to analysis as an ideology. The rhetoric of the war relied heavily on the immediate appeal of images of topography and domesticity to rally the public to the nation's defence. This was merely an exaggerated manifestation of a discourse of national identity which, arguably for several centuries, had invested much in topographical and architectural images as the definitive vocabulary of notions of Englishness.[5] The end of the war witnessed an intensification of interest in defining and consolidating conservative notions of national identity, in which literary representations of land and home became symbolic sites of contest and struggle. But, increasingly through the postwar period, what begins to register on this imaginative landscape of England are the 'small disturbances', the faultlines and fractures of class, gender, culture, race, and sexuality, which interrupt and contend with discourses of national identity. When we focus on a selection of the literary productions of one year, we can mark the recurrence of this particular set of narratives and ideas: home, nation, culture, place, belonging. And we can pay attention to the emergence of the 'small disturbances' which interrupt, contest and fracture such narratives and ideas. In doing so, we encounter the doubled time of literature, which appears, as North argues, to stage the opposition between synchronic and diachronic modes of historical engagement. Under this micro-historical analysis, 1945 appears a liminal time in English literary history, neither a beginning, nor an ending, but an interstitial time, which returns us inevitably and necessarily to the temporality of literary representation, to the effects of literature's passing through time.

Notes

1. See 'Weather News Again', *The Times*, 9 May 1945, 2.
2. See, for a discussion of annualised literary history, Michael North,

'Virtual Histories: The Year as Literary Period', *Modern Language Quarterly*, 62:4 (December 2001), 407–24.

3. For a recent revision of influences on the early Larkin, see Stephen Regan, '*In the Grip of Light:* Philip Larkin's Poetry of the 1940s', *New Larkins for Old: Critical Essays*, ed. James Booth (Basingstoke: Palgrave Macmillan, 2000), 121–9.

4. An interesting contrast to both Waugh's and Mitford's novels in the depiction of upper-class homes as icons of Englishness is Henry Green's *Loving* (1945), which focuses on the lives of English servants living in a country mansion in neutral Ireland during the war. The servants remain suspicious throughout of the alien country surrounding them, but are also seeking refuge in Ireland from conscription and German bombing raids.

5. John Lucas analyses the construction of Englishness in these terms from as early as 1688 in *England and Englishness: Ideas of Nationhood in English Poetry 1688–1900* (Iowa City: University of Iowa Press, 1990). David Matless argues that the symbolic association of Englishness with topographical features is particularly intense in the immediate aftermath of the Second World War, in *Landscape and Englishness* (London: Reaktion Books, 1998).

2 'After History': time and memory in postwar writing

'The destruction of the past, or rather of the social mechanisms that link one's contemporary experience to that of earlier generations, is one of the most characteristic and eerie phenomena of the late twentieth century. Most young men and women at the century's end grow up in a sort of permanent present lacking any organic relation to the public past of the times they live in.'

Eric Hobsbawm, *Age of Extremes* (3)

We live in a post-historical age, in which the past has apparently disappeared and been replaced by the 'permanent present'. Despite the fact that the teaching of 'history' in schools and colleges expanded enormously throughout the postwar period, that researchers and academics know more than ever before about the past, that new technologies have enabled more accurate estimates of how past societies lived and worked, that the bestseller lists of book sales in contemporary England reveal a popular taste for historical narratives, factual and fictional, the belief that we live in a post-historical age has gained considerable currency. It has manifested itself in various ways, from Francis Fukuyama's well-known celebration of the collapse of Eastern European communism as 'the end of history', to Fredric Jameson's argument that late capitalism has transformed the past into a commodity for consumption.[1] Hobsbawm's alarm at the lack of historical consciousness among young people indicates the ethical implications of the 'destruction' of the past (particularly for a generation raised to intone the undertaking 'lest we forget'), just as Lyotard's celebration of the end of grand historical narratives suggests contrary ethical imperatives (Lyotard 1984).

In contemporary England, the past is continuously presented

through various forms of cultural production, as tourist attraction, heritage site, collectible artefact, recreational hobby, or as exotic other to the present. Paradoxically, however, it is the very pervasiveness and popularity of the past in contemporary cultural production that has brought about crises in our relationships with the past. 'The past has undergone the usual consequences of popularity', writes David Lowenthal, 'The more it is appreciated for its own sake, the less real or relevant it becomes. No longer revered or feared, the past is swallowed up by the ever-expanding present' (Lowenthal 1985, xvii). The past is displayed everywhere – in museums, architecture, interpretative centres, internet sites, television documentaries, period dramas, literary texts and other forms of cultural representation – but, Lowenthal suggests, its meanings for the present, the precise nature of our relationships to the past, have become more difficult to read. This is the problem that, I will argue in this chapter, has been a persistent concern of contemporary writers in England: what is our relationship with the past? How are our experiences and cultural identifications connected to the past? How do we read the past? How have the extensive social and cultural changes in postwar Britain affected our understandings of the past, and our ability to read the past? These are some of the questions that are central to postwar writing in England, and that form the basis for a more general intellectual inquiry in contemporary England into the meanings of the past. I will argue that contemporary literature registers a profound shift in England's sense of historical identity, at the same time as it reflects on history as a narrative construct.

The anxiety that history has come to an end found expression in some of the best-known literature of the postwar period. It is, of course, central to Orwell's nightmare vision of England after the war in *Nineteen Eighty-Four* (1949). 'Do you realise that the past, starting from yesterday, has been actually abolished?', Winston Smith asks Julia:

> Every record has been destroyed or falsified, every book has been re-written, every picture has been re-painted, every statue and street and building has been re-named, every date has been altered ... History has stopped. Nothing exists except an endless present in which the Party is always right. (Orwell 1989, 162)

Winston knows that the past has ceased to exist, because it is his job continually to rewrite and falsify the past. *Nineteen Eighty-Four* has been read frequently as a satire upon totalitarian government, the propaganda society, but it is perhaps more accurately a modern fable about the elision of the past, the dangerous malleability of memory. Winston is 'the last man', who makes a last desperate attempt to preserve the memory of the past, to retain the last vestiges of humanity against the soulless tyranny of the 'endless present'. Winston treasures the only surviving artefact he has of a knowable past, a small glass paperweight, perhaps more than a hundred years old, which symbolises the endurance of the past, but which is symbolically shattered when Winston is arrested. The novel explores contemporary anxieties about historical amnesia and the capacity of modern societies to manufacture myths of their historical identity and coherence, amply demonstrated for Orwell not just in the revisionist tendencies of Nazism and Stalinism, but the myth-making in which capitalist and imperial societies also continually engaged. *Nineteen Eighty-Four* identifies memory as the site of political and cultural contest, the new battleground of modern forms of power, and presents a dystopian vision of the loss of memory as effectively the end of history.

Orwell's novel is an example of the contemporary anxiety about the veracity of memory. For much of the twentieth century, psychoanalytic theories have explored memory as a process, not merely of storage and awareness, but also of invention, substitution, displacement and revision. Memory is a faculty we associate habitually with authenticity – through memoirs, testimonies and autobiographical writings – but it is also the source of considerable cultural and political disquiet. Alan Sinfield cites the story of people who had endured the bombing of English cities in the 1940s, whose later recollections of the 'blitz spirit' of endurance and defiance did not tally with mass observation evidence revealed in the 1970s of the 'fear, helplessness and disaffection' felt at the time of the blitz (Sinfield 1997, 32).[2] Mass observation had recorded one contemporary version of the blitz, while the survivors later recalled a contradictory version. The clash of stories, of memories, as Sinfield suggests, has much to do with powerful myths forged in postwar England about the blitz as a test of national history and the national character. To remember the blitz as anything other than a tale of heroic, defiant endurance, then, is to come into conflict with a potent national myth.

An even more contentious debate about memory arose in the 1980s and early 1990s, when public awareness about recovered memory reached a peak. The recovered memories of men and women who had been physically and sexually abused as children, and who had subsequently repressed all memory of these experiences, opened new ground in thinking through the relationship between subjectivity and the past. Roger Luckhurst explains that the debates about recovered memory syndrome charted 'the emergence of a new structure of subjectivity, oscillating between memory and forgetting, with the prospect that another self, attached to a wholly occluded memory-chain, might lurk in the interstices of a life-story. In the instant of recovery, the technique proposes, we can become strangers to ourselves' (Luckhurst and Marks 1999, 86). Orwell's Winston experiences this very process of confronting the stranger within himself, as his torturer, O'Brien, promises that in Room 101, 'you shall see yourself as you really are' (283). O'Brien shows Winston to a mirror, where, after systematic abuse and torture, Winston can see that he has come to resemble his worst nightmare, the rat. This is Winston's most horrifying discovery, the appalling disparity between the stories he has told himself of his identity and past, and the wretched vision of himself and his society presented to him in Room 101. At the heart of Orwell's novel is the fear of the new sciences of psychology and psychoanalysis, the very premise of which is that memory is false, identity is constructed, and that the truth of our identities and pasts can only be revealed by trained, authoritative analysts.

If memory is the key agent in maintaining and negotiating our relationship to the past, its current predicament reflects the more general crisis of representation in Western societies. Richard Terdiman argues that since the nineteenth century, there has been a steady erosion of the dependence on 'live, organic memory', and an increasing shift to models of 'artificial or archival memory' (Terdiman 1993, 30). Print culture is itself a manifestation of artificial memory – the book an early instrument of expanded memory – while, in the late twentieth century, computer technologies exemplify this process in a more accelerated form. The idea that 'organic' memory, and with it what Hobsbawm calls our 'organic relation to the public past of the times [we] live in', is disappearing, to be replaced by archives, machines, and cyberspace, may be the cause of consternation, nostalgia, celebration or crisis in modern society. If 'organic' memory has been discredited throughout the twentieth century, so too archival and artificial means of memory are repeatedly treated with suspicion and anxiety.

As such, then, all forms in which the past might be re-presented (the concept of representation itself is dependent upon notions of memory and repetition across time and space) are subject to the scepticism and distrust of our post-historical age. It is not just, as Hobsbawm suggests, that young men and women lack any sense of historical connectedness, but that the means by which they might connect with the past have become increasingly troubled. This is by no means a unique facet of life in England at the beginning of the new millennium. Jimmy Porter, in John Osborne's *Look Back in Anger* (1956), complains that history is what has happened to the previous generation 'in the thirties and the forties', and that the postwar generation has no 'good, brave causes left', just the 'big bang', the 'Brave New-nothing-very-much-thank-you' (Osborne 1957, 84–5). There is, according to Jimmy, no history for the postwar generation to take part in, no sense in which the young share common purpose or experience with older generations. Jimmy contemplates the romantic imagery of England's glorious past, but concludes that it is 'phoney'. 'Still', he says, 'even I regret it somehow, phoney or not. If you've no world of your own, it's rather pleasant to regret the passing of someone else's' (17). Baffled early reviewers of Osborne's play wondered what Jimmy's 'anger' was about, but, apart from an obvious and disturbingly violent tendency to blame women, Jimmy's anger appears to stem from a failure to connect with the past, and a failure to find meaning and purpose in the present. Jimmy cannot empathise with England's imperial or aristocratic past, rejects the historical traditions of the church and the military, and finds the new, 'American age' dreary. This, it seems, is the constitutive anxiety of the postwar generation, which Jimmy Porter was supposed to represent, a past with which they can find no sense of belonging or identification, a present that is vacuous and futile without meaningful connections to the past.

Revisioning History

One consequence of such an anxiety is that literature in postwar England has been preoccupied with exploring and revising the meanings of the past. This is evident in the vogue for historical themes in postwar fiction: in the mock-Victorian narratives of John Fowles's *The French Lieutenant's Woman* (1969) and A.S. Byatt's *Possession* (1990);

in postmodern fictions of history such as Jeanette Winterson's *The Passion* (1987) or Salman Rushdie's *Midnight's Children* (1981); in the preoccupation with disquieting historical themes in Sebastian Faulks's *Birdsong* (1993) and *Charlotte Gray* (1998), Melvyn Bragg's *The Soldier's Return* (1999) and Barry Unsworth's *Sacred Hunger* (1992); in the more popular series of historical novels written by Patrick O'Brian and Bernard Cornwell; and, not least, in the numerous multi-volume novels which explore historical change, and the relationship between subjectivity and history, such as Doris Lessing's *Children of Violence* series (1952–69), Paul Scott's *The Raj Quartet* (1966–75), Anthony Powell's *A Dance to the Music of Time* (1951–75), Jocelyn Brooke's *The Orchid Trilogy* (1948–50), Olivia Manning's *Fortunes of War* (1960–80), and C.P. Snow's *Strangers and Brothers* (1940–70). This latter sub-genre of multi-volume historical novels seems to be concerned particularly with understanding and revising the meanings of the past, and, in paying attention to the processes of temporal change and mnemonic representation, the most susceptible to issues of historical identity and coherence. Two trilogies, in particular, I think, exemplify the problems of history as a mode of understanding and as a narrative construct in postwar culture: Evelyn Waugh's *Sword of Honour* (1952–61) and Pat Barker's *Regeneration* (1991–95).

Waugh's trilogy may appear an absurdly modest and reticent treatment of the Second World War. Bernard Bergonzi observes that the first two books of the trilogy, when they were published in the mid-1950s, did not seem to amount to much, and were inconclusive (Bergonzi 1993, 117). As the fictional story of an officer's experiences of the war, it is notable for its lack of action, its farcical treatment of military operations, and its despondent observations on the lack of honour and courage in modern warfare. This may be a symptom of what Arthur Marwick claims is a pervasive tendency in postwar British writing to represent the war as 'a little local affair, without epochal significance' (Marwick 1990, 97). But the war does have epochal significance for Waugh, not as the ultimate battlefield on which the fate of European politics would depend, but for its final eclipse of a past populated with heroism, glory and honour. The protagonist of the novel, Guy Crouchback, searches for 'honour', for the historic, chivalric role of the 'man-at-arms' in a time of national emergency, but what he finds instead is banality, lies, folly, and disgrace. *Sword of Honour* is not short of deaths and injuries, but they are almost always the consequence of senseless accidents or mechanical failures. Nor is it short on 'heroes', but their heroism is invented by war propaganda out of trivial, often farcical, mistakes.

Guy Crouchback enters the war full of naïve expectations of the gallantry and heroism of battle, acutely conscious of the weight of history. He is the last male descendent of an ancient and aristocratic Catholic family, heir to the Broome estate, which we are told is 'almost unique in contemporary England, having been held in uninterrupted male succession since the reign of Henry I' (Waugh 1984, 16). What crystallises his sense of purpose in the war, his feelings that it is a crusade, is the pact between Germany and Russia, which seems to him an alignment of the forces of grotesque modernity against the defenders of tradition and honour: 'the enemy at last was plain in view, huge and hateful, all disguise cast off' (11). This sets the scene for what seems to Guy an epic war, a war of good against evil, of Christian virtue against modern tyranny. Guy's thoughts in the novel turn frequently to a medieval antecedent, Sir Roger de Waybroke, an English knight, whose remains lay buried in the parish church of the Crouchback's holiday home in Italy. Before he goes to join the war in England, Guy visits the tomb of the ancient knight, and requests of his spirit 'pray for me ... and for our endangered kingdom' (12). The knight, who we are told was on his way to join the second crusade, serves as a frequent reminder to Guy of the historic notions of chivalry and codes of aristocratic honour. Indeed, much of Guy's initial thinking about the war is inflected with the language and imagery of the medieval crusades. But the knight is, as the trilogy turns out, an omen as much as a symbol, for his story, researched by Guy's uncle, is prescient of Guy's experience of the war:

> Waybroke, now Waybrook, was quite near London. Roger's manor had long ago been lost and over-built. He left it for the Second Crusade, sailed from Genoa and was shipwrecked on this coast. There he enlisted under the local Count, who promised to take him to the Holy Land but led him first against a neighbour, on the walls of whose castle he fell at the moment of victory. The Count gave him honourable burial and there he had lain through the centuries, while the church crumbled and was rebuilt above him, far from Jerusalem, far from Waybroke, a man with a great journey still all before him and a great vow unfulfilled. (Waugh 1984, 12)

It is significant, of course, that the knight was due to fight in the second crusade, which itself achieved nothing. The knight's bravery, in other words, was futile, all for no purpose, and met with disaster upon disaster. Guy enters the war filled with the romantic spirit of an unfulfilled crusade, then, but finds, in the phoney war, in the abject misery of Dunkirk, and, most central to the novel, in the failure at Crete, that he is living in a very different age.

The war is not a moral crusade, but a modern, bureaucratic muddle. To begin with, Guy's war is full of false starts. His regiment, the Halberdiers, are constantly sent off to battle, only to be recalled or diverted. Much of the trilogy shows Guy at training camps, regimental barracks, bureaucratic offices, or off duty. Steven Trout rightly argues that the trilogy is characterised by recurrent anti-climax, and tends towards reducing its vista of world war into a handful of miniature moments of farce (Trout 1997, 125–43). Guy sees little action – the only enemy soldier he sees is a motorcyclist in Crete at a distance – and his 'war wound' stems from twisting his knee while playing football with a wastepaper basket. The epitome of the modern hero in the novel, Ritchie-Hook, is a comic caricature, whose heroism is deeply ambivalent. He risks the lives of his men, including Guy, on the coast of North Africa in order to acquire a 'war trophy' – the severed head of 'a Negro' (178). Finally, in one of the few action scenes in the trilogy, he is killed pathetically and futilely while charging at a blockhouse manned not by Germans but Croat nationalists. Ritchie-Hook is absurdly brave, unlike many of the officers Guy encounters, but he is also exemplary of the farce which surrounds Guy throughout the war. The other acts of heroism in the trilogy turn out to be inflated or, worse, concocted. Ivor Claire, to whom Guy looks as a hero at one point, is awarded a Military Cross for 'shooting three territorials who were trying to swamp his boat' at Dunkirk, an act of dubious heroism, as Guy later suspects (232). This casts a suspicious outlook on the ways in which the panic and chaos of Dunkirk, the terrible failures and defeats of the war, are remade into myths of national glory. Guy encounters the invention of myths of heroism in the workings of the propagandist, Ian Kilbannock. Kilbannock rewrites the stupendous error by which a wayward unit of soldiers, including Guy, bound for an uninhabited island near Jersey, ended up briefly and fearfully in France, as the heroic assault on occupied Europe by a brave band of commandoes (310). Guy is told that he is too upper class to be popularised as a hero, and instead the cowardly Trimmer is elevated to heroic status. The people need their heroes, it seems, and Guy finds that in an age of no heroes, the military bureaucracy simply invents one out of farce and incompetence.

Waugh explains in his synopsis of the first two volumes of the trilogy that *Sword of Honour* is the story of Guy attempting to find his place in the battle, a moral crusade, in which he takes the 'opportunity to re-establish his interest in his fellow men and to serve them' (395). Guy fails to find his role in the battle, fails to find the war capable of producing situations in which honour, dignity or bravery might be possible or recognisable. Every apparent act of honour in the trilogy turns out to be deeply ambivalent. Guy's chivalrous or honourable deeds are much less public, less perceptible, than any of the brash, farcical actions which become myths of heroism in the war. He marries Virginia, his former wife, who is pregnant by Trimmer, in order to save her honour, for example. This stands out as a private act of honour, very different from the ideal of public honour which Guy has idolised (misguidedly) in Roger de Waybroke or Ivor Claire. It is the last recourse of the honourable man, it seems, in the modern age, and, like much of the trilogy, suggests that the contexts for honourable or moral action have shifted beyond recognition.

Sword of Honour is, in this respect, a melancholic, but also bleakly comic, narrative. It is deeply ironic, and indicative of Waugh's black humour, that the only tragic deaths to occur in the trilogy are those of Virginia and Guy's uncle Peregrine, who are killed by rocket bombs at the end of the war. This, for Waugh, seems to epitomise the changed moral contexts of the modern age, in which war becomes impersonal, mechanical, and purposeless. The rocket bomb, or doodlebug (as in Roy Fuller's poem, discussed in Chapter 1), symbolises this new world of mechanistic, bureaucratised war:

> Flying bombs appeared in the sky, unseemly little caricatures of aeroplanes, which droned smokily over the chimney-tops, suddenly fell silent, dropped out of sight and exploded dully. Day and night they came at frequent, irregular intervals, striking at haphazard far and near. It was something quite other than the battle scene of the blitz with its drama of attack and defence; its earth-shaking concentrations of destruction and roaring furnaces; its respites when the sirens sounded the All Clear. No enemy was risking his own life up there. It was as impersonal as a plague, as though the city were infested with enormous, venomous insects. (Waugh 1984, 533)

The randomness of death from a rocket bomb, its absence of purpose or pattern, troubles Guy's attempt to give order and meaning to the events of the war (or, more often, to the non-events of the war). The problem presented by a mechanised, bureaucratic war, it seems, is that it lacks drama; it lacks the tragic force of the 'just' war, and the narrative compulsion of a human struggle for good and honour. The moral story of heroism and tragedy, of good and evil, of triumph and martyrdom – familiar from history – is sadly lacking for Guy from the disappointing realities of modern war. It is lacking too, of course, from his medieval model of the warrior, since we know that Sir Roger's crusade ended pathetically, even if honourably. At this point, Waugh's trilogy seems to be identifying a gap between the dramatising, elevating tendencies of historical narrative, and the bleak, chaotic experiences of the real, in all its banality and lack of meaning.

In many ways, Waugh's depiction of the war is disturbing because it represents as without purpose, meaning or event a war in which there were millions of deaths, many tragic events and dramatic shifts of power, and a grave struggle against mass genocide and human misery. Waugh depicts a war, however, in which the allied war effort is far from righteous, in which Jewish people are abused and massacred by both sides, in which the allies resort to dishonourable methods and lies. The significance of Waugh's trilogy is that it shows sufficient conviction in the ingloriousness of the war, and the moral vacuity of the modern age, to depict what has been constructed historically as one of the most tumultuous and decisive events in human history as a pointless, dishonourable muddle. The tragedy for Waugh's protagonist is that he has joined a war which he believes is the end of his way of life, the end of all his beliefs. Waugh's defensive reaction to the gloomy consequences of this narrative of decline was to represent it ironically. Early in the trilogy, as Guy Crouchback has just signed up, he slumps off to his billet, a house ironically called Paschendael, and he reflects mournfully on the painful irony of his own war effort:

> The occupation of this husk of a house, perhaps, was a microcosm of that new world he had enlisted to defeat. Something quite worthless, a poor parody of civilization, had been driven out; he and his fellows had moved in, bringing the new world with them; the world that was taking firm shape everywhere all about him, bounded by barbed wire and reeking of carbolic. (Waugh 1984, 73)

Later, Guy finds the untrustworthy Ian Kilbannock selling this idea of a 'new Britain that is being forged in the furnace of war' (362), but it is a new world founded on lies and disgrace. The war signifies for Guy the end of history, the end of his connection to the past. This is signalled not least by the fact that the Crouchback's long line of descent, the family tradition which weighs so heavily upon Guy, is brought to an end during the war. Guy senses this impending sense of ruin as he enters the war, glumly aware of the ironic consequences of his own actions in the war, and of the disappearance of the traditions and values he enlisted to protect. The realisation of this irony does not, of course, make the consciousness of decline any less effective, for Crouchback in acknowledging the irony of his situation is also recognising its irreversibility.

Waugh epitomises to some extent the tendency in postwar British writing to represent the present as a pale shadow of the past, or indeed to see the present through the spectral lenses of the past. Waugh shared with his friend Anthony Powell an interest in the ways in which the present was 'ghosted' by the repetition of events and the spectral recirculation of scenes and moments, the effect of which in the writings of both is not to testify to the eternal recycling of time, but instead to make the contemporary seem always to be a pale imitation of the old. There is nothing necessarily nostalgic about this tendency, however, even in Waugh's writing. In *Sword of Honour*, Waugh shows that Guy Crouchback conceives of his experiences in the Second World War as indistinguishable imitations of his older brother's experiences in the First World War. Moreover, in comparison to the tragic desperation of the First World War, Guy finds the British war effort in the 1940s a pathetic and grotesque parody. As Steven Trout argues, Waugh's trilogy becomes 'the ultimate antiwar novel ... not through the emotional polemics and shock tactics of its World War I precursors; rather, Waugh refuses to grant modern warfare even the dignity of tragedy or horror' (Trout 1997, 140). The war is symbolic not merely of the end of aristocratic decadence, but the way that it is conducted is itself a symptom of the deteriorating circumstances and character of Waugh's England. Waugh thus represents the war through the forms of irony, farce and deflation most appropriate to its character. Paul Fussell wrote of the ironic and melancholic aspects of Waugh's trilogy in order to argue that the First World War, the Great War, dominated the mentality of the generations that followed (Fussell 1975, 318), but equally it registers the

Second World War as the final, pathetic eclipse of history, of the grand narratives of English civilisation and glory. If the first war was the great, engulfing tragedy of human history, *Sword of Honour* suggests that the second war was the point at which history became inhuman, and war became merely a matter of systematic destruction and systematic deception. This is not tragic for Waugh, merely contemptible.

The relationship between literature and history in *Sword of Honour* is of a peculiar character. The historical novel usually pays homage to the greatness or decisiveness of an event, or uses the symbolic significance of the event to reflect on the triumphs or tragedies of its protagonists. Waugh's trilogy shows its historical setting to be farcical, a pale shadow of what a historical event should be. If the historical novel usually borrows the symbolic weight of its setting to add authority and significance to its own story, Waugh's trilogy instead turns all the force of literary modes of satire and irony against its historical setting. The trilogy was published at a time when the British film industry was busy mythologising the war, with films such as *The Dambusters* (1954), *The Cockleshell Heroes* (1955), *The Bridge on the River Kwai* (1957), *Sea of Sand* (1958), and *Ice-Cold in Alex* (1958). Such films consolidated the myth of an inventive, defiant people, fighting with moral purpose against a superior force. Waugh's trilogy, seen in this context, is an act of historical vandalism, which, in its capacity to vilify the national memory of the war, is perhaps the literary precursor of the anarchist protestors who, in 2000, are alleged to have defaced the memorial statue of Winston Churchill in London.

Pat Barker's *Regeneration* trilogy, in comparison, is considerably more respectful of the public memory and historical significance of the First World War. The war represents a watershed in historical consciousness for Barker, an horrific vortex in which the Victorian sense of progress and civilisation is thrown into crisis, and the modern age of scepticism and irony emerges. The trilogy revolves around the character of the anthropologist and psychotherapist, W.H. Rivers, and his patients at Craiglockhart hospital, which include the poet, Siegfried Sassoon, and the fictional Billy Prior. As such, the war is represented through its psychological effects, rather than as an event in itself. Barker dramatises a confrontation between the authority and rationalism of psychoanalysis and the disturbing, haunting effects of war. Rivers experiences a profound crisis in the authority of his position as analyst, first by having to treat Sassoon's perfectly rational criticisms of the war as manifestations of mental illness, then by the ferocity of some of his patients' physiological reactions to the war, and, then, finally, by the return of his own repressions and ghosts. A central concern of the trilogy is the effect of the war as a traumatic, incomparable event on Rivers as an analyst. Is psycho-analysis capable of explaining and rationalising all forms of psychic disturbance? Or are there events and experiences so unique, so intense, so powerful, that they change the way in which we see and explain the world?

In the *Regeneration* trilogy, history throws up such a unique event, the effects of which tend to manifest themselves in figures and tropes of haunting. Sassoon in *Regeneration* sees corpses rotting in the streets of central London (Barker 1992, 12), and wakes to find the ghosts of dead soldiers in his hospital room (188). Burns, another of Rivers's patients in the same novel, continually relives the smells and tastes of finding his nose and mouth filled with the decomposing flesh of a German corpse (19). So too, in *The Ghost Road*, Wansbeck is visited in hospital by the ghost of the German prisoner he murdered, who becomes more and more decomposed with every visit (Barker 1996, 26). Prior in *The Eye in the Door* becomes his own ghost, by splitting into two opposing personalities (Barker 1994, 242), and the trilogy closes in *The Ghost Road* with Rivers encountering the ghost of a witch-doctor he knew in Melanesia. The recurrent figures of haunting in the trilogy serve to underline the potency of history experienced as traumatic event. Haunting signifies the repetition of time, the refusal of the past to stay in its place. This is, in many respects, what Rivers must confront in each of his patients – an excess of memory, of history, the disturbing eruption of the past into the present.

The excess of memory and history experienced by Rivers's patients is also, Barker's novels suggest, the proto-typical temporal condition of the twentieth century. Barker traces our contemporary concerns with recovered memory, hidden subjectivities, forgotten stories – the exclusions and elisions of history – to the 'Great War'. The effects on memory and consciousness of the war is so great as to induce a re-imagination of the experience of time and space. The landscape of Barker's trilogy, set around Craiglockhart and London, is pervaded with the haunting imagery of the trenches. Her characters are constantly visualising and hearing the effects of trench warfare as they walk around the hospital, the fields around Craiglockhart, or the streets and wastelands of cities. In one memorable scene, the traumatised Burns finds refuge from a violent storm in the ruins of a moat, reliving the security of the trench against the battery and thunderous noise of war. The medieval moat and the modern trench are here collapsed into one image of the attempt to burrow into some security in the face of war. This folding of one historical image into another is a recurrent trope in Barker's work. It features too in a conversation between Owen and Sassoon in *Regeneration* about their experiences of time as ghostly:

> [Owen:] 'Sometimes when you're alone, in the trenches, I mean, at night you get the sense of something *ancient*. As if the trenches had always been there. You know one trench we held, it had skulls in the side. You looked back along and ... Like mushrooms. And do you know, it was actually *easier* to believe they were men from Marlborough's army than to to to think they'd been alive two years ago. It's as if all other wars had somehow ... distilled themselves into this war, and that makes it something you ... almost can't challenge.'
> [...]
> [Sassoon:] 'I had a similar experience. Well, I don't know whether it is similar. I was going up with the rations one night and I saw the limbers against the skyline, and the flares going up. What you see every night. Only I seemed to be seeing it from the future. A hundred years from now they'll still be ploughing up skulls. And I seemed to be in that time and looking back. I think I saw our ghosts.' (Barker 1992, 83–4)

Both Owen and Sassoon articulate here the sense of history transforming into myth, of a war which is the distillation of all wars, of a war which is already the ghostly imitation of itself. Owen sees the war as the inevitable culmination of all wars – the end of history, in one sense – while Sassoon describes his experience of the present as history in the making, as the future anterior. Barker is here drawing our attention to the displaced temporality of the war, the sense that the time of the war is never self-present, but must always be filtered through its mythic resonances or its future significance. The war is, at one and the same time, the repetition of the 'timeless' mythic story of Abraham and Isaac,[3] and the decisive moment of epochal shift from the Victorian faith in progress and civilisation to the postmodern scepticism of the twentieth century.

Barker's trilogy, in this sense, registers the displaced chrono-consciousness of the late twentieth century, for one paradoxical consequence of living in an age which defines itself as post-historical is that we are both free to be 'timeless' (the permanent present noted by Hobsbawm), and we are condemned to live in everyone else's past (like Jimmy Porter). The problem for Barker's characters is that time is constantly displaced, the past endlessly invading the present, usually with disturbing consequences. *Regeneration* explores the familiar psychoanalytic theme of the return of the repressed, but it does so in contradistinction to the premises of psychoanalysis. Where psycho-analysis emphasises a temporal trajectory towards healing and progress, *Regeneration* suggests instead that, after the First World War, historical consciousness has been structured around the temporality of loss, absence and mourning. In such an age, the trilogy suggests, the very possibility of rational analysis, and therefore the possibility of scientific or historical knowledge, is thrown into crisis in the disturbed and unstable temporalities of our postmodern, post-historical sensi-bility. Barker's trilogy concludes with Rivers visualising the Melanesian witch-doctor, Njira, performing the dance of the living dead. It suggests that Rivers now belongs, like all his patients, like us, to the land of the living dead, to the haunted time of post-history.

History is over, then, according to these two, distinguished histori-cal trilogies, which is a hyperbolic way of saying that the twentieth century has witnessed a profound shift in our sense of historical consciousness and belonging, that the means and forms of our connections with the past have altered radically. The heightened attention in contemporary literature to problems of memory, to the disturbing meanings which lie buried in the past awaiting present discovery, to the malleability and equivocation of history, are all mani-festations, of one form or another, of this crisis in our sense of history. The effects of such attention are not simply to be found in the variety of historical settings and themes in contemporary literature, but also in the ways in which contemporary writers interrogate the framing axioms of historical narrative and representation. In the next section of the chapter, I will examine the implications of this emphasis in postwar writing on the frames and forms of historical representation.

Revisiting History

One important realisation of the new historical emphases of much contemporary critical theory is that literature does not simply reflect or respond to an external reality, but instead participates in a complex process of negotiation and exchange with other forms of representation. 'History' is neither a given context against which to measure the veracity or representativeness of a literary text, nor is it merely another text. It is, instead, according to Fredric Jameson, 'an absent cause ... inaccessible to us except in textual form ... [Our] approach to it and to the Real itself necessarily passes through its prior textualization' (Jameson 1983, 35). History is always mediated, always the subject of prior representation and narrativisation, and one form in which history becomes accessible to us, in very particular ways, is through the medium of literary representation. Literary texts articulate and mediate forms of historical experience, and attempt to conceptualise the experience of social, cultural and political change. This is arguably true of all genres and periods of literature, but never more so than when the prevailing forms of literary invention tend towards sociological or realist models. Then, we are obliged to confront two misconceptions of the relationship between literature and history: first, that literature passively reflects actual social and historical conditions; and second, that literary texts belong, in some fundamentally modern fashion, to a particular chronological moment. Jameson provides useful ways of thinking about the productive and constitutive function of literature in relation to historical experience. He argues, for example, that narrative might best be conceived as 'a "form of reasoning" about experience and society' (Jameson 1977, 543), in which narrative constructs models for understanding social and historical change. Such is the case, I will argue, in two key 'sociological' literary texts of the postwar period, Alan Sillitoe's novel, *Saturday Night and Sunday Morning* (1958), and Tony Harrison's poem, *v.* (1985).

Sillitoe's novel appears to register a particular moment of social change in English history, a time in the 1950s of full employment, national military service, increased earnings and improved standards of living for the working class. The novel's central character, Arthur Seaton, a young factory worker in Nottingham, describes in meticulous detail the economic, social and cultural conditions of a newly emergent 'affluent working class'.[4] Seaton earns fourteen pounds a week, enough to be considered rich by some of his relatives, enough to keep him in good quality Italian suits, in beer and cigarettes through the week. The industrial community in which he lives now boasts 'a television aerial hooked on to almost every chimney, like a string of radar stations', although Seaton observes also that these are 'each installed on the never-never' (Sillitoe 1985, 31). The novel depicts the routine experiences of a single, working-class man – the minutiae of daily factory work, Saturday nights spent in pubs and chasing casual sex, and fishing on Sundays. There is unusual precision about the industrial process in which Seaton is engaged, about the wages he earns and what he spends his money on, and about the particular feel, voice and character of his local community. It is hardly surprising that, when the novel was published in 1958, it was praised largely for its documentary qualities, for the accuracy of its depiction of contemporary working-class life (Ritchie 1988, 198–200). The anarchic energies and opinions of the novel's hero earned the novel a place too in the emerging pantheon of 'angry young men', who were supposed to signify a new form of youthful dissent from the postwar establishment.

The particular 'time' of the novel, the historical moment of the late 1950s which reviewers felt it reflected, is more complex than it initially appears, however. Arthur Seaton's view of working-class life in the 1950s is constantly filtered through the contrasting experiences of the 1930s, for example, so that the experience of postwar affluence is perceived always from the perspective of someone who has a prewar consciousness of poverty and unemployment. The ease with which Arthur acquires money, sex, entertainment and material goods, the sense of what Harold Macmillan famously referred to as the era in which Britons had 'never had it so good', sits oddly with Arthur's feeling of having to fight 'every day until I die', which seems to reflect working-class experiences of the 1930s more closely:

> Why do they make soldiers out of us when we're fighting up to the hilt as it is? Fighting with mothers and wives, landlords and gaffers, coppers, army, government. If it's not one thing it's another, apart from the work we have to do and the way we spend our wages. There's bound to be trouble in store for me every day of my life, because trouble it's always been and always will be. Born drunk and married blind, misbegotten into a strange and crazy world, dragged-up through the dole and into the war with a gas-mask on your clock, and the sirens rattling into you every night while you rot with scabies in an air-raid shelter. Slung into khaki at eighteen, and when they let you out, you sweat again in a factory, grabbing for an extra pint, doing women at the week-end and getting to know whose husbands

are on the nightshift, working with rotten guts and an aching spine, and nothing for it but money to drag you back there every Monday morning. (Sillitoe 1985, 254–5)

Arthur doesn't have any fights with mothers, wives, landlords, gaffers, or any state authorities. He is beaten up by two soldiers for having sex with one of their wives, a consequence of his determination to have a good time, or, in a phrase used recurrently in the novel, to 'make hay while the sun shines'. He doesn't have to fight to earn a living, although he does work hard. Instead, he has to be careful not to work too hard, for the piecework process at his factory discourages over-production. He has no landlord to fret about, his gaffer pays him what Arthur acknowledges is a decent wage, and his mother is pleased with his contribution to the household earnings. Yet, Arthur *feels* as if he is fighting against an authoritarian system, and has an anarchic attitude towards the state. Partly this is an ingrained, individualist resentment at having to pay tax or conform to laws, and perhaps presages the emergence in the 'affluent society' of the new consumerist individual-ism, which came to prominence in the conservative governments of the 1980s. But partly too, it is the product of an older, working-class culture, 'dragged-up through the dole and into the war', which is reflected in the novel's evocation of close community spirit and common feelings of hardship, self-help and dissent.

The 'yard' of terraced housing, which is the residential setting of Sillitoe's novel, has its stalwart characters and routines, emblematised most clearly in the figure of 'fat Mrs Bull the gossiper', 'a tight-fisted defender of her tribe' (31). The community is structured around such knowable, familiar characters, around the daily routines of its men going to the factory, and its women performing household chores. It is anchored in specific experiences shared in common, and specific networks of familial and community support. It is a community with common cultural reference points, forms of dress and entertainment, modes of speech and behaviour. Arthur's higher earnings place him in a potentially disjunctive relationship with this community, however, and the prospect of marriage at the end of the novel sees him imagined in a new light as a 'young man of the world ... who had been a good soldier and who was now a good worker', and whose earnings will probably take him and his wife-to-be, Doreen, to a new suburban house. But Arthur has no sense of himself as part of this newly emergent class formation. Instead, he continues to think and feel as a kind of anarchic class warrior, despising as oppressors the capitalist 'boss-class', yet at the same time capitalising individually on the fruits of a boom economy. To put it more starkly, Arthur seems to represent the mind of a 1930s communist trapped in the body of a 1950s consumer.

Once we try to locate this novel historically and chronologically, then, it is immediately apparent that there is a kind of time-lag embedded in the structure of the narrative, whereby the working-class culture of the 1930s is continually present in Sillitoe's representations of the 1950s. This is easily explained as the product of the lengthy gestation period of the novel, given that Sillitoe had worked on the short stories which comprise parts of the novel as early as 1950. Then, the war and the depression, stories of desertion and unemployment, were much more fresh in the memory, and were repeatedly invoked in the election campaigns of 1945, 1950 and 1951. This would account for what Stuart Laing calls the 'occasionally unstable sense of period in the novel' (Laing 1986, 66). There is more to this temporal disjunction in the novel than simply the confused product of a lengthy period of composition, however. It may be that the novel reflects a condensed or refracted image of contemporary working-class culture, drawing into its frame the economic conditions of the 1950s with the cultural identity of the 1930s. If so, we need to rethink the notion of mimeticism in the realist novel, for *Saturday Night and Sunday Morning* is not a synchronic reflection of youthful rebellion, but a diachronic fusion of divergent times and identities.

This is evident once we explore the concepts of time and temporal rhythm which are foregrounded in the novel, even in its title. Saturday night and Sunday morning symbolise two different times and modes of behaviour, two cultures. Saturday night sees Arthur pursuing pleasure with the same vigour, energy and speed with which he pursues his work. The novel opens with Arthur falling down the stairs of a pub, having consumed eleven pints of beer and seven small gins (9). His consumption of beer, his aggressive pursuit of casual sex, his sense of competition with other men, and his responses to violent and disciplinary stimuli all correspond to the patterns which dictate his working life, but are also, paradoxically, part of the process of purging himself of mechanical time. In contrast, Sundays find Arthur in a different temporal order, fishing patiently on a riverbank. Sillitoe's prose in this passage is at its most contemplative, most lingering pace:

> Arthur's eyes were fixed into the beautiful earth-bowl of the depthless
> water, trying to explore each pool and shallow until, as well as an
> external silence there was a silence within himself that no particle of
> his mind or body wanted to break. Their faces could not be seen in
> the water, but were united with the shadows of the fish that flitted
> among upright reeds and spreading lilies, drawn to water as if they
> belonged there, as if the fang-like claws of the world would come
> unstuck from their flesh if they descended into its imaginary depths,
> as if they had known it before as a refuge and wanted to return to it,
> their ghosts already there, treading the calm unfurrowed depths and
> beckoning them to follow. (Sillitoe 1985, 240)

Sillitoe depicts here a moment of spiritual unity between Arthur and
the natural world, an originary coming together which is figured as
birth and death, as a process of recirculation quite distinct from the
mechanical time of factory work and Saturday nights in the pub. It is
only when Arthur goes fishing, we are told, that he has any sensory
experience of seasonal time, while his working life obeys a distinctly
weekly cycle of time. As Ian Haywood observes, Sunday morning does
not just symbolise a time of repose and restitution (which might in
that case be conceived simply as the necessary extension of the labour
process), but also represents a redemptive time, in which Arthur
grows and remakes his own identity (Haywood 1997, 103). It is not
then an alternative mode of being, but an alternative mode of becoming, for Arthur, in considering whether he is fish or fisherman, decides
that 'taking the bait' (by which he means settling down to marriage
and the discipline of labour) is part of a necessary process of change
and renewal. 'If you went through life refusing all the bait dangled
before you, that would be no life at all', Arthur says, which verges on a
dialectical notion of the relationship between fish and fisherman,
between acquiescence and aggression (252). This, at least, is his imaginary resolution to his paradoxical self-image as both wage-slave and
self-determining individual, and it allows him to decide to take new
directions in his life.

Sunday morning, then, signifies a temporal order not of recovery
but of flux. It functions in the novel as a symbolic moment of transformation, by which time lags into an organic, slow movement – the
movement of seasonal time – and enables Arthur to reflect on the
narrative of his own life and experiences, to see himself within a life-
trajectory. He moves from the mechanical logic and temporality of

repetitive production into the lagged time and space of contemplation. He reminds us, however, that such contemplation, such
processes of reflection and change, take place right at the heart of the
industrial process:

> Time flew while you wore out the oil-soaked floor and worked furi-
> ously without knowing it: you lived in a compatible world of pictures
> that passed through your mind like a magic-lantern, often in vivid
> and glorious loonycolour, a world where memory and imagination
> ran free and did acrobatic tricks with your past and with what might
> be your future, an amok that produced all sorts of agreeable visions.
> (Sillitoe 1985, 44)

Arthur is found here contemplating the play of time within consciousness, the productive engagement through memory and imagination
with modes of past being and future becoming, with narratives of self-
identity. What Sillitoe figures in this passage, then, is the divergent
temporal modes of machine and consciousness, so that Arthur is
compelled on the one hand to obey the rhythm of the industrial
process, but he is also engaging imaginatively with a different temporal rhythm. The movements between action and contemplation,
which occur throughout the novel, indicate a significant process of
exploring the relationship between time and narrative.

Saturday Night and Sunday Morning is noteworthy for its complex
shifts in narrative perspective, between Arthur's own self-narration
and the multiple points of view of the narrator and other characters.
But it is also significant for its shifts in temporal modes, from register-
ing the lived time of the present, to refracting the present through
images of the past, to the lagged time of contemplation. The consequence of these shifting temporal orders in the novel is that *Saturday
Night and Sunday Morning* implies a very different relationship
between narrative and history than the one routinely offered up in
praise of its documentary qualities. Arthur Seaton is constructed not
as the representative of a particular class formation at a particular
time, but as a self-conscious participant in historical and social
change, who embodies the disjunctive temporalities of cultural identity, and who shapes as well as obeys the narrative logic of identity
formation. Perhaps most importantly, Sillitoe places his working-class
hero not within the conventional linear time-frame which would
imply a sense of progression to the social changes represented in the

novel, but, through multiple time-frames, suggests instead a fractured sense of history. Arthur Seaton may have emblematised to some readers the emergence of an affluent working class, but he remains an ambivalent agent of that emergence, steeped still in the class consciousness of the 1930s, deeply critical of the notion that history is unfolding towards a classless utopia.

In *Saturday Night and Sunday Morning*, then, we have an instance of a novel which constructs itself in relation to a knowable, social reality, but which also problematises the idea that we can isolate and 'fix' its historical or temporal location. It does the latter by focusing attention on what Peter Osborne calls 'the constitutive role of the subject in the formation of temporal experience' (Osborne 1995, 48), which is to say that any historicising analysis of the novel must take into account its shifting and fractured senses of time, its filtering of historical perspectives through the consciousness of its characters, or, to put it another way, how the novel historicises itself. It is perhaps inevitable that working-class writing in the postwar period should dwell upon its own historicity. After all, Sillitoe was writing at a time which supposedly saw the emergence into English literary history of the modern industrial working class, and in which working-class writing became a significant organising category (at least for marketing purposes) of contemporary literature. The sense of historical change, which has enabled working-class writing to earn some forms of cultural recognition, clearly raises issues about the lack of educational opportunities and lack of access to means of representation which were common experiences for previous generations. Hence, Arthur Seaton lives with the constant feeling that his life, his achievements, must be measured in relation to the experiences of his father's and grandfather's generations. The theme of an inter-generational class-consciousness is taken up in Tony Harrison's *v.*, a poem which created much controversy when it was first televised.[5]

Harrison's poem begins with a quotation from Arthur Scargill, which reflects on this sense of inter-generational consciousness: 'My father still reads the dictionary every day. He says your life depends on your power to master words' (Harrison 1989, 5). The opening verse of the poem continues this theme, imagining Harrison's grave 'behind the family dead ... adding poetry to their beef, beer and bread' (7). The quotation from Scargill, and Harrison's opening lines, evoke issues of inheritance and tradition, and register the significance of linguistic self-consciousness. Scargill is citing his father's wary hoarding of words as evidence of his awareness of the power of representation. Harrison's poem dwells upon the words of 'skinhead' graffiti which have been written over the inscriptions on his parents' gravestone, and reflects on the resemblances between graffiti as a form of palimpsestic writing, and his own writings as a poet. Where his family have been renowned for 'beef, beer and bread', now he adds 'poetry', at once a form of labour equal to theirs, and a mark of the education and cultural authority which seems to distance him from them. The poem poses a difficult moral problem for the poet, who steers blame for the defacement of the graves away from the 'skinheads' and towards his own shameful neglect. He compares his father's routine weekly visit to honour and tidy the family graves, to his own occasional, sometimes annual, visit – a product of his problematic removal from the society and culture of his upbringing. He returns to the graves now as a middle-class revisitor, no longer part of his parents' community and class, and, although he defends his poetry as a vehicle for the voice of the disenfranchised ('to give ungrateful cunts like you a hearing!' (19)), he must also confront the notion that his education and his poetry place him at a distance from the culture which produces such graffiti.

This is the substance of an imagined conversation between himself and the skinhead author of the graffiti on his parents' grave. Harrison constructs the imaginary persona and voice of the skinhead in order to gain insight into the reasons for such vandalism, and, more importantly, into the social and cultural contexts which might explain the graffiti as the product of educational and economic deprivation. The skinhead functions as much, however, as Harrison's alter ego, a parallel version of what he might have been, perhaps, had he not been educated away from his class, had he found expression through the aerosol rather than the pen. This is suggested by the fact that the poet and skinhead share the same name. The skinhead accuses the poet of selling out – '*now yer live wi' all yer once detested*' (21) – which leaves the poet feeling alienated from his roots, and leaving for a home, far removed, which he thinks of as a safe sanctuary. His flight from the city of his upbringing is a frightened reaction to his inability to read its changed environment and culture. *v.* is a poem about crossing and recrossing class divisions. This is figured perhaps most clearly in the altering modes of the poet's speech, which crosses from an educated discourse in which French and Greek words are adopted liberally in conversation, to a dialect, 'street' language, in which the poet shortens his vowels and uses the same expletives as the skinhead, in order to 'reveal' that beneath the mask of his education lies the voice and identity of his rearing. The poet's identity and sense of belonging has been shaped by a working-class upbringing, but has then been transformed by education and by his achievements as a poet. *v.* is his attempt to read himself back into the working-class culture of his home city, but he finds that the dereliction of employment and educational opportunities which characterise the poor of 1980s Leeds are far removed from the full-employment 1950s in which he grew up. Employment, in particular, seems here to mark the difference between two generations, for where Harrison can locate himself in a genealogical line of working men, the skinhead is unemployed, and his motive for defacing the memories of the dead is his anger on '*reading on their graves the jobs they did – butcher, publican and baker ... . When dole-wallahs fuck off to the void what'll t'mason carve up for their jobs? The cunts who lieth 'ere wor unemployed?*' (18).

The defacing of memorials to the dead in *v.* symbolises not just the destructive capacities of a generation without hope, then, but also the sense of a break from the past. Harrison blames his own neglect in part for their destruction, indicating that he has allowed his own sense of continuity with his parents' generation to lapse. In the void created by this neglect, a new, desolate generation, with no sense of continuity with the past, with resentment against the emptiness of the present, engage in seemingly mindless acts of vandalism. They are seemingly mindless, Harrison implies, until one reads the underlying symptoms of a generation abandoned, with neither tradition nor future to believe in.

The poet leaves the graveyard with a grim sense of loneliness, but this is soon reworked into a determination to heal divisions and inter-generational conflicts. The two words of graffiti on his parents' grave that stick in his mind are remnants of a football slogan, 'united v.'. The poet considers that 'united', written across the names of his mother and father, may unintentionally signal their aspirations towards unity in some spiritual after-life, or indeed, it may articulate the desperate cry of the skinhead's generation who feel the tragic loss of any sense of social, cultural or political unity. Hence, too, the divisive resonances of 'v.', which symbolises for the poet all those oppositions in life and society which abound in our daily existence and are screened every night on the television news. The world described in Harrison's poem, then, is a world structured by division, conflict and opposition, but aspiring towards unity, and this is what the poet endeavours to do at the end of the poem. This itself is a sign, however, of his alienation from the culture of the 1980s skinhead, as Terry Eagleton has suggested, for the skinhead knows too well that 'the talk of "peace" and "unity" which so haunts his creator is in political terms an insulting mystification' (Eagleton 1991, 350).

v. manufactures a sense of purpose, of progress, at its conclusion, by showing the poet determined to cry out for unity in a nation riven with conflict, and by miniaturising the grief and strife of modern times as so much grist to the mill of the 'vast, slow, coal-creating forces' of nature and history (32). The poem tends towards the illusion of potential harmony, then, either forged momentarily in the poet's imagination, or seen from the widest historical panorama. It tends, in other words, to want to elide or ignore the differences between the poet and the skinhead, to walk away from those differences, rather than confront their meanings and manifestations. At this point, *v.* seems to cast poetry as the retreat from history, with the poet shrinking away from his confrontation with the hard, half-answered questions of the skinhead. If, as Neil Roberts argues, *v.* depicts the poet's attempt 'to gain privileged access to the world of the unemployed and alienated youth of the early 1980s' (Roberts 1999, 165), it is a poem which registers failure at every turn. The poet fails to find the voice and sense of belonging of the skinhead, merely the angry, reproachful ghost of his own neglect and alienation. He fails too to register the significance of the tension and conflict between his generation and the unemployed youth of Thatcher's Britain, which crystallises around divergent notions of tradition, belonging, and the past.

If the graveyard connotes the poet's sense of identity and history, it is not only a space contested by the scribblings of disaffected youth, but it is also depicted as inherently unstable grounds of any sense of belonging. It sits precariously on top of 'a worked-out pit' (9). The mineworks, once the foundations for the vibrant, industrial working class from which Harrison hails, are now shown as the volatile foundations of its graveyard. *v.* is a poem which, like Gray's *Elegy in a Country Churchyard*, mobilises the graveyard as the symbolic space of the nation, but, unlike Gray, Harrison shows the modern graveyard which is Britain to be in danger of destroying its connections with the working-class cultures and identities of the past by its decimation of the working-class cultures and identities of the present. In its faltering attempt to connect with and understand the disaffection of the 1980s generation, the poem emblematises this crisis in the national sense of belonging and sense of continuity with the past to its core.

Both *Saturday Night and Sunday Morning* and *v.* address issues of social and political division, and exemplify the formal difficulty of representing historical change. Read as attempts to locate the specific social and cultural dynamics of an emergent generation – the affluent worker of the 1950s, the unemployed vandal of the 1980s – both texts denote the complex negotiation of subject positions, historical consciousness and modes of temporal experience which make such attempts problematic. Sillitoe's novel refracts the consciousness of a 1930s generation as it struggles to come to terms with the social changes of the 1950s, while Harrison's long poem depicts the cultural and political chasm between the 1950s and 1980s generations of working-class men. The difficulties in achieving inter-generational understanding in both texts, I have argued here, signify a wider problem in constructing historical narratives, and in attempting to locate the historical consciousness of the present. In the final section of this chapter, I will explore recent attempts to historicise the contemporary, to read the cultural life of the present.

Millennial Thinking

Notions of progress in the twentieth century have increasingly centred upon paradigms of speed and acceleration. In earlier times, progress may more often have been associated with movement across expanses of space, but in terms of our contemporary emphases on transport, technology, communication and processing, the dominant model for contemporary progress is one of speed. This paradigmatic shift requires us to rethink our understandings of how the world is structured and interlinked. If, according to the mode and speed of transport one is using, it is faster to travel from New York to London, than from Edinburgh to London, how does this change our conceptual 'maps' of the space that we live in? If, furthermore, with the 'instant' technologies of fax, email, text-messaging and mobile telecommunications, 'space' is abolished altogether, how are we to understand the relationships between time and space? Have such accelerated technologies of communication made notions of spatial distance irrelevant? One could argue that at the same time our sense of the past, of the temporal, has been displaced into spatial modes of thinking, as Roger Luckhurst and Peter Marks explain: 'architecture cannibalised all past styles and displayed them together as spatially adjacent; television channel hopping made the pictorial archives of history instantly and randomly juxtaposed, fatally dislocating the continuity of historical narrative' (Luckhurst and Marks 1999, 2).

For some commentators, as discussed at the opening of this chapter, this means that we are living in a truly 'con-temporary' age, in which the past in all its forms is experienced as simultaneous to our own time, and in which our almost instantaneous connections with people in distant places have made spatial distance almost irrelevant. *Almost*, because it is advisable not to extemporise from the privileged access to computer technology and telecommunications available in a handful of rich countries for the wealthier proportions of their populations to the social, economic and cultural conditions of the human population across the globe. Time, as both Sillitoe's and Harrison's texts testify, is experienced and constructed subjectively, and is conceptualised differently in relation to varieties of social and cultural factors. The turn of the millennium in the year 2000, itself much underlined as an artificial construct, afforded some opportunities, however, for reflection on our subjective experience of time, and on processes of historicisation. It represents, in one sense, a site of contest and conflict, not only in the competing political and religious meanings attributed to it, but also in a clash of temporal modes. On the one hand, the acceleration of time in the cultures of Western modernity places increasing emphasis on the ephemerality, contingency, and instability of historical narratives. On the other hand, the approach of a 'momentous' turn in chronological history generated much speculation about the grand narratives of historical evolution, about how we historicise our own sense of identity and belonging in relation to those narratives. Two texts published in 1999, and with special relevance to the millennium fever of that year, Simon Armitage's *Killing Time* (1999) and Peter Ackroyd's *The Plato Papers* (1999), may help us to understand better the particular conjunctions of time and narrative, identity and transformation, which this moment in the modern calendar was supposed to represent.

Armitage was commissioned in January 1999 as the 'official millennium poet', or, as he was soon mistakenly dubbed, 'the Dome poet'. The commission, funded jointly by the New Millennium Experience Company and the Poetry Society, entailed writing a thousand-line poem, which would be published in book form and broadcast on radio and television by the end of 1999. The result is *Killing Time*, in which Armitage reflects on the news events of 1999, and reports in verse on the 'state of the nation'. The poem is broken into sections – some are single quatrains, some are long cantos – which imitate the structure of a television news broadcast, using the language of news bulletin links ('meanwhile') and concluding with the familiar phrase 'and finally', the end piece of the ITN channel's 'News at Ten'. It considers events such as the Colorado high-school shootings, the Paddington rail crash, the solar eclipse, the London nail-bombings, Kosovo, and the preparations for celebration on the eve of the new millennium, while at the same time satirising and parodying the means by which news broadcasts convert daily occurrences into narrative entertainment. In this sense, Armitage is indebted to his poetic precursors, Louis MacNeice and W.H. Auden, who satirised the emergent forms of mass broadcast media in the 1930s, and whose voices and forms echo through Armitage's poem.

Killing Time combines an occasional foray into dreamy optimism – when the poet imagines the Colorado boys giving flowers to their classmates instead of shooting them, or when he imagines how much better life would look from a balloon – with a heavier and more pervasive note of cynicism. The latter note is present right from the prefatory poem, which imagines a sandwich-board man carrying the gloomy phrase 'NO NEWS IS GOOD NEWS' (Armitage 1999, i), and continues through persistent MacNeicean images of war and desolation: 'and the thing we are told / was a thing of the past is coming up once more like the dawn, / and it is dark, and it is cold' (7). Millennial thinking, in Armitage's poem, is more likely to dwell on the haunting return of the horrors of the past than on the achievements or progress of humanity. War, with its attendant images of bombed cities, emaciated bodies, and columns of straggling refugees, is the dreaded spectre casting its dark shadow over millennium celebrations. This is no trite moral caution against celebration. The deliberate inflection of images towards death, starvation, poverty, and war casts a cold, grim light on what all the millennium celebrations are about. Armitage may send up a few optimistic balloons of his own, but, for the most part, his poem repeatedly punctures the balloons of millennial contentment.

In the cantos, *Killing Time* can sometimes mime too closely the journalese which it satirises, and it lapses occasionally into

Larkinesque cliché ('we could do worse' (18)) and wry amusement ('last week in a West Yorkshire village / nothing happened at all' (52)). In contrast, the pithy quatrains which punctuate the cantos exercise savage twists out of the language of reportage, turning a statistic or a statement suddenly into grim irony or sardonic wit:

> This season, luggage containing terrible thoughts
>   was left in Brixton, Soho and Brick Lane,
> the kind which scatters the baggage of one man's mind
>   into the public's brain. (Armitage 1999, 28)

These lines allude to bombs placed in parts of London renowned as centres of either gay or ethnic minority cultures, bombs which the poet imagines as the explosion of racist and homophobic thoughts into public discourse. Such lines are engaging in a process of thinking through the wider implications and meanings of newsworthy events, and this, in part, is what Armitage's poem is doing – telling the news, but with the length and depth of perspective, and with the metaphorical and symbolic resonances of a literary text. The poem is 'timely', in this sense, for its allusion here to the brief, one-man bombing campaign in London is indicative of the way that it feeds off topical events. It may depend too closely, in other words, upon its contemporaneity with the events it represents, and function as a kind of poetic review of the news highlights of the year.

The sense of time, of temporal flow, in the poem is somewhat more complex than its parody of news bytes would suggest, however. Armitage pauses for contemplation about the nature of time, imagining it (after Heaney, perhaps) as 'the great geology', packed tight in layers, awaiting us to 'uncurl the stubborn fist of what is gone' (30–1). So too, even those topical images occasionally glimpse into the greater cosmological or historical abyss. A 'silver spoon' at the table of millennium celebrants 'collects the constellations in its palm' (45). The wreck of the train crash outside Paddington station suddenly bears the imprint of the holocaust, with 'its ghostly freight of warm, weightless ash' (27). *Killing Time* is rooted firmly in the events of 1999, but, in keeping with its brief, the poem steals furtive glances at what it calls 'the great, revolving permanence of humankind' (32). There, the poet finds that one war resembles another, one image of refugees tracks seamlessly into the next, one century bleeds its dead onto the pages of the next century's history. If the millennium festivities encourage confidence in the 'permanence' of humankind, the poet is also remarking on the grim repetitiveness of its violent history, as if the revolving globe defined the condition of our history. This explains the prevalence of metaphors of flight in the poem, as the poet struggles to imagine ways of escaping from the spinning maelstrom of history.

At times, as in Tony Harrison's *v.*, the poet seems to want to step outside of history, to rise above 'the sink estates and the island tax-havens' (18), to miniaturise the turbulent, messy events of human life by looking down upon them from a distant vantage point. This is implied too in the poem's affirmation of the biblical view that 'one day is with the Lord as a thousand years, and a thousand years as one day' (39). Armitage has fun with this idea by imagining various figures of human history – Hitler, Attila, Stalin, Shakespeare, Florence Nightingale – spliced into ironic situations in contemporary culture. So too, the images and events of the past collide and metamorphose into one another – a 'bright star over the Middle East' is 'the burn of a cruise missile' (5), for example. The poem continually folds moments in time into one another, representing imagistically the local and temporal particularity of a topical event only then to collapse it into a protracted, historical jumble.

The news images of Armitage's poem rush past, imitating the accelerated narratives of a televisual culture, in which history has become a seamless, randomly sequenced blur. Poetry seems antithetical to this culture, on one level, especially in this commission, which was intended to create a pause for contemplating the meanings of a particular moment amidst frantic celebrations. But the poem imitates the speed of the postmodern hyperreal, not the slow time of contemplation. Its rhythm has it rattling through the year, through the millennium, with only occasional pauses to ask, 'what if?' or 'couldn't we just?'. Imitation and parody are its modes of operation, not distant reflection, and hence, in the penultimate section of the poem, Armitage takes as the final register of the millennium an escaped lyre-bird, another refugee from the Balkans. The lyrebird impersonates surrounding sounds, like the poet, and, 'when finally caught and put on the spot', it blurts out the following sequence of sounds:

> boots marching on tarmac,
> razor wire shredding the breeze,
> the onward grinding of tank-tracks
> through deserted streets. (Armitage 1999, 50)

Armitage's poem records and blurts out the same discomforting impersonations of human history, and proffers an image of the present that bears haunting resemblances to the horrors of the past. The relationship between poetry and history in *Killing Time* is one not of reflection or mimesis, but mimicry, as it parodies the history of a millennium as a series of grim, tawdry news bytes. Like the lyrebird, the poem displays that striking capacity of mimicry to disturb and delight us, simply by stepping in time with its subject, parroting its every utterance, chirping away the sounds of our daily tragedies and body counts. It is against this sound of incessant chirping that Armitage optimistically imagines that at the moment of cork-popping revelry, the revellers 'detect instead':

> a silence so profound it figures on the Richter scale,
>   as if the dead
> from every age had risen from their hundred billion graves
>   to speak a word
> so soundlessly and noiselessly, that even in deep space
>   it was heard. (Armitage 1999, 46)

The grand narratives of human history constructed around the approaching millennium celebrations are also considered and parodied in Peter Ackroyd's *The Plato Papers* (1999).

Plato is an orator in the city of London in c.AD 3700, who gathers the citizens to listen to his narratives of the city's ancient history and cultures, and to debate with them the meanings of the past, especially the 'Mouldwarp' era, AD 1500–2300. Ackroyd plays with the fiction of examining our society and culture from a distant future, with Plato reading the fragments of nineteenth- and twentieth-century writings for evidence of the poverty and folly of how we perceive the world. This includes a delightful reading of *On the Origin of the Species* as a satirical novel by Charles Dickens, a lecture on E.A. Poe's gothic tales as histories of American culture, and one on *Jokes and their Relation to the Unconscious* as 'a comic handbook', authored by the famous comedian, Freud. Plato's comic readings of our contemporary culture function partly by applying the same method of speculative extrapolation from fragmented texts which characterise our own historiography. They function partly too by applying a kind of 'Martian' naïvety to twentieth-century phrases, so that 'rock music' is interpreted as the 'sound of old stones', 'sunstroke' as 'the death of the sun', and 'common sense' as 'a theory that all human beings might be able to share one another's thoughts, so that there would in reality be only one person upon the earth' (Ackroyd 2000, 24; 25; 13). Such devices enable Ackroyd to satirise modern modes of historical knowledge, and to ridicule the pretensions of late twentieth-century society. They also highlight the interdependence of history and textuality. Ackroyd reveals the twentieth century to itself here in textual form, parodying what a 'thick description' of the textual fragments of the present might look like. *The Plato Papers*, for this reason, resembles the allegorical fictions of Samuel Butler's *Erewhon* (1872) or H.G. Wells's *The Time Machine* (1895).

Plato, of course, is not just a fictional orator of a distant future, but resembles the ancient philosopher. The novel imitates the forms of Plato the philosopher's discourse – dialogues, oratory and definitions – and suggests therefore the ways in which past and future are interchangeable. So too, the London of the future is one in which the place names of its constituent villages appear to have been reconnected to their original referents, and the shape of the city appears to resemble its medieval form. The city appears to be flowing backwards in time. Ackroyd proposes an alternative model of temporal experience than the chronological one which dominates modern discourses of knowledge. Plato is both a distant ancestor and a remote descendant, and he comes to the shocking realisation towards the end of the novel that the laughable Mouldwarp civilisation is also contemporaneous with his own, hidden, like Wells's 'Morlocks', in a vast subterranean cavern. *The Plato Papers* collapses temporal and spatial distance here, so that cultures and civilisations which appear to be remote from each other are suddenly contemporaneous and coexistent. This is a consistent feature of Ackroyd's writing, a concern with temporal flow, with the ways in which 'the past is penetrating the present ... [and] manifests itself in the present' (for example Gibson and Wolfreys 2000, 229). Time in *The Plato Papers* is neither linear nor cyclical, but interchronistic, in which past, present and future are constantly relocated in relation to each other, often in spectral, psychodynamic forms. Plato first becomes conscious of the contemporaneity of the Mouldwarp peoples when he encounters their presence as ghosts. In part, Ackroyd seems to be responding to the possibilities explored in contemporary theoretical physics on temporal reversibility, parallel states of time, and other forms of temporal disruption, and creating from these possibilities the notion of a present which is constantly interconnected to, and contemporaneous with, forms of the past and future. Plato's growing realisation in *The Plato Papers* is that the world he inhabits is neither synchronic nor as self-present as its citizens arrogantly presume. When he is tried in court, on charges of corrupting the young with talk of his visions of other worlds, he issues a caution against such arrogance: 'I know that other ages, like that of Mouldwarp, refused to countenance or understand any reality but their own' (133).

Like Armitage, then, Ackroyd bears a sobering parable of the limitations of contemporary culture, a refracted image of its faults and conceits. Ackroyd does this through a fiction of the future anteriority of our culture, and then he further subverts the conceptions of progress and historical perspective which give the lie to millennial pomp and complacency. The historical perspective in Ackroyd's novel is presented as a fiction of seeing the past as a finished product, which is gradually subverted when Plato realises that the past is both seamlessly continuous with the present, and, paradoxically, irreducibly 'other'. History in *The Plato Papers* is far from over. In fact, it appears that we are only beginning to see the diverse, paradoxical forms in which what we have conceived as 'the past' continues to affect and disturb the time of the present. Ackroyd presents us with a conception of time and history which does not resolve into a vacuous 'permanent present', but is instead a radically disjunctive, interchronistic notion, which begins to delineate the complexity of temporal experience. In historicising our own time, he shows the necessity for re-imagining the relationship between the past and the present, between history and identity. The past has not disappeared, as Plato discovers, but its dislocated, shifting modes of presence in contemporary culture have found expression, and have begun to be conceived and articulated in many forms of postwar literature.

Notes

1. See Francis Fukuyama, *The End of History and the Last Man* (London: Penguin, 1992) and Fredric Jameson, *Postmodernism, or the Cultural Logic of Late Capitalism* (London: Verso, 1991).
2. Sinfield is referring to evidence produced by Tom Harrisson in *Living Through the Blitz* (Harmondsworth: Penguin, 1978), 323–27.
3. See Catherine Lanone, 'Scattering the Seed of Abraham: The Motif of

Sacrifice in Pat Barker's *Regeneration* and *The Ghost Road'*, *Literature and Theology*, vol. 13, no. 3 (September 1999), 259–68.

4. The myth of a new class structure, in which a new class formation, the affluent worker, had emerged, became widespread in the 1950s and early 1960s. See J.K. Galbraith, *The Affluent Society* (London: Hamish Hamilton, 1958), Vernon Bogdanor and Robert Skidelsky (eds), *The Age of Affluence 1951–1964* (London: Macmillan, 1970), and John H. Goldthorpe, David Lockwood, Frank Bechhofer and Jennifer Platt, *The Affluent Worker: Cambridge Studies in Sociology Vols. 1–3* (Cambridge, UK: Cambridge University Press, 1963–9). See also my chapter on working-class writing of the 1950s which contested this myth in *Literature, Culture and Society in England, 1945–1965* (Edwin Mellen Press, 2002).

5. See the second edition of the poem, published in 1989, which includes extracts and quotations from the media response to the poem. Much of the controversy centred around the abundant use of words like 'fuck' and 'cunt' in the poem, and prompted arguments about the role of poetry.

3 A Literature of Farewell: the condition of England and the politics of elegy

> And that will be England gone,
> The shadows, the meadows, the lanes,
> The guildhalls, the carved choirs.
> There'll be books; it will linger on
> In galleries, but all that remains
> For us will be concrete and tyres.
> Philip Larkin, 'Going, Going' (1972)

In *Midnight's Children* (1981), Salman Rushdie uses the metaphor of the ticking clock, or what he describes as 'the metronome music of Mountbatten's countdown calendar' (Rushdie 1995, 106), to mark the final hours of British rule in India, before the midnight hour, when Nehru steps forward to proclaim that while the world sleeps, 'India awakens to life and freedom' (116). The 'tick tock' of Indian independence, its 'year zero', Rushdie implies, is the countdown of demise for Mountbatten and the British Empire: 'English-made, it [Mountbatten's clock] beats with relentless accuracy. And now the factory is empty; fumes linger, but the vats are still' (106). The manufacturing metaphor is especially apt, as the imagery of industrial closure and waste has become central to the portrait of England in decline. Rushdie here contrasts, and suggests a causal link between, the nascent narrative of post-colonial nationalism and the valedictory narrative of the post-imperial nation. Post-imperial 'time' obeys a distinct and doleful rhythm compared to the vibrant, youthful beat of the post-colonial clock, and while dawn breaks over the new India, another sun sets on the British Empire. The consequence for discourses and narratives of post-imperial English identity is the generation of a language and literature of 'farewell', in which the past becomes not merely the source for the legitimation of present cultural identities, but becomes the lost 'home' of those cultural identities. Far from legitimating modern expressions of Englishness, representations of the past in contemporary British fiction tend to make such expressions seem remote, alien and anachronistic. In the course of this chapter, I want to examine not only fictional representations of this process in which the past renders Englishness obsolete, but also those fictions which depict the contemporary anomic state of Englishness.

Contemporary British fiction, according to Ian Jack in his editorial for *Granta* in winter 1996 (the issue entitled 'What Happened to Us?'), has become preoccupied with themes of loss, disappearance, remembrance and nostalgia. Jack was one of the Booker prize judges in 1996, and commented on how surprised he was 'by how many new English novels (and new English novelists) were preoccupied with the past ... with the country and people that seemed to be there a minute ago, before we blinked and turned away' (Jack 1996, 8). Jack called this new wave of English writing, which signalled the passing of a way of life, a nation, a culture, unsentimentally and casually, 'the literature of farewell'. Yet entangled in this literature is a paradox which seems also to ensnare Rushdie's *Midnight's Children*. Rushdie's narrator, Saleem Sinai, writes out the history of his life, which is also the history of his nation, precisely at the moment that he believes he and his nation are falling apart. So too, Ian Jack's argument implies, contemporary British fiction has become obsessed with telling stories of Englishness and the shadows of England's past at exactly the moment that England is disappearing. Never has the gaze of the English writer been stronger, but she or he now surveys the landscape of the post-imperial aporia – the ubiquitous signs of slippage, decline, corruption and lost prestige – with a mournful, backward stare. That writers such as Graham Swift, Pat Barker, Kazuo Ishiguro and Martin Amis began to do this at a time when 'official' Englishness was reasserting and re-staging its lost imperial identity, when Thatcherism seemed to be defined, as Simon Gikandi argues, 'by the need to take stock of that which no longer exists' (Gikandi 1996, 21), gives added impetus to inquire into the *politics* of the 'literature of farewell', which I will pursue later in this chapter.

While post-colonial writers may treat, however sceptically, of the newness which emergent nationalism seeks to bring into being, contemporary British writers are, according to Malcolm Bradbury, picking over the traces and rubble of history. Bradbury laments the fact that contemporary fiction has settled into a tone of 'retrospective poeticized nostalgia', or, where nostalgia has been supplanted, a diet of 'constant bitter battles of generation, gender, class, ethnic and regional identity, new wars over representation, all presided over by an anxious atmosphere of disorder, terror or gothic extremity' (Bradbury 1994, 458). Bradbury is not alone in diagnosing the current preoccupation with the irretrievable security of England past, or with the intolerable aporia of the present, as the most lamentable cultural symptoms of the decline in political power and national identity. Others have ascribed the reasons for this 'literature of farewell' to the apathy of writers who are content to add to the myths of 'the world we have lost' (McCrum, *Bookseller* 1980), or to the time-warp conservatism of the British publishing industry (Buford, *Granta* 1980), or simply to the fact that contemporary British writers cannot achieve the cultural certainties and literary prowess of the Victorians (Taylor 1994) or the Modernists (Lodge 1977). But the apathy, conservatism or the technical mediocrity of writers and publishers, if this was indeed the case, does not yet explain the preponderance in contemporary British writing of elegiac prose, condition of England novels, historical fictions and valedictory narratives. It is a further aim of this chapter, then, to explore the reasons for the forms of storytelling which contemporary British fiction has adopted and preferred, to explain therefore why contemporary writers are preoccupied with themes of history, memory, death, and disorder.

Among the English

According to D.J. Taylor in *After the War* (1994), the defining characteristic of the literature of the postwar period is its consciousness of decline, a characteristic which Taylor sees reflected not merely in the tone and content of postwar fiction, but also in its lack of technical and formal skill, so that for Taylor to read postwar fiction is 'to become conscious of a precipitous decline' (Taylor 1994, 75). The reason for this sense of decline is evident from Taylor's view of postwar literature, which he caricatures as 'a debased and decadent animal, creeping along in the shadow of mighty ancestors' (Taylor 1994, 289). In short, Taylor imagines the writers of postwar Britain overshadowed and stifled by the weight and power of English literary and cultural tradition. The dead weigh down on the backs of the living, or as Harold Bloom wrote in *The Anxiety of Influence*, our 'precursors flood us, and our imagination can die by drowning in them' (Bloom 1973, 154). But if we accept Bloom's affirmation of Borges's aphorism that every writer creates his own precursors, the tradition of 'mighty ancestors', to which Taylor refers, is invented and fostered by the very postwar writers who appear to be overshadowed by it. The 'consciousness of decline', then, is as much a fiction created and promoted by postwar writers as it is the consequence of comparing their supposedly meagre talents with that of their ancestors.

The 'tick tock' of English nationalism as it appears in contemporary British fiction is, then, the sound of a last gasp, like the apocalyptic rhythm which beats through Martin Amis's *London Fields*. But with this last gasp comes the desire to seek out and find the embodiment of contemporary Englishness, and for a number of contemporary writers, this takes the form of seeking out the representative identity, the atomised, oblivious individual who encompasses and defines for his age the meaning of late twentieth-century Englishness. Amis's narrator in *London Fields*, Samson Young, for example, claims to understand the English by understanding Keith Talent, the darts-playing, beer-drinking, street-trading protagonist of the novel. Talent is a study in the emerging class of ambitious, enterprising con-men who embrace wholeheartedly the consumerist logic of Thatcherite capitalism, and yet are also its victims. In his antipathy to 'cheating' (indeed, he heralds darts as one of the few games which cannot be cheated), he appears to embody the 'traditional' English values of decency and fair play, but this is an ironic depiction, as Keith Talent is also a compulsive, if not altogether successful, crook. Keith is also shown to apply himself energetically to various tasks, seeming to represent the virtues of hard work, but mostly his tasks include burglary, philandering and darts. There is much humour, particularly ironic, in Amis's depiction of the new model of English working-class masculinity which seemed to prosper in the 1980s, but there is also a great deal of contempt, which is channelled through the American narrator in order to construct the appearance of coming from an external, anthropological perspective:

> I wish to Christ I could do Keith's voice [the narrator says]. The *t*'s are viciously stressed. A brief guttural pop, like the first nanosecond of a cough or a hawk, accompanies the hard *k*. When he says *chaotic*, and

he says it frequently, it sounds like a death rattle. 'Month' comes out as *mumf.* He sometimes says, 'Im feory ...' when he speaks theoretically. 'There' sounds like *dare* or *lair*. You could often run away with the impression that Keith Talent is eighteen months old. (Amis 1990, 26)

There is, of course, a degree of wonder and condescending affection in the narrator's description of Keith Talent, as there might be of any description of a cute and curious new species, but mostly Keith Talent is the butt of ferocious, class-ridden caricature. He is, in many ways, a comic exaggeration of middle-class fears of the lurking violence and shiftiness of the urban proletariat, the darker side of the 'Del boy' stereotype. Through the dying eyes of the American narrator, Keith becomes the 'John Bull' of his generation, the defining image of Englishness, and, furthermore, set in the apocalyptic contexts which the narrator is constantly evoking, the scapegoat for everyone else's moral decrepitude. The narrator comments on how even the babies in England are dressed as if they are old; everything in the novel, in fact, appears to be preparing for death, with the exception of Keith, who constantly displays his zest for life, but whose every move and word ultimately, as D.J. Taylor argues, is borrowed from tabloids and soaps, or indeed manipulated by Amis's femme fatale, Nicola Six (Taylor 1994, 192).

Amis's construction of Englishness through the character of Keith Talent is deeply ambivalent, not least because of the complicated series of ironies and caricatures which go into his making. It is, at the end of the novel, not Keith who is either the murderer or the child-abuser, as he is suggested to be at various points in the novel. He is, in short, not all that bad, and at the conclusion, is as much an object of pity as of scorn. He is, after all, only a mild version of a more extreme prototypical English male who became the subject of much political and media attention in the last two decades – the 'thug', or soccer hooligan. Bill Buford describes his search for this phenomenon in his book, *Among the Thugs* (1991), which begins with the notion that across England every Saturday a ritual took place which was central to contemporary English culture – so central in fact that it went unremarked – the habitual looting, rioting and violence which surrounded the customary football match. As an American living in England, Buford is able to achieve the same sense of disinterested anthropological curiosity in England as Amis channels through his American narrator, and it allows him to establish from the beginning how odd it is that the football hooligan – the purveyor of weekly anarchy – seemed to melt anonymously and invisibly into English society and culture, unexamined. Buford's own anthropological quest, then, uncovers the following specimen, who is treated as representative of a section of people who have become synonymous with English working-class culture:

> He had a fat, flat bulldog face and was extremely large. His T-shirt had inched its way up his belly and was discoloured by something sticky and dark. The belly itself was a tub of sorts, swirling, I would discover, with litres and litres of lager, partly-chewed chunks of fried potato and moist, undigested balls of over-processed carbohydrate. His arms – puffy, doughy things – were stained with tattoos. On his right bicep was an image of the Red Devils, the logo of the Manchester United team; on his forearm, a Union Jack. (Buford 1997, 25–6)

Mick, as Buford calls him, is not as predisposed to violence as some of his fellows, whom Buford meets later, but he encapsulates the lifestyles and attitudes of his class. The side of this prototypical 'hooligan' figure that we see here is merely the unhealthy and tasteless, but Buford trawls through its nasty sides – the relentless violence, aggressive racism and voracious appetite for destruction – at first in order to explain it as the understandable consequence of poor material circumstances, but finally he can only catalogue the depth and strength of aggression and leave with the impression of the dark crudity of what he calls the 'miserable nationalism' of late twentieth-century England (Buford 1997, 317).

In John King's trilogy of novels on football hooligans, the 'thugs' embody the most energetic expressions of national identity in contemporary England, particularly in the final novel, *England Away* (1998). King projects a vision of contemporary meanings and manifestations of Englishness through the thoughts and actions of three characters, two of whom, Harry and Tom, are travelling with an 'army' of football fans across Europe, while the other character, Bill, sits in a pub contemplating his experiences as a veteran of World War Two. Harry and Tom imagine their violent rampages through Holland and Germany as the echoed spirits of the English troops fighting fifty years earlier, echoes which help to establish Tom's conviction that

Englishness is a militant, proud stubbornness in the face of adversity. Like Keith Talent in *London Fields*, Tom's characterisations of Englishness are borrowed from tabloid editorials and easy clichés – the English are 'fair and square', 'don't make a fuss', and are 'an island race' – and his expressions of patriotism are churned out like advertising slogans – 'England united shall never be defeated', 'Come and have a go if you think you're hard enough', and 'Two world wars and one world cup'. What perhaps distinguishes both Tom and Harry from Keith Talent is their own awareness of the process by which media imagery and political rhetoric shape and manipulate their consciousness. Indeed, part of their enjoyment of being 'away' from England is that they can escape the media bombardment which they consider to be part of the claustrophobia engulfing England. Even though Tom's patriotism is borrowed from tabloids, and Harry's from old war films, both recognise the hypocrisy of the media which incites the worst excesses of xenophobic expression from them, breeding into them a national self-consciousness which is predicated on the myth of the natural island race, yet also denounces their kind as Nazi thugs who soil the name of Englishness. Beneath Tom's resentment of the media image of 'thugs' lies also a suspicion of class prejudice, whereby 'it's okay for the Spice Girls to wear Union Jack dresses and for magazines to put it on their covers, and for the knobs who go to the last night of the proms, but if it's us lot with the Union Jack or the Cross of St George, then we're automatically Nazis' (King 1998, 44). King's 'thugs' imagine themselves as the heirs of the spirit of Britain evoked from the Second World War, thus as the rightful ambassadors of the legend and reputation of England, and not the vandals and fascists which they are represented to be. But the novel also sets the behaviour of Tom and Harry against the context of World War Two in order to signify that England's 'thugs' are an inevitable consequence of its past, the last vestiges of a post-imperial hangover, in which its citizens can only express their patriotism through racism and violence.

King constructs his characters principally through interior mono- logue, and, in contrast to Amis and Buford, these latter-day 'John Bulls' are not judged morally by a narrative perspective external and superior to them. There is, nevertheless, a series of external perspec- tives within the novel, including the implied attitudes of the media and the refraction of Tom and Harry's behaviour abroad through the lens of Bill's war experiences, which enable the reader to set Tom and

Harry within moral and political contexts other than the ones they offer themselves. In Amis and Buford, distance is maintained between the narrative and the subject by sustaining a controlled narrative posture of ironic observation, which lends itself to the genre of anthropological study, or even, more simply, to that most imperial of genres, travel writing. The particular manifestations of contemporary Englishness which are scrutinised by Amis's narrator and by Buford emerge in consequence as the alienated and eccentric objects of a tourist's gaze, an effect which Ian Bell has noted in contemporary travel writings as the 'transformation of Britain into a kind of theme park' (Bell 1995, 25), and which in turn Julian Barnes satirises in *England, England* (1998). In contrast, King's characters, because they are narrated from an interior perspective, tend to resist the impression of England as a dying force, even when other perspectives in the novel construct them as symptomatic of post-imperial degeneracy.

The interiority of King's characters gives his narrative the force of a testimony, a testimony to the state and meaning of Englishness. England, Harry tells us, is in his blood (King 1998, 103); it inhabits him, but it is most exposed and animated only when it is forced into conflict with otherness. In retracing the meanings of Englishness 'away', King therefore reconstructs the imperialist formation of 'England' through the perpetual imagination of England's 'others'. But perhaps what is most exposed in King's narrative is, to borrow Fredric Jameson's phrase, the 'situational consciousness' of his characters (Jameson 1986), their incessant need to relate their own individual identities to the collective, to tell their story through the group identity. This, ultimately, is the vulnerability of King's characters, not their shallow addiction to the aggressive consumption of sex, alcohol and violence, but their compulsive dependence on the authority of a mythic national identity.

Kazuo Ishiguro explored a very different sense of Englishness in *The Remains of the Day* (1989), but used a similar interior perspective to construct (and indeed, like King, to deconstruct) the insular voice of national belonging. Ishiguro's novel functions as an allegory of the state of Englishness, not merely in the knowing detail of exchanging an English master for an American one after the war, but also in the ways in which the first person narrator, Stevens, defines his own character in relation to the characteristics he associates most with England – dignified, undemonstrative, understated, and dutiful. The language he uses, the behaviour he adopts, even his faithful devotion to the requirements of his narrative exhibit these characteristics, and so appear to conserve in impeccable form (as a museum piece, perhaps) a working example of a dying character. Stevens's narrative, of his life as a butler in a great English house, is often stiflingly restrained, incapable even with the distance and security of time to break the habit of reserve, politeness and modesty. As Miss Kenton acknowledges when she asks why Stevens must always pretend, Stevens's identity is comprised of a mask which is now indistinguishable from his self. Indeed, the very notion that it is a mask is merely the benevolent speculation of Miss Kenton, and perhaps also of Ishiguro, the only evidence for which comes at the end of the narrative when Stevens breaks down in tears when telling the story of his life to a stranger he meets on a pier at Weymouth. Stevens is preoccupied in his narrative with the meaning of 'greatness', and the dignity of his service to his master, but fails to confront the legacy of his master's collaboration with the Nazis in the war. Lurking somewhere in Stevens's consciousness is the knowledge that his master has betrayed the very ideals of loyalty, service and dignity, for which he, Stevens, has sacrificed any ounce of his self-worth. This, Salman Rushdie argues, is the power of Ishiguro's narrative, the magnificent balance of a narrative that is perfectly, stiflingly 'still', and yet at the same time seems to burst with the awful truth that Stevens is conscious of his whole life as a futile, servile lie.

The implications of the national allegory are, at the same time, hard to avoid. Stevens serves his American master in a house which employs a skeleton staff to do no more than preserve the house in order. The old skills and traits of character which Stevens prizes above all, and believes are responsible for the success of the house prior to the war, prove to be redundant. His American master does not want dignity, nor duty, nor reserve, it seems, merely what Stevens calls 'banter', which Stevens finds difficult. Once the house has ceased to be great, the whole edifice of character, lifestyle and heritage crumble. Without its greatness, Darlington Hall loses its very identity, as it spirals in stature from the house at which is decided the business and politics of Europe, indeed the fate of the whole continent prior to the war, to the isolated, occasional holiday retreat of an American businessman. The allegory is poignant, as Stevens tours England for the first time in his life, and finds that instead of the busy hub of a global empire, England has become the sum total of what its landscape can offer to visiting tourists – 'the very *lack* of obvious drama or spectacle that sets the beauty of our land apart' (Ishiguro 1990, 28). And if the greatness of the English landscape is defined by an absence, so too is, in Stevens's mind, the greatness of English identity dependent on an absence – the absence of anything but the performance of an identity. Stevens measures the greatness of the English butler as opposed to the Continental or Celtic in terms of a racial distinction between the capacity of Englishmen to 'inhabit their professional role', and the inability of the foreigner to 'maintain a professional demeanour' at all (Ishiguro 1990, 42–3). Englishness, according to Stevens, is characterised by dissimulation, by the pretence of absence, a fitting description of an identity which Ishiguro depicts, akin to Dean Acheson, of being lost without its imperial power.

Stevens's own sense of loss and bewilderment is exacerbated when he tours the English countryside in his master's car. Like the prototypical English traveller, he sets out to discover England as it is represented in a travel book, *The Wonders of England* by Mrs Jane Symons, which has clearly fed his imagination of the English landscape and habitat while he has been isolated in Darlington Hall. The journey which he undertakes, ostensibly to discover if his former housekeeper, Miss Kenton, will agree to be re-employed in the house, causes him some degree of discomfort, not least because he is frequently filled with the feeling of being lost, or disorientated. He compares this feeling with that of finally losing sight of land on a sea voyage, and on other occasions with being a stranger in a wilderness, both of which serve as metaphors for his sense of dislocation. While this has the effect of turning his travels through the beauty spots of the English landscape into a voyage of discovery, this is nothing compared to his disorientation on meeting some of the local people of these far-flung English villages. In the most sustained encounter between Stevens and such locals, Stevens's stiff sense of what it means to be English meets with an uneasy contrast in a cottage in Devon. One of the locals, Harry Smith, defends vociferously the right and duty of every Englishman to exercise his freedoms, and declares that 'there's no dignity to be had in being a slave' (Ishiguro 1990, 186), a libertarian definition of 'dignity' which runs contrary to Stevens's equation of dignity with service and loyalty. On more than one occasion, Stevens finds his own sense of Englishness disturbed and contradicted by the English villagers and farmers he meets on his travels, not least when in this same encounter the locals have the impression, conveniently overlooked by Stevens, that he is a master, not a servile butler. At stake in the competing definitions of dignity offered by Harry Smith and Stevens is the social and political status of the English, as citizens on the one hand, or subjects on the other, and Ishiguro implies a dangerous and slippery continuity between Stevens's acceptance of the authority of his superiors, and his master's collaboration with Nazism. If Stevens begins the novel as the familiar voice of a certain type of Englishness, the reserved, restrained gentleman, he concludes the novel, as Steven Connor has argued, with 'the possibility that there is no plausible addressee at all to his narrative' (Connor 1996, 112):

> The hard reality is, surely, that for the likes of you and I, there is little choice other than to leave our fate, ultimately, in the hands of those great gentlemen at the hub of the world who employ our services. (Ishiguro 1990, 244)

Stevens is ultimately so out of joint with his own time, so anachronistic a characterisation of Englishness, that Ishiguro depicts him ironically, pathetically, addressing a reader who could only be the mirror image of himself. Ishiguro perhaps demonstrates, as Doris Lessing remarks in *In Pursuit of the English* (1980), that whenever one tries to bring the English under scrutiny, they seem to vanish (Lessing 1980, 7).

The 'thug' and the butler are, perhaps, idiosyncratic expressions of particular versions of twentieth-century Englishness, which caricature the national stereotype in the way that they telescope the perceived meanings and manifestations of Englishness into an exaggerated and fixated representation. The effect in each case, arguably, is the production of an over-determined identity, which seems always to announce itself as a false consciousness, as a mask which has been adopted and appropriated unconsciously from the available discourses of national identity. In Graham Swift's first novel, *The Sweet Shop Owner* (1980), it is an understated national stereotype which is explored and disclosed, the myth of the nation of shopkeepers. Willy Chapman devotes himself to running his sweet shop earnestly, modestly and cautiously, maintaining a steady stock of reliable lines of sweets, and introducing new ideas and ranges gradually and carefully. He is the embodiment of the conservative, prudent caretaker, who nurses his business into slow, humble growth without any show of excess, zeal or enthusiasm. The sweet shop symbolises more than the caretaking conservatism of postwar England, however. Willy's wife buys him the shop with the money she has inherited from her uncles, who died, she tells him, like skittles in the First World War. The shop is thus described by Willy as a memorial, an inheritance which is ghosted by the sacrifice of a generation. Willy's narrative is punctuated by such sacrifices, and by the heavy burden of indebtedness which they bequeath on the living. And beneath the feeling of indebtedness is also the uneasy suspicion that the dead generations of the past have left nothing but their money to the living. The world of Willy, and his wife Irene, and their daughter, Dorry, appears to be strangely absent of love. Irene's gift to Willy of his shop is represented as a transaction which substitutes for love, their love-making itself the obligation of a contract between them. Willy asks of Dorry in his ponderous narrative to her: 'If the word love is never spoken, does it mean there isn't any love?' (Swift 1997, 116), a question which reverberates through Ishiguro's *The Remains of the Day* also.

Swift's novel depicts the England which emerged out of both the First and Second World Wars as spiritually and mentally exhausted, a world in which nothing remained to be imagined or dreamed, in which, as Willy says, everything is a performance. Willy constructs himself as a plausible shopkeeper, whom his customers can believe in as a guarantor of order, of security, as the purveyor of newspapers, chocolate, cigarettes. He sells them the useless, trivial consumables which are the very emblems of ephemerality and transience, while he stands like a mannequin in what he has crafted for himself as his memorial. Memorials 'don't belong to us', he tells Dorry, 'They are only things we leave behind so we can vanish safely. Disguises to set us free' (Swift 1997, 221). His life, as with the life of his wife, Irene, has been merely a preparation for the disappearing act of death, a mournful passage of the empty time left in the wake of war. While Willy's narrative marks the passing of historical events – the wars, assassinations and crises, the slumps and the booms of the postwar economy – it is the steady litany of the dying which beats out the rhythm of his narrative more faithfully, overshadowing his own life with the unending obligations of remembrance and homage, and anticipating his own death. But Willy is a ghost throughout his narrative, apparently speaking from his death bed, but actually speaking in the language of the already dead – 'You touch nothing, nothing touches you' (Swift 1997, 44). He becomes, by his very spectrality, his sense of the ghostly absence of meaning and action, a metaphor for the disembodied, ethereal subjectivity of the atrophied nation – England's ruined and haunting Greece to America's imperial Rome, to adapt Macmillan's famous characterisation of postwar England.

In Swift's novel, then, the nation of shopkeepers has become the nation of shop window mannequins, the performance of an identity behind which there is nothing but the empty, frivolous legacy of the past. Willy Chapman lives in what Benedict Anderson describes as the 'homogenous, empty time' of the present (Anderson 1991, 204), entangled in the peculiar contradiction of narratives of identity, their '[a]wareness of being imbedded in secular, serial time, with all its implications of continuity, yet of "forgetting" the experience of this continuity' (Anderson 1991, 205). This contradiction, Anderson explains, 'engenders the need for a narrative of "identity"', yet in Swift's novel, it engenders instead the need for a narrative of absence, of non-identity. In contemporary 'condition of England' fiction, then, the compulsion to tell the story of the collective is also the compulsion to narrate the dissolution of the collective identity, to unfold the conditions by which England has come to the limits of its own existence. For each of the symbolic figures of contemporary Englishness – the 'thug', the butler, and the shopkeeper – time, it seems, is running out, and the heat of living in the moment becomes increasingly indistinguishable from the consuming fires of history. The 'tick tock' of post-imperial history is counting down, and the most appropriate mode for contemporary narratives of identity seems to have become the elegiac.

English elegies

In his book, *Literary Englands*, David Gervais argues that nostalgia and retrospection have become part of the 'staple cultural diet' of late twentieth-century England, and warns that 'Modern England is in danger of becoming a museum of itself' (Gervais 1993, 271). The poetry of Geoffrey Hill, John Betjeman and particularly Philip Larkin had helped to secure the central place of the elegy in contemporary English literature, and 'England' seemed to be defined for such poets by its antipathy to the modernity of the present. Larkin's instinctive reaction to what he depicted as the race to become the 'First slum of Europe', with its 'greeds and garbage ... too thick-strewn', was to evoke nostalgically an insular, provincial England of the imaginary past, against the alarming realisation that 'it isn't going to last' (Larkin, 'Going, Going'). English literature in the postwar period, as Hugh Kenner argued in *A Sinking Island*, seemed to be defined by 'a common devotion, in utterly disparate idioms, to the past of England' (Kenner 1987, 245). It is a devotion which in contemporary fiction has frequently taken the form of confessional narratives from the deathbed, of reviewing a life of survival in the midst of ruins, of evoking an England which is in the process of disappearing from view.

Angela Carter's *Wise Children* (1991) acknowledges that the elegiac tendency of its own narrative may be the inevitable effect of having an elderly narrator, Dora Chance, who tells us that 'nostalgia [is] the vice of the aged', and that she and her twin sister, Nora, 'watch so many old movies our memories come in monochrome' (Carter 1992, 10). Dora and Nora are the illegitimate heirs of a great thespian, Melchior Hazard, illegitimate in the circumstances of their birth, and illegitimate in that they have spent a life in the music halls and dance clubs, rather than the high-brow Shakespearean extravaganzas of their father. As with many contemporary novels, Carter's narrative weaves back and forward in time, juxtaposing the exciting, romantic years of Dora and Nora's stage performances with the stationary, antique-filled setting of their sunset years. In the process, Dora reconstructs the parameters of their imagination and consciousness to reflect what she tells us is the feeling that 'we're stuck in the period at which we peaked' (Carter 1992, 5). The past, contrary to what she tells us about its monochrome tones, remains vivid and real to Dora, while the present is merely the occasion for reflecting back on the passage of decline. The present is thus constructed as the imaginary 'outside' of time, not in continuity with the past, nor even worthy of contrast with the past, but merely a vacant platform from which the narrator can launch into nostalgic reverie. The fact that Dora's reminiscences frequently turn to the dead art form of the music hall help to establish this absolute break with the past, as if the exploits of 'Gorgeous George', the patriotic comedian with the map of the world, the British empire marked in bold red, tattooed on his torso, existed in an alien, fantasy world.

The nostalgia of Carter's novel, however, is self-consciously constructed, as is evident in the way that Dora's narrative frequently exhibits fairy-tale devices – chapters which begin with 'Once upon a time', for example, as well as the pantomime knights and dragons who caricature the various members of the Hazard family, and the quest at the end of the narrative for a 'happy ending'. Dora and Nora exchange lovers and hatch plots in farcical scenes which mimic the pantomime format to which they are both so attached, just as Melchior Hazard, the great Shakespearean actor, unconsciously parodies and acts out the confused paternal and filial relationships of Hamlet and Lear in his own life. Dora's narrative is populated with other narratives, her nostalgia suffused with the nostalgia of dead generations, and the complicated narrative of the lines of descendence and inheritance, biological and cultural, is, perhaps, an ironic deflation of contemporary anxieties about legitimacy and heritage. For Dora, Shakespeare is father both to the venerated institutions of national theatre, and the bawdy underside of entertainment, represented in the music hall, the dance hall, the TV game show and the circus.

For all that *Wise Children* may parody the contemporary tendency towards nostalgia, however, it may also be a victim of it. Dora has little time or passion for the diverse offerings of television, and is immersed instead in her ecstatic memories of monochrome film, extinct music hall acts and the lost spectacle of the pre-war theatre. It is the past which seems always to contain the real vitality of her narrative, not the commentary, ironic or otherwise, on the state of contemporary culture. The interweaving of her family history with Shakespearean plot, or indeed with fairy story – the intertextuality which characterises the self-conscious fictions of postmodernity – may be less a matter of playful parody than a revealing symptom of the exhaustion of modern culture, that it is incapable of creating anything but echoes and repetitions of the culture of the past.

In this case, John Barth's description of postmodern fiction as the 'literature of exhaustion' may refer not only to what Frederick Bowers called the attempt 'to explore the rules of language and form as far as they extend' (Bowers 1980, 154), but also to the particular condition of writing in a period which constructs itself around the notion of an impending 'end' (whether this is the end of modernity, history, the planet, the empire, Englishness, the West, time, civilisation, or any of the other identities which are threatened with extinction in the discourses of decline which have held currency in the last few decades). As Jean-François Lyotard argues, the notion of an impending end engenders the production of an art and architecture in which the dominant mode is not the 'new', but the repetition and quotation of the styles and forms of the past, a mode which he characterises by the term 'bricolage' (Lyotard 1993, 47). But such a mode is better represented in modern British fiction by such works as A.S. Byatt's *Possession* (1990) or John Fowles's *The French Lieutenant's Woman* (1969), which both exercise faithful parodies of the language and forms of the past, than the fictional works I talk about in this section, which dramatise the ways in which the past presents itself and is constructed in the narratives of the present.

Such a moment of dramatic realisation occurs in Ian McEwan's *Amsterdam* (1998), for example, in which Clive Linley's heroic struggle to wrestle from his creative consciousness the symphony which will commemorate the passing of the end of the century and the millenium produces 'a shameless copy' of Beethoven's *Ode to Joy*. McEwan's novel narrates the impact of the death of wild-child turned successful magazine editor, Molly Lane, on three of her former lovers – Clive Linley, a successful composer, Vernon Halliday, the editor of a tabloid newspaper, and Julian Garmony, the Conservative government's Foreign Secretary. In the complicated twists in the events which follow Molly's death, Clive and Vernon end up dead, having made a pact to organise each other's euthanasia in an Amsterdam clinic should they fall into the state of chronic loss of memory and control which befell Molly in her final months of life. A bizarre series of circumstances occurs when Clive objects to Vernon's attempts to damage the Conservative government by publishing scandalous photographs of Julian Garmony dressed as a woman, and when Vernon discovers that Clive has ignored an attempted rape that he witnessed while trying to gather inspiration for his unfinished millennial symphony; circumstances which lead them both to suspect the other of having gone mad, having lost the power of memory and reason, and thus to orchestrate each other's deaths. It is the loss of memory which Clive and Vernon fear most, the incapacity to access and rehearse the past, and in their dying reveries, it is the ghostly figure of Molly whom they both envisage arriving to nurse them. *Amsterdam* thus dramatises the power of the dead over the living, and equates living with the power to remember. That Clive unwittingly plagiarises Beethoven's *Ode to Joy*, in what he thinks of as his elegy to the dead century (McEwan 1998, 20), and on another occasion as a 'representation of himself' (156), reveals a creative mind which is as exhausted by the burden of cultural tradition and history as the landscape he roves over for inspiration is eroded by walkers and trampled by tourists (80, 83).

The middle-aged professionals of McEwan's novel are less conspic-uously allegorical of a particular collective identity in a period of post-imperial and post-industrial decline than, for instance, Ishiguro's butler, or Swift's shopkeeper, but the tone of *Amsterdam* nevertheless reflects and contributes to the elegiac mode of contemporary English culture in its preoccupation with themes of death, loss of memory, euthanasia, cultural exhaustion, moral decay, and the alienation and fragmentation of contemporary society. There is, as might well be expected in a McEwan novel, no redemption or salvation from the relentless tone of moral ruin and impending death. Graham Swift's *Last Orders* (1996), on the other hand, tempers the elegiac narrative of Jack Dodds's death, with the often cheerful reveries of the friends he has asked to scatter his ashes from Margate pier:

> We head on past the gas works, Ilderton Road, under the railway bridge. Prince of Windsor. The sun comes out from behind the tower blocks, bright in our faces, and Vince pulls out a pair of chunky sun-glasses from under the dashboard. Lenny starts singing, slyly, through his teeth, '*Blue bayooo ...*' And we all feel it, what with the sunshine and the beer inside us and the journey ahead: like it's some-thing Jack has done for us, so as to make us feel special, so as to give us a treat. Like we're off on a jaunt, a spree, and the world looks good, it looks like it's there just for us. (Swift 1996, 18)

Jack's funeral procession to Margate becomes a day trip for his friends, an occasion for celebration rather than mourning, and in this passage Ray expresses the sense that Jack's ashes have the redemptive power of bringing his friends together on a rare expedition, and what turns out to be a rare opportunity to reflect back on their life stories. By its very nature, Swift's novel is predominantly elegiac, but its nostalgic qualities tend to be uplifting rather than maudlin. The narratives of Ray, Vic, Lenny, Vince, and Jack's wife, Amy, frequently turn to blithe nostalgia for the raucous camaraderie of the East End London markets, or the pastoral idylls encountered while hop picking in Kent, or the heady excitements of seaside holidays in Margate. The life of Jack Dodds has been marked by tragedy and decline, in his refusal to reconcile himself to the infant mind to which his daughter has been confined for all of her fifty-year-old life, and in the steady disintegration of his marriage and his business. There is no hopeful future implied or offered in the conclusion of the narrative, merely the scattering of ashes, and the novel is told relentlessly and irrefutably in the tone of 'retrospective poeticized nostalgia' that Bradbury argues is characteristic of contemporary British fiction, but its nostalgia is also untrammelled by regret or bitterness. As is proper to a 'literature of farewell', the mood in Swift's *Last Orders* is one of acceptance, of reconciliation with the past – a mood which is reflected in the acts of homage to the dead which Jack's friends make on their way to Margate (at Canterbury Cathedral, and the memorial to the men killed at sea at Chatham).

Swift's characters are conscious of being the last in a generation scarred by memories of the Second World War. In Jack's case, this manifests itself in the lingering feeling that he ought to have been killed in the war, were it not for the fact that his friend, Ray, whom he calls 'Lucky', had saved him. Jack thus imagines a tombstone waiting for him in the Libyan desert, and has the uneasy sensation that he is living on borrowed time. The same sensation is felt by other charac-ters too, by Ray, for example, who, just as he is overawed by the longevity of England's heritage exhibited in Canterbury Cathedral, is also made conscious by the disintegrating pier and coastal front of Margate of the slow, steady erosion of the England of his youth. In *Wise Children* and in *London Fields*, characters attempt to arrest the process of decay with video technology, giving them the illusion of freezing time, of capturing in suspension what Keith Talent calls the 'action'. But time is running out for all of these characters, a process which the narrator of Amis's *London Fields* believes is the ultimate sign of our own unique contemporaneity:

> We used to live and die without any sense of the planet getting older, of mother earth getting older, living and dying. We used to live outside history. But now we're coterminous. We're inside history now all right, on its leading edge, with the wind ripping past our ears. (Amis 1990, 197)

To be 'inside history', in this sense, means to be conscious of our own historicity, of the process of our own demise and extinction, a process which Jean-Luc Nancy calls the 'contemporary suspension of history' (Nancy 1990, 150). It is a condition reflected in contemporary fictions by the refusal of chronological order, and the retelling of the past as if it is contemporaneous. In Swift's *Last Orders*, just as in Pat Barker's *The Century's Daughter* (1986), the past is the daydream of the present, not its ordained ancestor. For Liza Jarrett, lying in her deathbed in a condemned house in a northern working-class street, the past is relived in her telling. Born on the stroke of midnight at the beginning of the twentieth century, Liza's ebbing narrative is punctuated by the First World War, the depression, the Second World War, and thereafter the gradual erosion and dissolution of the community in which she grew up. The quality of her narrative is not nostalgic, or reminiscent, however, but, more properly, anamnetic – recovering the spirit and sensation of living in the past in order to reconcile the psychic disturbances of the present. Liza's narrative is, thus, a kind of healing, both for her and the social worker, Stephen, who listens to her stories with increasing compulsion as the community around them disintegrates.

The Century's Daughter depicts urban England in a state of near anarchy, a society littered with condemned houses, disused factories, redundant workers and dysfunctional families. Thatcherist economics have succeeded in destroying Liza's community more effectively than the two world wars or the depression, and Stephen finds his job as a social worker almost futile. He thinks of himself as caretaking the unemployed, or helping them to find less destructive ways of passing the time. Initially, Liza's animated stories of the past are pleasant distractions for Stephen from the failure of the local community centre, and the lynching which he almost receives at the hands of local youths, but the troubles of the community slowly and inevitably impinge on Liza. She becomes the victim of violent robbery in her own home, even her memory box disturbed and its contents scattered across the room. The demolition teams move in on her street too, knocking down the empty terraced houses of which she is the last occupant. Her dead husband, Frank, a disturbed veteran of the First World War, who spent his life communing with dead spirits and trying to heal the living with anamnesis, appears to her on her death bed, as does her mother, beckoning her away as the clock strikes midnight.

'I gave the dead breath', says Liza's husband, Frank, reproaching her for locking away the past in a box (Barker 1986, 276). Barker's novel, like other elegiac novels in contemporary British fiction, treads a thin line between the redemptive implications of prosopopoeia, the ascription of life to the dead or the past (which Frank practises), and the regressive and maudlin implications of remaining trapped in a fixed and truncated past. Towards the end of *The Century's Daughter* the metaphors of regeneration and resurrection gather pace, a theme which became the central focus, obviously, of Barker's more recent trilogy on the First World War. As Stephen walks away from the waste-land which Liza's street rapidly becomes after her death, he notes how 'the wind blew, bending the dead flowers, and from one or two of them seeds began to disperse, drifting down across the wasteland, like wisps of white hair' (Barker 1986, 284). Liza's stories may have performed a similarly redemptive function for him, in inspiring him with the will to breathe new life into the generation which he defines as 'a people without hope' (219), but the imagery of seeds drifting 'like wisps of white hair' may also suggest that they will disperse and die without giving life, just as Frank's seances with the dead have merely edged him closer to death himself. As Frederick Holmes argues in his short study of the historical imagination in contemporary British fiction, 'a fear shared by [contemporary British writers] is that the exercise of the historical imagination might have the unintended, perverse effect of casting a deathly pall over the living, rather than resurrecting the dead' (Holmes 1997, 80). A similar paradox, I would argue, is discernible in the cultural politics of the last two decades, particularly in the specific forms of nationalism and conservatism which have prevailed in England since 1979.

The politics of 'farewell'

'Britain has not changed'. This was the lesson which Margaret Thatcher drew for the people of Britain following the victory of British troops in the Falkland islands in 1982, victory which was instrumental in bolstering her image as a leader of Churchillian dimensions, who was determined, as she proclaimed in her 1979 election campaign, to put the 'Great' back into Britain. Arguably, the Falklands War won the 1983 election for the Conservative party, and thus helped to secure the power base needed for the cultural crusade which the party embarked on throughout the 1980s and well into the 1990s. As Ivor Crewe argued in an analysis of the values of the 1980s, Thatcher became such a focus for intellectual as well as political attention, partly because of the longevity of her stay in office, but partly also because she was the first prime minister in this century to articulate and develop a cultural campaign designed to change the values of the society she governed (Crewe 1989, 239). Her avowed desire to lead Britain back to the glories of empire, the values of Victorian society and the order and stability of the 1950s established her as a crusading figure, but she was only the most vocal and visible agent of a discourse of nostalgia and decline which crossed over conventional social and political divisions, from the preservative language of the right to the 'what went wrong?' retrospective focus of the left. Even the Labour government in place since 1997 is, as Tom Nairn argues, merely a more aggressively managerial version of the politics of managing decline (Nairn 2000). But the campaigns to return Britain to a mythic idealised past, to the Victorian values of self-reliance, or the orderliness and conformity of the 1950s, are also signs of disturbance in the implications such campaigns held for the state of contemporary Britain. In the anxious repetition of the desire to return to the values of the past, modern conservatism contradicted its own image of the deep continuity of the essential core values of 'Britain'. To dream of the order and security of the 1950s was, at the same time, to acknowledge the radical discontinuity of British society; instead of the aspired progress towards what Chambers calls the 'imaginary modernity' of 'financial independence, profitability and enterprise culture' (Chambers 1990, 17), Thatcher's cultural crusades seemed to imply that Britain was steadily regressing into anarchy, disorder and bankruptcy. And perversely, the vigorous march which conservative politics proposed into the 'great' future paradoxically appeared to resurrect the dead, and, as Holmes puts it, cast 'a deathly pall over the living' (Holmes 1997, 80). Margaret Thatcher could call for the return to the Victorian values of industry and hard work, and yet presided over the widespread decimation of the coal mines which were the engine of Victorian industry. She attempted to project the imagery of Victorian diligence and prudence onto the growth of financial services in the 'city', yet the other legacy of Victorian society, slum housing and homelessness, returned to haunt this vision. Ghosts returned from the past, it seemed, especially for the Thatcher governments, and arguably led to Thatcher's downfall when that spectacular failure of the fourteenth century, the poll tax, appeared in the twentieth century, riots and all. Not all of these ghosts worked against the politics of conservatism, either. Shortly after the victory celebrations of the Falklands war, crowds gathered to watch the raising of Henry VIII's flagship, the 'Mary Rose', from Portsmouth Harbour, which Simon Barker argues was an ideological performance 'quite as powerful as the Falklands Parade itself' (Barker 1984, 17). The politics of conservatism attempted to harness the imagery and power of the past to its own vision of the future, with some success, but the spectres of history, as Derrida shows, have a treacherous tendency to choose their own provenance.

The contradiction between the claim that Britain had not changed, and the crusades to return to the values of a lost past, are, however, necessary to the conservative political ideologies of the last two decades, not least because the threat of serious and terminal decline is required in order to justify the radical departures from the postwar consensus which Thatcherism embraced. My concern here, though, is not with the function of this paradox within conservative ideology, but with the apparent proximity between the retrospective, lamenting tone of contemporary fiction and the nostalgic imagery of decline and decay which feed the conservative vision of the future. In noting this tendency among contemporary writers to represent 'the phase of history into which they were born [as] already ended', for example, Margaret Scanlan warns of the dangers of fiction collaborating with our desire to escape the responsibilities of the present by taking refuge in images of a mythic past (Scanlan 1990, 195). D.J. Taylor also endorses this view, maintaining that what characterises postwar literature as a whole is the 'unspoken assumption that present circumstance is of no account when compared to the agreeable playgrounds of the past' (Taylor 1994, xxii). Neither critic is unaware of the left-wing aspirations of many contemporary novelists, yet the implication of the perceived nostalgia of contemporary British writing is that an instinctive conservatism lurks in the preoccupation with the past. In a survey of the impact of Thatcherism on literature and the arts, Brian Appleyard is less coy about such implications, and argues that 'in reacting to various perceived problems of our recent past, politics and art have advanced along broadly similar paths' (Appleyard 1989, 314).

The analyses of contemporary British writings offered above do not suggest the argument that literature in the 1980s and 1990s countenanced and sanctioned the values of late twentieth-century conservatism, however. They do indicate, on the other hand, that the foundations of the conservative cultural revolutions – none articulated more succinctly, or failing more dismally, than John Major's 'Back to Basics' campaign – overlap significantly with the elegiac, 'condition of England' focus of contemporary fiction. In literature as in politics, Englishness seemed to be imagined in the 1980s and 1990s within a discourse of decline and impending crises, which, for writers as for politicians, prompted a revival of interest in visiting and re-imagining the past. The turn to history as the source of a lost home of identity, as the location of 'Englishness', was not confined to the disciplines of politics or literature either, but, as Robert Hewison argues, England in the 1980s became a heritage-saturated society, trafficking in history to supply the compulsive narrative of national identity (Hewison 1987).

As a response to the narrative of national decline and post-imperial malaise, Catherine Hall argues for the cultural imperative of imagining Britain anew, of imagining British identities without an empire, without the stifling myths of cultural homogeneity and timeless traditions (Hall 1996, 76). But Hall is just one among many critics, including Homi Bhabha, Paul Gilroy, Simon Gikandi, Ian Baucom and Iain Chambers, among others, who have located the agency for the cultural renegotiation and re-imagining of Englishness in the work of post-colonial writers such as Salman Rushdie, David Dabydeen, or Hanif Kureishi. By reconceptualising Englishness through histories and narratives that read racial difference and colonial stereotypes back into the 'centre' of English identity rather than the margins, and by shifting notions of the multiplicity and hybridity of English identities into the foreground, post-colonial writers have contested conservative myths of national identity and belonging repeatedly and forcefully. But equally important, as Iain Chambers acknowledges, is the task of critically revising the heritage of England's past within the terms of the discourse of decline itself:

> It is not possible to deliberately abandon such an inheritance, to cancel it as though it were a page that can now be torn out of the history book. One is forced to come to terms with such a heritage, to revisit it, to live in its ruins and there in the gaps, openings and fragments to grasp a wider sense of the possible. (Chambers 1990, 50)

The writings discussed in this chapter embody such a critical revision of the legacy and myths of Englishness in the late twentieth century. They 'live in its ruins', sometimes all too literally, depicting the conditions of England's paralysis, not in order to evoke nostalgically the return to a mythic ideal of the past, but instead to lay to rest, to 'wake', the ghosts of England's pasts. They do so not in the spirit of 'forgetting', or absolving, the past – which in any case, the novels of Peter Ackroyd and Iain Sinclair teach us is a conceited delusion of the modern age – but instead to embrace historicity as the precondition of deconstructing narratives of national identity.

The 'tick tock' of England's atrophied, hemiplegic death, as depicted in contemporary British fiction, then, signals the very possibility of its transformation, or regeneration. In place of the deep continuity of an immemorial spirit of national identity, or the timeless presence symbolised in the remains of England's heritage, contemporary British writers stress the historicity of England, the sense of its continual, relentless, imminent disappearance. To Ishiguro's butler, Stevens, the halls and villages of England become strange figures of his own sense of 'absence'; when he goes in search of England he discovers only the scattered, tourist-trail beauty spots which substitute for the missing, 'real' England. To Amis's narrator in *London Fields*, England is caught in a prolonged process of suspended annihilation, waiting like him to die of exhaustion and disintegration, and yet enduring in the compelling disclosure of the narrative. In Swift's *Last Orders*, the threatened disappearance and erosion of England, fused with the dissolution of Jack's ashes in the wind, is the final image of the novel. Swift's characters watch their friend dissolve into nothing as they stand on a pier which is crumbling and vanishing into the sea. Paul Theroux concludes his travel narrative, *The Kingdom by the Sea* (1983), written in the midst of the Falklands War, with a similar image, of the coastline crumbling, and writes that 'The endless mutation of the British coast wonderfully symbolized the state of the nation ... . The British seemed to me to be people forever standing on a crumbling coast and scanning the horizon' (Theroux 1984, 360). It is an image which he uses to contest the notion of a timeless, unchanging nation, suggesting that it is at the English coast, at the symbolic borders of 'the island race', that we can best testify to the historicity of 'England'. Homi Bhabha argues much the same point at the end of his essay, 'Dissemination', using the quirkiness of English weather 'to invoke ... the most changeable and immanent signs of national difference' (Bhabha 1994, 169).

Contemporary literary representations of the condition of England place the presence and continuity of Englishness under erasure, returning repeatedly to images and tropes of absence and disappearance. In using the arsenal of conservative metaphors and projections of national identity, they overlap significantly with the terms of conservative articulations of 'Englishness', but open up the conceptions of national belonging and heritage to criticism. Contrary to what

Julian Wolfreys terms 'the idea of national identity as a metaphysical category beyond critique' (Wolfreys 1994, 2), writers such as Swift, Ishiguro, Amis, Carter, Barker and McEwan lay open the discourse of national identity to the recurrent trope of disappearance or death, thus posing the question of non-identity, or indeed the performance of an identity which is absent or anachronistic. To present Englishness with figures of its own historicity is, finally, to expose it as a construction, as an effect, for, as the late Antony Easthope argued, to show 'that Englishness is an effect is to show that it can be faked, replicated, impersonated. For if Englishness is an effect it can be changed' (Easthope 1995, 156).

Part II

Making New Maps

4 'Common Ground': feminist fictions and the cultural politics of difference

'... literature is no one's private ground; literature is common ground. It is not cut up into nations; there are no wars there.'

Virginia Woolf, 'The Leaning Tower' (168)

For the author of those influential lectures contained in *A Room of One's Own*, which ponder the 'unsolved problem' of the relationship between women and fiction, the statement that 'literature is common ground' is surely aspirational rather than descriptive. That literature might serve as a utopian space of equal representation is certainly the assumption behind the arguments of *A Room of One's Own*, but Woolf attests to the many material and cultural disadvantages that have made this ideal far from practicable for women in the past (Woolf 1977). Literature, Woolf shows, has been a contentious space of representation for women, in which, as Susan Watkins argues, 'there is no space between the beautiful, virtuous, angelic heroine and the ugly, wicked, demonic villainess for the diverse versions of femininity about which we may wish to read' (Watkins 2001, 14). Woolf's argument hovers between the materialist demands of financial and spatial independence for women, and the idealist vision of women and men writing on 'common ground', free of the constraints of gender difference.

'[It] is fatal for anyone who writes to think of their sex ... . It is fatal for a woman to lay the least stress on any grievance; to plead even with justice any cause; in any way to speak consciously as a woman' (Woolf 1977, 112). For Woolf, equality for women in literature could be achieved, but only at the unacknowledged cost of their distinctive identities as women. Equality was thus synonymous for Woolf with androgyny, and was incommensurable with the articulation or construction of gender difference. Woolf is in no sense representative of feminist writing and thinking of her time, or since, in this matter, however. In the work of near contemporaries and later women writers, such as Elizabeth Bowen, Jean Rhys, Rosamund Lehmann, Lettice Cooper and Phyllis Bottome, the notion of a 'common ground' in gender relations is contested, complicated and doubted at every turn. It is the politics of difference, rather than the politics of equality, which is the subject of this chapter, which argues that women's writing since 1945 has rehearsed and tested the intersecting discourses of social, racial, sexual and cultural identities. Margaret Drabble once wrote that 'Arnold Bennett tells you things Virginia Woolf simply didn't know' (Alexander 1989, 17). 'Difference' is problematic in some forms of feminist thinking, perhaps most visibly for feminism in the 1950s, which, in focusing too narrowly on the perspectives of educated, middle-class women, opened more widely the ideological gap between women of different classes, races, cultures and sexualities.[1] For many other women writers, 'difference' is an empowering, radical concept, instead of simply a constraint. But it is also a disquieting category of thought for contemporary feminism, and according to Robyn Wiegman, may even explain the rise of pronouncements on the death of feminism: 'it is safe to say that, at the beginning of the new century, academic feminism finds itself so deeply troubled about the internal dynamics of "difference" that women's very incommensurabilities with one another serve as one of the most powerful forces in narrating feminism's apocalyptic end' (Wiegman 2000, 808).

If feminism is in crisis at the beginning of the twenty-first century, the reason Wiegman offers for this is its historic dependence on the teleology of narrative, its tendency to plot feminist agency within a progressive movement between tradition and futurity. Thus, feminism acquires origins and foundations, a logic of succession and debt, and a teleological imagination of an ideal resolution of gender conflicts in the future. To infuse such a narrative with the demands of 'difference', to recognise the proliferation of micro-narratives of identity, is to acknowledge that the infinity of 'feminisms' can no longer be gathered into a single, progressive narrative. As Wiegman rightly believes, this should not so much spell the end of feminism, and the supposed arrival of the 'post-feminist' era, as the re-visioning and re-imagining of the narrative structures and historical logic of feminism (Wiegman 2000, 822–3). The argument of this chapter is that postwar women's writing in England has been centrally concerned with imagining the meanings of feminism(s) for contemporary women, and has experimented with fictional modes for representing women's experiences in relation to prevailing ideas of gendered identity. My use of the term 'feminist fiction' here indicates a refusal to give up on the term 'feminism' as a mode of political engagement with gendered structures and identities, and an underlying argument that many of the women writers considered here, although they problematise feminism in relation to other forms of cultural difference, are also working to articulate the complexities of feminist politics of difference. With Gayle Greene, I share the view that 'Feminist fiction is the most revolutionary movement in contemporary fiction – revolutionary both in that it is formally innovative and in that it helped make a social revolution' (Greene 1991, 2). Women writers have adopted the conventions of liberal realism as well as generated the self-reflexive, revisionary terms of postmodern narrative, and have explored feminist politics through and with both forms of literary representation. Feminist fiction, I argue in this chapter, seeks to conceptualise the cultural and political dynamics of the dialogic relationship between women and fiction – the original terms of Woolf's lectures – and works to conceive both terms anew.

Gendered Ground

The problems with Woolf's conception of 'common ground' are apparent in the relationship between feminism and literature in the 1950s. One of the most pervasive myths of the immediate postwar era, according to Elizabeth Wilson, is that the political demands of feminism had been met, and that, consequently, the sex war had ended (Wilson 1980, 2). This appeared to be a common opinion not merely among academics and officials of the time, but also among feminist writers and thinkers, such as Pearl Jephcott, Alva Myrdal, Viola Klein, Judith Hubback and Vera Brittain.[2] Feminism was far from dead, but it is perceived to shift its emphases from campaigning for political rights to constructing a moral agenda for women within the so-called social consensus established after 1945. The Birmingham Feminist History Group argue that feminists of the 1950s 'could not escape

from the social democratic stress on the "equality" already achieved
and the rights won – "mopping up" was all that was required'
(Birmingham 1979, 63).[3] Arguably, this shift had less to do with the
supposed liberating effects of the Second World War on women, than
the emergence and consolidation of the welfare state in the late 1940s.
The demands which the pre-war feminist, Margery Spring-Rice, made
in her book on working-class wives, published in 1939 – family
allowance schemes, housing subsidies, wage increases, improved
health services, universal extension of health insurance, and
increased access for women to educational and recreational facilities
– had already been met to various degrees in the social welfare legisla-
tion introduced by the postwar Labour government (Spring Rice
1939). As far as these political demands were concerned, equality had
been achieved, or was at least believed to be imminent. In response,
postwar feminism recoiled from the confrontational image of early
twentieth-century suffragettism, and remained within the ideological
parameters of the social consensus. Myrdal and Klein articulated the
uneasy awareness that postwar feminism was embracing values and
moral codes which had dubious inferences for earlier feminists: 'The
maxim "Children First" must therefore be regarded as axiomatic, even
though it has very often been used in the past as a means to impede
the emancipation of women' (Myrdal and Klein 1956, 116).

Ironically, this shift of focus for feminism occurred at the very time
that debates about femininity and motherhood moved into the foreground of a powerful nexus of government, religious, sociological and
academic discourses. According to official reports on population,
marriage, delinquency, education and sexuality, which appeared
throughout the late 1940s and 1950s, the role of women as housewives
and mothers was materially and symbolically central to the stability,
harmony and durability of postwar British society.[4] So too, for the
emergent consumerism of the mid-1950s, the housewife was the
indispensable pivot of what H. Hopkins calls 'the new arts of continuous consumption' (Hopkins 1963, 324). This was especially evident in
the popular media of the time, in women's magazines, in particular,
which were devoted to presenting women as the self-confident,
professional managers of their home and children. There was an
acknowledgement in such magazines that women could achieve
anything – they could be rocket scientists and engineers if they
wished to be – but that women *should* choose to be housewives and
mothers for the good of social and family life, and, at the same time,

for their own good. As the Birmingham group argue, 'girls and women were surrounded by representations of themselves which focused on the satisfactions they would achieve through their marriages and their children' (Birmingham 1979, 63). The grounds of debate had shifted for women from what they were capable of doing, to the morality of what they should choose to do. Conservatives argued that the emancipation of women was contributing to the moral decay of the nation, while liberals accepted that women's equal status was desirable but that women fulfilled their potential better as housewives and mothers.

As Niamh Baker argues, in *Happily Ever After*, if critical opposition to the postwar orthodoxy on femininity was not available in feminist academic writings, it could be found in fiction written by women writers (Baker 1989, 20). The period saw its conservative women writers too. In the fictions of Angela Thirkell, Barbara Pym and Nancy Mitford, women who transgress the moral codes of middle-class society are usually depicted as licentious and untrustworthy. But women's writing of the 1950s tended to represent women's roles as housewife and mother as unfulfilling, family life as troubled and unstable, and the moral proscriptions of feminine behaviour anachronistic. Rose Macauley's *The World My Wilderness* (1950) and Elizabeth Taylor's *At Mrs Lippincote's* (1945) show marital disintegration, in which family life is increasingly dissatisfactory, and in which men play little or no role in child rearing, preferring instead to present the bond between mother and child as sufficient and complete in itself. The early novels of Doris Lessing's *Children of Violence* quintet, *Martha Quest* (1952), *A Proper Marriage* (1954) and *A Ripple from the Storm* (1958) are forthright in their depictions of marital dissatisfaction, and of the myths and delusions of femininity. Lessing's heroine begins as a teenager imagining the delights of married life, but she is left unfulfilled when she does marry and continually searches for happiness and freedom through other means. Such fictions, I would suggest, rehearse contemporary feminist arguments about the relationship between femininity and the social institutions of motherhood and child-rearing. In this section, I consider in particular two fictional explorations of single motherhood – Lynne Reid Banks's *The L-Shaped Room* (1960) and Margaret Drabble's *The Millstone* (1965) – which play out contemporary debates on independence, maternity, and sexuality which were central to postwar constructions of femininity.

The L-Shaped Room and *The Millstone* present similar stories of an educated middle-class woman who becomes pregnant in her first sexual encounter, and after considering the moral issues of abortion, adoption, child-rearing outside of marriage, and the duties or responsibilities of the father, decides to accept the life of a single mother. In Banks's novel, Jane Graham loses her 'cumbersome virginity' pathetically and indifferently to a man for whom she feels nothing (Banks 1962, 128). She becomes pregnant, is thrown out of her house by her father, loses her well-paid job, and decides to live in a tenement flat as a form of self-punishment. Jane knows that she does not have to live in the bug-ridden attic room, in a house with prostitutes in the basement, and an assorted collection of bohemian artists in between, but considers that since her condition makes her morally equivalent to prostitutes in the eyes of her father, she might as well live like one. The *L-Shaped Room* combines fictional exploration of the trials and tribulations of single motherhood in 1950s England with a kind of anthropological curiosity about how people like prostitutes, bohemians and black musicians live outside of Jane's middle-class social world. The novel includes exploratory depictions of a black dance hall, of the life and feelings of one of the prostitutes, and of the experiences of pregnancy and childbirth. Perhaps in keeping with the emergent authority of sociological and psychological studies of class, femininity and sexuality, Banks's novel offers fictional depictions of ordinary experiences as a kind of documentary journey into hidden lifestyles. As a result, *The L-Shaped Room* oscillates between pioneering the validation of previously underrepresented experiences as worthy of literary and cultural attention, and offering portraits of the lives of the working class, prostitutes and ethnic minorities to the voyeuristic amusement of the middle-class reader.

Pregnancy brings Jane Graham into contact with a wider social and cultural circle than she has so far encountered, and this reflects a pervasive concern in literary and cultural representations in the 1950s with themes of social mobility and accessibility. For Drabble's heroine, Rosamund Stacey, this is also the case. Aloof and detached from people of other social and cultural backgrounds by her education and class, Rosamund finds that pregnancy and motherhood places her in new relationships with people from other classes and races. She explains the effect of this experience on her to one of her friends, Joe, after she has given birth:

> I tried to explain the other day to somebody, no less than Joe Hurt himself in fact, about how happy I had felt, but he was very contemptuous of my descriptions. "What you're talking about", he said, "is one of the most boring commonplaces of the female experience. All women feel exactly that, it's nothing to be proud of, it isn't even worth talking about".
>
> I denied hotly that all women felt it, as I knew hardly a one who had been as enraptured as I, and then I contradicted my own argument by saying that anyway, if all other women did feel it, then that was precisely what made it so remarkable in my case, as I could not recall a single other instance in my life when I had felt what all other women feel. (Drabble 1968, 103)

Joe dismisses peremptorily Rosamund's feelings of connection with 'all other women', but this connection has an important function in the novel. Motherhood brings her into contact with women whom she describes as 'representatives of a population whose existence I had hardly noticed' (37), which itself is indicative of the myopic social existence to which Rosamund has been raised and educated. Motherhood is, thus, for Rosamund, a point of connection with an imagined community of women, a levelling experience which brings her into notional equality with other women, and which appears to establish Rosamund as a representative figure of contemporary motherhood. This representative tendency in Drabble's work has led Elaine Showalter to argue that 'Drabble is the novelist of maternity, as Charlotte Brontë was the novelist of the schoolroom' (Showalter 1999, 305). Motherhood enables Drabble's heroine to encounter and witness the lives of other classes and races, and to feel 'the blows of fate and circumstance under which they suffered ... in my heart' (Drabble 1968, 68). *The Millstone* dramatises, in fact, the tension between the Victorian ethics of individual self-reliance, which has been an important part of Rosamund's liberal Protestant upbringing, and the egalitarian ethics of a welfare society, represented in the novel by Rosamund's anxious encounters with the National Health Service and with people of other social and cultural backgrounds.

Rosamund places great emphasis on her independence, and avoids having a committed, intimate relationship, but remains trapped between the desire for some kinds of human connection and the fear of intimacy. Patricia Waugh argues that *The Millstone* tells the story of

Rosamund's attempt to overcome her emotional and psychological inhibitions:

> In *The Millstone* ... [Drabble] presents a heroine who does, *partially*, resolve her defensive need to erect boundaries and is able to acknowledge her repressed desire for connection without fear of subjective dissolution or loss of self in other. The resolution is confined, though, to her relationship with her infant daughter. She remains at the end fixated in what is essentially a pre-oedipal union which offers only the as yet unrealized *potential* for a satisfactory adult relationship. (Waugh 1989, 128–9)

Motherhood, according to Waugh, is not the means by which Rosamund overcomes her emotional insularity, but rather an extension of her cocoon-like existence. Her own parents have insisted on raising her to be self-sufficient emotionally and psychologically, but her relationship with her infant daughter seems to promise instead an emotional dependence between mother and child. Waugh's analyses of Rosamund suggest that we need to be cautious about celebrating Drabble's novel, as Gail Cunningham does, as a feminist articulation of the experiences of independent intellectual women (Cunningham 1982, 130–52). Rosamund's narrative shifts between self-revelation and the intimation that she is essentially unreliable as a self-aware narrator. *The Millstone* is, according to this view, the portrait of a woman who has become chronically self-detached, despite her obsessive concern with being self-reliant.

At the heart of Drabble's novel is the conflict between the Victorian preoccupation with the morality of individualism and the postwar construction of a cohesive, welfare society. Rosamund tells us that her parents 'had drummed the idea of self-reliance into me so thoroughly that I believed dependence to be a fatal sin' (Drabble 1968, 9). In this, *The Millstone* shows early signs of Drabble's interest in the 'representative' novel, of representing definitive (or at least illustrative) moments in the condition of society and culture. Drabble recalled that her novels published in the 1960s 'had unwittingly tuned into a mood that was spreading through the country. Far from being isolated, I was part of a movement ... . The times were changing. The captive housewife spoke' (Greene 1991, 54). Her iconic status as novelist of, and contemporary commentator on, issues of motherhood is one way in which she 'captured the mood', but her early novels are equally concerned with contemporary moral issues and problems. Drabble contrasts the Victorian moral codes which are evoked throughout *The Millstone* with the new morality of the welfare state. Rosamund fears the reactions of her parents and peers to her pregnancy, particularly as her lifestyle could not be further from the taint of irresponsibility and sexual promiscuity with which the condition of single motherhood was associated. '[B]eing at heart a Victorian', she thinks of her pregnancy as 'the Victorian penalty', as retribution for her sins (Drabble 1968, 18). The sins are not, however, ones of sexual immorality, but instead the 'brand new, twentieth-century crime' of sexual abstinence, which the novel seems to suggest goes against the prevailing expectations of postwar femininity. Rosamund confesses to her 'suspicion ... fear ... apprehensive terror of the very idea of sex' (17), which is rooted, Waugh argues, in her desire to avoid the experience and feelings of femininity (Waugh 1989, 130). In this sense, her pursuit of academic learning is constructed as a masquerade of her gender, a means by which she can shelter from the physical implications of her femininity in the androgynous mask of the literary scholar. She considers pregnancy, then, as punishment for 'having been born a woman in the first place. I couldn't pretend I wasn't a woman, could I, however much I might try from day to day to avoid the issue?' (Drabble 1968, 16)

The Millstone was published at a time in which the contraceptive pill had become widely available, and was not yet associated with any health risks or side effects. In the mid-1960s, the pill was perceived to have liberated female sexuality, enabling women to gain greater control over the relationship between sex and pregnancy. For Rosamund Stacey, and for Jane Graham in *The L-Shaped Room*, pregnancy is, at least initially, an undesirable but undeniable sign of the physical constraints of the gendered body, an unmistakable mark of biological and social difference which frustrates and contradicts the aspiration to equality and freedom. This is why both characters consider the option of abortion, before re-assessing the meanings and values of motherhood. For Rosamund, motherhood becomes an indication of an acceptance of responsibility, of social duty, and, more importantly, of living out a meaningful, material relationship between tradition and futurity. This is even more manifest in Banks's novel, in which Jane Graham becomes conscious at the end of the novel of her experience as both a repetition and anticipation of the experiences of other women. As she vacates her 'L-shaped' room to take up her inherited cottage, she meets the young woman moving in, and stops to savour 'an uncanny feeling of omniscience. I could see the future as clearly as if I were sitting through a film for the second time' (Banks 1962, 269). Thus, Banks's novel seems to suggest a continuum between women's experiences, an imaginary unity between Jane, her prostitute neighbours, her mother who died giving birth to her, the preceding and succeeding occupants of her room, the other women in the house – Doris and Mavis – who sympathise in various ways with her condition, and other women whom she encounters during her pregnancy.

The problem with this imaginary unity of women is that it is inter-rupted and contradicted at numerous points in the novel by differ-ences of class and race. Jane's lurking fear of her black neighbour, John, whom she constantly views through a racial stereotype of animality, emotional instability, and intellectual limitation, clearly problematises the existence of a common, cross-racial feminism. Jane describes one of her first encounters with John as being 'assailed by an almost overpowering warm, animal smell'; John's room is depicted as having a 'powerful negro odour' surging from it; Jane asks the reader 'Do negroes have more teeth than other people? I'll swear they do' (51; 65; 89). When we encounter John in the novel, his blackness precedes him, or rather, Jane's racial assumptions and 'atavistic buried fear' of blackness determines her relationship to him (108). The racial codes and barriers in the novel immediately complicate its feminist narratives, since the narrator seems to construct a series of identifications and stereotypes which invite readers to identify with white, English prejudices. A similar vein of suspicion of Jewishness runs through the novel too, which takes the form of Jane's distrust of her Jewish employer, and her fascination with Toby's looks. He is described at one point as a 'Jewish leprechaun' (80). This is meant to be comic, no doubt, but depends too heavily upon inscribing into the narrative an implicit set of white, English, Christian subject positions. The fairy-tale ending of *The L-Shaped Room*, in which Jane inherits a cottage and is able to move away from the squalid conditions of her tenement flat, reinforces too the class distinctions which serve to make her status as an unmarried mother less difficult. So too, Drabble's heroine acquires a secure academic post at the end of *The Millstone*, and a professional title 'which would go a long way towards obviating the anomaly of Octavia's existence' (Drabble 1968, 155). The privileged social status of both characters enables them to control and negotiate the degree to which their biological identities interfere with their aspirations towards independence. The heroines of both novels are conscious of their privileged social position, and of the less fortunate women who have to endure the privations of single motherhood in poverty. Nevertheless, the extent to which these novels might offer a radical critique of the moral strictures on femininity and motherhood in postwar society is severely curtailed by the implications of their representations of social and cultural differences, which recur frequently in both novels, and from the implicit subject positions that the narratives construct for us as readers. As realist novels, *The L-Shaped Room* and *The Millstone* seem to promise a mimetic construction of contemporary social situations and problems, but in the course of doing so they constantly raise issues about forms of representation, and about the subject positions of the narrator and reader. In the meantime, as Elizabeth Wilson has argued of feminism in general in the 1950s and early 1960s, the pervasive concern with the problems of middle-class femininity masked the perennial problems of poverty and loss of freedom for women further down the social ladder (Wilson 1977, 63).

The L-Shaped Room and *The Millstone* gave expression to the ambivalent status of motherhood in postwar society – as the biological marker of difference that qualified and limited the extent of female independence and equality, and simultaneously the creative and emotional fulfilment of human love and responsibility. Both novels also articulated experiences of independent femininity and unmarried motherhood in ways which presented such experiences as worthy of literary and cultural celebration. But, as Maroula Joannou argues, 'the rebellion in both [novels] is qualified and decorous. In many respects their heroines are disappointingly more conservative and less adventurous than women in the late nineteenth-century "new woman" novels of Olive Schreiner, George Egerton and Sarah Grand' (Joannou 2000, 60). In representing maternal women outside of the consensus orthodoxies of marriage and feminine passivity, Banks and Drabble offered important counter-narratives to the prevailing discourses of femininity and motherhood in the postwar period, but for both novelists the idea of social and gender equality is constantly shown in their fictions to be undermined by the disruptive implications of 'difference'.

Form and difference

Banks and Drabble belonged to that postwar generation of writers who adopted the conventions of documentary realism in order to represent the social changes introduced in Britain after the war. This, at least, was the critical consensus of the time – that where John Braine and John Osborne had represented the working class, or Colin MacInnes had fictionalised the new youth culture, or Sam Selvon had presented the lives of England's most recent immigrants, so Banks, Drabble, Lessing, and other women writers were giving voice to the hopes and dilemmas of postwar femininity. The retreat from modernism in such writings, it is argued, represented also a retreat from form to the political expediency of representing a changing social organism. Such realist fictions were strategically important, one might argue, in expanding the literary repertoire of female characters and roles, and in providing a public forum in which to explore the meanings and values of femininity in the changed social climate of the decades after the war. This is to argue that the social realist litera- ture of the 1950s and early 1960s diverts our attention away from the literary, away from issues of *how* it represents, to focus instead on the social content within its fictional frames. The realism of Banks and Drabble's novels is, of course, a construct, an achievement of the appearance of mimeticism. This appearance is carefully crafted through such devices as first-person narrative, which simulates the authenticity of personal experience, through the roughly chronologi- cal sequence of the narratives, through the narrowness of the range of tropes and figurative language used in the novels, and through the adherence to coherent subject positions that attempt to stabilise our identifications and interpretations of what the novels depict. For this reason, it is crucial to recognise the constructedness of feminist realist fiction, and to acknowledge its political efficacy as a form. The realist novel might serve feminist culture, as Rita Felski argues, 'as a medium for working through contradictions in women's lives and as a source of powerful symbolic fictions of female identity' (Felski 1989, 78). Yet, as Felski acknowledges, realism has had its feminist detractors, too, who have critiqued its innate conservatism and its complicity with existing ideological frameworks. Realism, Catherine Belsey argues, for example, 'is a predominantly conservative form. The experience of reading a realist text is ultimately reassuring' (Belsey 1980, 51). For Belsey, realist fictions create the illusion of a knowable and coherent world, presented through a transparent medium, by effacing the marks of 'their own textuality, their existence as discourse'. Thus, realism as a form conspires to conceal the existence of ideology, of discourse, and works to smooth over the cracks of ideological division. Belsey, of course, is addressing this critique of realism from a post-structuralist perspective, one in which realism seems to lag, dozily and naïvely, behind the more astute, sophisticated forms of postmodern fiction. We might question, too, the teleology of Belsey's narrative, which perhaps overlooks the potential evident in Banks and Drabble's novels to appropriate the universalising subject position of liberal realism for a feminist politics of representation (even if its universal assumptions are deeply problematic).

These issues – central to the debate about the cultural politics of realism as a form – are foregrounded in Doris Lessing's novel, *The Golden Notebook* (1962). Lessing had already written several novels in realist style, although even her first novel, *The Grass is Singing* (1950) hinted in its conclusion at the limitations of liberal realism, when the narrator acknowledges an inability to disclose what the shadowy black character, Moses, is thinking. Realism, Lessing seems to suggest even at this early stage in her career, can never fully transgress the limits of its cultural and social origins. Lessing's central character in *The Golden Notebook*, Anna Wulf, articulates a more developed view of the function and values of the contemporary realist novel:

> The point is, that the function of the novel seems to be changing; it has become an outpost of journalism; we read novels for information about areas of life we don't know … . Most novels, if they are successful at all, are original in the sense that they report the existence of an area of society, a type of person, not yet admitted to the general literate consciousness. (Lessing 1993, 75)

The Golden Notebook offers a critique of this type of novel, not just in Anna's self-reflexive critical comments on writing and literate culture, but in its very form. Anna divides her life into four notebooks – black, red, yellow and blue – each of which represents and contains different aspects of her experience and self-awareness. The fifth notebook, the golden notebook of the title, is her attempt to resolve her diffused and fragmented identities into a meaningful whole. These notebooks are themselves interspersed with a realist narrative entitled *Free Women*, a novel within the novel, which tells the story of Anna and her friend,

Molly, and their attempts to find love and happiness. As Susan
Watkins argues, however, it is difficult to settle the status of *Free
Women* within *The Golden Notebook*: 'is it a parody of the type of
conventional realist novel Lessing has previously written but now
rejects, or is it something to which she thinks we ultimately have to
return?' (Watkins 2001, 65)

   This is a question which might be asked more widely of the novel's
critique of realism. Lessing seems to draw our attention throughout
the novel to a postmodern sense of the fragmentation and incoherence of human subjectivity, yet central to the narrative is an attempt
to resolve rather than celebrate such incoherence. The attempt by
Anna to explore her identity beyond the realist narrative of *Free
Women* produces multiple realist narratives, of her life in Africa, her
pursuit of communist politics, her life as a fiction writer, and her
quest for some sort of psychic balance or harmony. These narratives
are realist in varying degrees, ranging from the romance conventions
which permeate the yellow notebook, to Anna's desperate attempt to
document reality by pasting newspaper headlines and reports into a
scrapbook. Each of the narratives in *The Golden Notebook* attempt to
make sense and order out of what Anna perceives to be the chaos of
her life. Lorna Sage argues that this is the theme of the novel, which
contains within its form a critique of the attempt to make sense and
order out of chaos:

> Gradually, we realise, this filing system undermines its own purpose –
> each notebook spells out the same message, that putting yourself in
> order is the problem, not the solution. Joining the Party, or finding a
> genial Jungian analyst, or making up stories to live inside are all
> strategies for denying the underlying incoherence of things. Or
> rather, their common ground in violence and diversity. You *represent*
> the world best by letting yourself fall apart, crack up, break down.
> (Sage 1992, 15)

For Sage, as for other feminist critics such as Gerardine Meaney and
Patricia Waugh, Lessing's novel ultimately deconstructs the liberal
humanist notion of a coherent, stable identity (Meaney 1993, 36;
Waugh 1989, 203). In its place, we have Anna Wulf, who learns
through her various attempts to write her own identity, and to fix her
place in the world, that identity is shifting, unstable, disordered and
incoherent. She learns, in other words, to acknowledge 'difference' as

the defining principle of subjectivity, rather than sameness. Waugh argues that this acknowledgement is in a sense the logical outcome of 'her marginal status as a left-wing woman and an anti-colonial ex-colonial', which manifests itself 'in a series of desperate pastiches, parodies, and stylistic experiments' (Waugh 1989, 201–2). The parodic form of *The Golden Notebook*, its reflexive and metafictional structures, intimates an important and critical difference from the ideological underpinnings of the realist narrative. Realism, as Anna Wulf observes, is too easily complicit with the consumerist demands of a literate culture, serving up doses of informative docu-fiction to satisfy the sociological curiosity of the middle-class reader. The point of *The Golden Notebook* is to offer up the experiences of Anna Wulf for reflexive interrogation, to shift the perspective of the reader from privileged voyeur to self-conscious subject. It does this by teasing the reader constantly with the expectation of coherence, of resolution, and supplying instead an openness to contradiction, to fragmentation and to disorder.

This explains, to a large extent, what Gayle Greene observes as the novel's 'transformative power' (Greene 1991, 26). *The Golden Notebook* juxtaposes the closed, predictable conventions of realism in *Free Women* with the irreconcilable differences evident throughout the notebooks. When Anna talks about seeing people 'in a sort of continuous, creative stream', for example, in *Free Women* (Lessing 1993, 243), this reflects the narrative construction of *Free Women*, which narrates the experiences of Anna and Molly as a coherent, continuous stream. But the notebooks show that Anna's experience of time is disjunctive and incoherent, quite unlike how the narrative shapes her experience. The notebooks take on different narrative forms – diary, memoir, scribbled ideas, fragments of thoughts, introspective questioning, and so on – and are frequently punctuated by lines, subdivisions, and editor's notes commenting on changes of style or form. The notebooks assemble Anna's experiences into some kind of order, then, but it is less coherent, less accessible than the realist conventions of *Free Women* suggest. The disjunction between the two styles constantly throws into question what we learn about Anna, and constantly disrupts the subject positions within the novel. The effect of the combination of styles and forms within the novel is to pose more questions than it answers, befitting Lessing's sense of political disillusionment when she wrote it, and indeed the disillusionment felt by Anna and Molly throughout the narratives. It has disquieting implications, not just for the fate of left-wing commitment in a world dominated by capitalism, but also for liberal feminism. If, as the novel seems to suggest, identity is incoherent and unstable, if the power of self-representation and self-knowledge is elusive, then how might it be possible to formulate the kind of grounded, assured subject position necessary to feminism, and indeed any oppositional politics? 'What price any feminism that cannot tell what a woman is?' Ruth Robbins poses rhetorically (Robbins 2000, 212). In this sense, *The Golden Notebook* can be read as a prolonged meditation on the discursive strategies and formal dilemmas of oppositional politics, be that feminism or communism. *The Golden Notebook* poses the difficulty of effecting change to a system using the linguistic and literary forms which have been produced within that system. Is it possible, then, to construct a radical feminist aesthetics using the tools of a patriarchal system? This is a question which, I want to argue, is pertinent not just to Lessing's novel, but to other feminist fiction too. It is especially relevant to Jean Rhys' late novel, *Wide Sargasso Sea* (1966), for example, which returns to Charlotte Brontë's *Jane Eyre* to follow the hidden story of Bertha Mason (Antoinette Cosway in Rhys' novel), the mad wife in the attic of the Rochester house (Rhys 1968).

Rhys attempts a feminist and post-colonial revision of Brontë's novel, explaining and contextualising Bertha/Antoinette's madness through the double displacements of femininity and colonialism. In doing so, she interprets Brontë's text as complicit in the patriarchal structures of colonialism, with Bertha functioning to symbolise the madness, instability and terror of the colonial 'other'. As David Leon Higdon argues, '*Wide Sargasso Sea* takes a situation which, to its author, epitomized the half-understood conflicts between diverse cultures. She felt that Charlotte Brontë was "beastly English" to Bertha Mason and to the problems of culture shock in general' (Higdon 1984, 112). For Rhys, then, *Jane Eyre* is a study in cultural myopia, in the lack of common understanding between women, in the fractious relations between feminism and colonialism. Antoinette, as a Creole woman in Jamaica, is from the beginning a hybrid figure, caught between the distrust of the coloniser and the contempt of the recently freed slaves. She suffers the violence of the colonised when an angry mob attacks and burns down her family home, and another kind of violence when her brother, Richard Mason, sells her into marital slavery to Rochester, and the two men conspire to have her committed so that they can obtain her inherited wealth. The conclusion to the novel implies that Antoinette does literally use the master's tools to dismantle the master's house, shielding a naked flame to where she will set fire to Rochester's house. This act, the novel implies, is the return of the violence bred by the coloniser to his own home, but it is also the fulfilment of the pervasive stereotype of demented femininity as a force for destruction. 'Why, what could she have done, being what she is?' Yeats asks of his own symbolic figure of terrible beauty, Maud Gonne: the same sense of historical inevitability and mythic force seems to ring through Rhys's novel (Yeats 1989, 185).

For Rhys, however, it is not so much a question of what Antoinette *is*, as what she is made to be. The narrative structure of the novel implies the loss of discursive power which underlies Antoinette's final, desperate fate. Her alienation is marked throughout the narrative, in the way, for example, that Rochester's narrative occupies the centre of the novel, and turns Antoinette into its subject. But even in Antoinette's narrative, we are given the perspective of a character watching her fate unfold from the sidelines, unable to alter the course of events that will lead to her subjugation. The novel is divided into three parts, the first of which is narrated by Antoinette and tells the story of her childhood; the middle section of the novel, by far the longest, is narrated by Rochester; and the final part returns to the disinherited, zombie-like narrative of Antoinette.

Throughout the novel, Antoinette is shown to be subject to various forms of power. Subjectivity is defined in post-structuralist thinking as that process of acquiring selfhood in and through language, and being subject to the effects of ideological, political, discursive and socio-historical forces. One of the most obvious ways in which our selfhood is inscribed in and through language is in the act of naming. Our names recognise that we are identifiable and subject to the call of others, and that our identities are inscribed within a social system, based upon patrilinear descent. In this sense, it is significant that Antoinette bears a similar, elongated form of the name of her mother, Annette. More significant, however, is Rochester's displacement of her name. Rochester recreates Antoinette as Bertha, a name which he insists upon as the stamp of her subjection to him. This displacement of names is indicative of an uneven relationship of power, in which the power to name is the privilege of patriarchy.

Names are sites of contest in the novel. Antoinette refuses to be called Bertha, but Rochester continues to insist upon her new name. The erasure of her name is part of that process by which Rochester

obliterates her history, her property, her identity, her freedom. She is
deprived of any sense of self-identity, so that when we encounter
Antoinette incarcerated in his home in England, she no longer recognises herself:

> There is no looking-glass here and I don't know what I am like now. I
> remember watching myself brush my hair and how my eyes looked
> back at me. The girl I saw was myself yet not quite myself. Long ago
> when I was a child and very lonely I tried to kiss her. But the glass was
> between us – hard, cold and misted over with my breath. Now they
> have taken everything away. What am I doing in this place and who
> am I? (Rhys 1968, 147)

This image of alienation, of non-recognition, is repeated several times
in that final section of the novel. She fails to recognise herself, and
fears the ghost that she has become. This manifests itself in another
mirror scene, in which she sees 'the woman with streaming hair. She
was surrounded by a gilt frame, but I knew her' (154). In the final
section of the novel, we find the dissolution of Antoinette's identity,
and the fulfilment of her earlier prophecy that 'I will write my name in
fire red' (44). Deprived of language, deprived of identity, deprived of
any other means by which to represent herself, she resorts to the only
language available to her, the language of fire, of destruction. This is,
of course, a mirror image of the fire which has raged through the
Mason home earlier in the novel, and invites us to consider the ways
in which Antoinette's condition of enslavement is comparable to that
of the angry mob. One image to which Rhys draws our attention in the
earlier fire scene is that of the parrot engulfed in flame, his wings
failing him and his falling, screeching, to the ground. This image
recurs in the final scene of the novel, in which Antoinette projects
herself as the parrot, with a voice calling to her 'Bertha, Bertha', as she
falls, screeching, to the ground. Antoinette has become the metaphorical equivalent of the parrot, the caged bird with clipped wings,
reduced to repeating the terms of her own subjection. If Antoinette's
subjectivity is shown throughout the novel to be shaped and determined by the social, economic and cultural forces around her, in the
final section of the novel we find her reduced to a state of abjection –
that is, the state which Julia Kristeva describes as one in which
meaning and identity collapse, in which the structure of
subject/object relations collapses. Hence, Antoinette becomes a force

of destruction, threatening to destroy the house of her own imprison-
ment. This, the novel implies bleakly, is the only power left to
Antoinette, once she is deprived even of her own name.

Names can be withheld, too, as means of exercising power. Daniel
Cosway's reason for writing his inflammatory letter to Rochester is
that his own father could never remember his name, and referred to
his illegitimate offspring as 'what's-your-name' (101). His revenge is
to represent Antoinette to Rochester as destined for madness, from a
sick and cursed family. But Rhys's narrative, too, exercises the power
of withholding names. It denies to Brontë's Rochester his own name;
at no point is the character who corresponds to Rochester given that
name in the narrative. As Gayatri Spivak points out, this is a deft
manoeuvre on Rhys's part, in denying to him 'the Name of the Father,
or the patronymic', the one thing which ties him to the security of
cultural inheritance and social status (Spivak 1999, 129). This withholding of the name from Rochester is itself indicative of the novel's
strategy: it does not depict Rochester without sympathy, without
recognition of the process of social marginalisation which has
produced his own subjectivity.

Rhys's novel, then, is concerned with power relations, and the
discursive construction of subjectivity. It undermines the very notion
that literature might be 'common ground', for it shows that literature
erects powerful structures of its own for disenfranchising women and
the colonised of the power to represent themselves. This is projected
metaphorically in the novel as the conflict between the imaginative
geographies of Antoinette and Rochester, between her vision of
England as an unreal, dream-like textual space, and his confidence in
the implacable reality of England in contrast to the conspiratorial arti-
ficiality of Jamaica. Christophine, Antoinette's servant, offers a further
contrast, as she cannot even believe that England exists – it belongs so
much to the realm of myth that it is a kind of blank space, about
which she has heard only that 'it cold to freeze your bones and they
thief your money' (92). Even the geography of this novel, then, the
ground upon which it is played out, is a matter of dispute and contradiction. *Wide Sargasso Sea* constantly returns us to the incommensu-
rability of gendered subject positions, which are also of course
colonial subject positions, and thematises the discursive power of
narrative and representation. This power, by which, for example,
Antoinette is appropriated and dispossessed through Rochester's
narrative, is explained by Romita Choudhury:

> Rochester's power resides exactly at this point when self-reflexivity intersects with the larger political and economic establishment that makes English presence possible in Jamaica; individual unease aligns with political and economic certainty to grant him central authority in 'reading' Antoinette's experiences and prescribing the 'proper' course of action. In correspondence with this process of usurpation, Antoinette's textual space gradually diminishes and her interpretive control over her story fades. (Choudhury 1996, 323)

Rhys depicts the shrinking of Antoinette's power of self-representation by returning her to the image constructed in Brontë's novel, of a ghostly figure who haunts the Rochester house. In contrast to *Jane Eyre*, however, in *Wide Sargasso Sea* the narrative explains and develops the contexts in which Bertha/Antoinette becomes this figure, and allows us to situate her final act of destruction within a network of discursive power relations. Dispossessed of the power to represent herself, her history and identity, Antoinette resorts to the only power available to her, the power of 'the revenant', the original title of the novel. *Wide Sargasso Sea* is a novel of ghosts, the ghosts of Brontë's novel, the ghosts of colonialism and slavery, the ghosts of Antoinette's mother and father. The final part of the novel finds Antoinette in an unreal state, in which dreams merge with reality, in which she has been robbed of her name, and in which she sees the ghosts of herself everywhere. She becomes the mad woman who haunts the house, the spectre of revenge and destruction, the 'other' who counters the masculine ideologies of property and colonialism with the memory of a wronged woman and a wronged people. She becomes, in more acute ways than Anna Wulf, a doubled, ghostly figure. Antoinette signifies the split, multiple identities and voices of the dispossessed, and, like Lessing's novel, this is reflected in the narrative structures of the novel, as Lorna Sage explains: 'In place of Brontë's robust all-encompassing first person, Rhys has first persons whose narratives are partial, baffled, cross-threaded' (Sage 1992, 51). In comparison to the realist forms adopted by Drabble and Banks, then, Rhys's novel constructs an altogether more complex representation of feminine identity, which, as Sage goes on to suggest, implies a more cynical assessment of the fate of women in a world determined by patriarchal structures. Antoinette, Sage writes, 'can symbolise ... a state of indeterminacy, a volatility and a vulnerability that suggest infinite regress' (Sage 1992, 52).

The same pessimistic note echoes through Ruth Prawer Jhabvala's novel, *Heat and Dust* (1975). Jhabvala's novel tells the story of two Englishwomen in India: Olivia, the wife of a colonial official, whose story is set in 1923; and the unnamed narrator, fifty years later, who arrives in India to retrace Olivia's life. As in Rhys's novel, the alienation of Jhabvala's characters is represented through their estrangement from the landscape and climate. India is experienced as 'heat and dust', as 'another world altogether ... another reality' (Jhabvala 1994, 85). The juxtaposition of the story of two women across a fifty year period invites comparisons about the degrees of freedom and opportunity enjoyed by both Olivia and the narrator. Olivia comes to India in the context of her marriage, and she is expected to bear and support a family for her husband. The narrator arrives as a single woman, not in devotion to a man, but in the cause of finding out the hidden history of Olivia, of whom she knows only the rumours of sexual trangression whispered among her family in England. Olivia becomes weary of the numbing routine of inactivity and domestic confinement which characterises her role as a dutiful wife, and begins instead to accept the invitations of the charming Nawab. The narrator is able to trace Olivia's life up to the point at which she forces a miscarriage of the child she bears from her transgressive affair with the Nawab, after which she disappears from our view, leaving no evidence of her life.

Increasingly as the narrative progresses, the narrator's experiences mirror Olivia's. She too has a relationship with an Indian official and becomes pregnant. They visit the same places, hear the same words from their lovers, and receive the same gifts and tributes, as if the narrator's life is a revisitation of Olivia's. Much has changed in the fifty years between Olivia and the narrator. Only the buildings retain any sense of the confidence and grandeur of the colonial past, and even they have been converted to other uses, or are in various states of decay or dereliction. What remains unchanged, however, is the social and sexual status of women, as objects of exploitation and manipulation. Olivia, it seems, is as much the victim of the Nawab's power games and ruses, as she is the transgressive heroine the narrator has come to believe. So too, despite the appearance that the narrator is a free, independent woman, who carries her own luggage and makes her own way in the world, she allows herself to be used for sex by Chid, the English boy seeking spiritual enlightenment in India (which the novel implies is a kind of new phase of Western 'uses' of

India). 'I have never had such a feeling of being used', says the narrator, 'I don't really know why I let him go ahead' (65). The narrator acknowledges that some degree of consent is involved in being used sexually by Chid, but that her consent is given joylessly, despite herself. She knows that she 'could easily keep him off', but she permits him to continue, as if it was her inevitable duty to serve his sexual needs. The way in which Chid abuses the narrator for his own pleasures in this scene, and her revulsion at being used, expose as a shabby deception the idea that Chid is in search of spiritual enlightenment, and the idea that the narrator is a 'free woman'. Jhabvala's novel is concerned here to represent the complexities and ambivalences of the 'sixties generation', of the notion pervasive in the West of 'free love' and universal equality. Chid achieves his spiritual and sexual liberation, but at the expense of the narrator's desires and needs, much like the relationship between Olivia and her husband, or indeed, Olivia and the Nawab. The implication is that the lives and opportunities of Olivia and the narrator are not so very different. The narrator may be free of the moral strictures which Olivia endures and transgresses in colonial society, but she nevertheless remains bound up in patriarchal discourses of power and sexuality which continue to figure women as objects.

Chid's abuse of the narrator, or the Nawab's exploitation of Olivia, might have been represented more acutely as rape, either literally or metaphorically, and thus, the novel echoes but refuses to repeat the scene imagined in Forster's *A Passage to India*. The key element in Jhabvala's novel which complicates the depiction of women's status in society is that of consent or complicity. Olivia is not forced to run off with the Nawab, but desires to do so. The narrator is bigger and stronger than Chid, and could resist his sexual cravings, but doesn't. Likewise, both women encounter what the colonial administrators call 'suttee' – the practice of widows burning themselves on the funeral pyres beside their dead husbands. This is dismissed by one colonial official as a 'barbaric custom', but both Olivia and the narrator find reverence and desire for the outlawed practice. Olivia challenges the colonial officials gathered around her husband at dinner, who unanimously deplore 'suttee', to think of it instead as 'a noble idea ... to want to go with the person you care for most in the world' (59). She declares her willingness to do the same, should her husband die. 'Suttee' represents a complex problem for Olivia and the narrator, for it suggests an act which is both the pinnacle of romantic love, and the extreme manifestation of female dependence on men. As Gayatri Spivak argues in 'Can the Subaltern Speak?', 'sati' is a site of intense conflict between imperial and nativist discourses, in which the practice is condemned on the one hand as barbaric, immoral and deserving of punishment, and celebrated on the other hand as a sacred act of self-sacrifice which testified to the sanctity of the love between the widow and her husband, and earned her spiritual reward (Spivak explains that 'suttee' constitutes a grammatical error on the part of the British since 'sati' meant 'the good wife', not the act of self-immolation itself). For Spivak, the conflict over the meanings of 'sati' is interesting not just from the postcolonial standpoint, but from the feminist perspective too:

> The abolition of this rite by the British has been generally understood as a case of 'White men saving brown women from brown men'. White women – from the nineteenth-century British Missionary Registers to Mary Daly – have not produced an alternative understanding. Against this is the Indian nativist argument, a parody of the nostalgia for lost origins: 'The women actually wanted to die'. The two sentences go a long way to legitimise each other. One never encounters the testimony of the women's voice-consciousness. (Spivak 1994, 93)

'Sati' is represented and imagined through various discourses of morality, colonialism, sexuality, ethics and feminism, but, for Spivak, it highlights most of all the absence of the subaltern voices of the women themselves. It underlines, in other words, the social and political status of women as the objects and effects of discourse, as interpellated through structures of power and meaning. In *Heat and Dust*, 'sati' emblematises the fate of women throughout the novel, signifying their complicity in discourses and forces which are ultimately self-sacrificing. The reasons why Olivia and the narrator consent to being used, to sacrificing themselves for men, remain unanswered, just as neither character can grasp fully the motivations of the 'sati' widows. It is questionable whether Olivia identifies with the 'sati' widows, or merely constructs their experiences through Western conventions of romance fiction. (Indeed, the question of whether Westerners can see India at all, rather than a heavily romanticised construction of it, is central to the novel.)

Nevertheless, there is a connection made between the English and

Indian women in the novel, which implies that Western women share common historical experiences of oppression and subjection with the colonised. Jhabvala's novel, in this sense, reflects a growing concern for the feminism of the 1960s and 1970s with the interrelations between gender, class, race, sexuality and culture. *Heat and Dust* seems to suggest provocative connections between structures of patriarchal and colonial power, and to invite the need for a feminism capable of explaining and resisting discourses of racism, colonialism, nationalism and class prejudice, as well as sexism. As such a feminist text, however, Jhabvala's novel is profoundly ambivalent. India, and Indian women, remain marginal, shadowy figures in the novel, suggesting that they continue to be inscrutable from the Western perspectives of Olivia and the narrator. Cultural differences problematise the notion of a common feminist perspective, in other words. In presenting continuity, or at least connections, between the experiences of Olivia, the narrator and 'sati' widows, however, the novel seems to imply a persistent paradox in the relationship between women and the structures of patriarchal power. Laurie Sucher argues that Jhabvala's novel 'confirms and illustrates the premise of feminism, the societal derogation of women. It even confirms feminism's imperative: that women resist that social and psychological derogation' (Sucher 1989, 9). The novel suggests, though, that women are condemned to repeat history, to continue to act out the parts prescribed for them in patriarchal myths, even as they are conscious of the possibilities of resistance and refusal.

Like Banks and Drabble's novels, *Heat and Dust* concludes with its narrator embracing the responsibilities and pleasures of motherhood, but where Banks and Drabble depicted the experience as a new beginning, a new kind of independence and freedom, the narrator of Jhabvala's novel lives too much in the shadow of ghosts to suggest any optimism for the future. Where Banks and Drabble depict a generation of women surviving and progressing, the novels of Lessing, Rhys and Jhabvala discussed above figure the experiences and conditions of contemporary femininity in tropes of breakdown, suicide, displacement, madness, dissolution and death. Such tropes may indicate a morose preoccupation in feminist fiction of the 1960s and 1970s with the destructive effects of male-centred discourses of power, but they do represent an important dispute with the cultural politics of consensus and consolidation in the 1950s and early 1960s. The self-reflexive structures of *The Golden Notebook*, *Wide Sargasso Sea* and

Heat and Dust encompass purposeful critiques of the discourses of patriarchal domination, foregrounding the ways in which gender is constructed discursively, and thus rehearsing the deconstructive transformation of contemporary gender relations.

Discourse and subversion

The problem which the novels of Lessing, Rhys and Jhabvala expose so lucidly is the problem of how change comes about. In *The Golden Notebook*, Lessing presents the stories of women who are acutely, often painfully, conscious of the structures and means of patriarchal oppression, yet who remain dependent on men. *Wide Sargasso Sea* studies the tragic cycle of violence and madness in which Antoinette is caught up, against which she can only respond with violence and madness. *Heat and Dust* depicts women's experiences across time as repetitive, as a continuation of historical abuse and powerlessness. How might this cycle be broken? How might a feminist utopia even begin to come into existence? How might the power politics of patriarchy be subverted? How might we move beyond the necessity of feminist fiction (and indeed feminist politics) into what Showalter imagined in 1977 as a future in which women writers entered into 'a seamless participation in the literary mainstream', an idea surely proximate to Woolf's ideal of 'common ground'? (Showalter 1999, 323) More importantly, how might we subvert the very notion of a literary and political mainstream? This question of subversion, of transformation, is the concern of the writers considered in this final section of the chapter.

The emphasis in second-wave feminism of the 1970s on the discursive and ideological foundations of patriarchy has depressing consequences for any possibility of feminist change. The fiction which follows second-wave feminism, written in the 1980s in which the highest political office in England was occupied by a woman, Margaret Thatcher, is charged with the complexity of post-suffragette politics. For many feminists, particularly on the left of British politics, the politics of Thatcherism offered ample evidence that the access to political rights – the right to vote, the right of women to achieve formal positions of power – was no guarantee of social and political change for women. The key to changing social and political structures, after second-wave feminism, was not a matter of getting women into positions of power. Rather, the structures of power them-selves had to be subverted. In this sense, as Patricia Waugh argues, post-1970s feminism has much in common with postmodernism. This is not to say that postmodern forms of feminist fiction have supplanted or made redundant realist forms of fiction – far from it – but Waugh considers the disjunctive, subversive formal strategies of postmodernism to enable a certain kind of feminist critique. For both, it is necessary to 'disrupt traditional boundaries: between "art" and "life", masculine and feminine, high and popular culture, the domi-nant and the marginal' (Waugh 1989, 6). For both, moreover, the adoption and subversion of traditional structures of meaning and identity is a central strategy of resistance.

This is the case, for example, in Fay Weldon's ninth novel, *The Life and Loves of a She Devil* (1983), which adopts the conventions of romance and Gothic fiction, and subverts the traditional ideological effects of those conventions. Ruth Patchett, a gigantic, Frankenstein figure, is the jilted wife of Bobbo, who has an affair and eventually runs off to live with the beautiful, romantic novelist, Mary Fisher. Ruth and Mary are at opposite ends of a spectrum of conventional stereotypes of femininity. Ruth lives in boring suburbia, with two chil-dren and a dog, pitied but neglected by her husband, while Mary lives in a converted lighthouse, unattached but adored and seduced by men, and thriving on the royalties from her successful novels. Ruth is the figure of the female freak, that powerful coercive image of grotesque femininity, which Gilbert and Gubar argue functions to police women's identities:

> The sexual nausea associated with all these monster women helps explain why so many real women have for so long expressed loathing of (or at least anxiety about) their own, inexorably female bodies. The 'killing' of oneself into an art object – the pruning and preening, the mirror madness, and concern with odors and aging, the hair which is invariably too curly or too lank, with bodies too thin or too thick – all this testifies to the efforts women have expended not just trying to be angels but trying *not* to become female monsters. (Gilbert and Gubar 1979, 34)

In Weldon's novel, femininity essentially entails these two poles of beauty and monstrosity, desire and neglect, power and oblivion, in which women must work to appear beautiful, to conform to the desires of the male gaze in order to attract love, money and power. Mary Fisher has it all, of course, while Ruth predictably struggles against the rigid confines of her domestic enslavement. Bobbo ultimately blames Ruth's gigantic, freakish body for the failure of their marriage: 'How can one love what is essentially unlovable?' he asks, and proceeds to insult her as 'a bad mother, a worse wife and a dreadful cook. In fact I don't think you are a woman at all. I think what you are is a she devil!' (Weldon 1983, 46–7) When Bobbo calls Ruth a 'she devil', she acquires the power the name signifies. Naming, as Gerardine Meaney has argued, is the game of creation, the inscription in language of the power to create, and ultimately Weldon's novel is a story of self-generation, of Ruth acquiring the power to name and create herself (albeit within heavily prescribed limitations) (Meaney 1993, 68). Instead of trying to be the good wife, Ruth realises that if she is a 'she devil', 'I can take what I want' (49). According to Anne Cranny-Francis, Bobbo succeeds here in alerting Ruth 'to the only kind of power she has – as the transgressive woman – a she-devil, who takes her destiny into her own hands and becomes an active, oppositional subject' (Cranny-Francis 1990, 189). The story from this point on becomes a kind of fantasy revenge, in which Ruth sets out to destroy the new relationship between Bobbo and Mary Fisher, and, in essence, to win her husband back. In the course of doing this, she adopts several fantastic personae, carries out extraordinary feats of deception, and, perhaps most significantly of all, reinvents her appearance with drastic and dangerous procedures of cosmetic surgery. Ruth is thus somewhat problematic as the 'active, oppositional subject' of feminist politics, since she uses the technological apparatus of late twentieth-century patriarchy – cosmetic surgery – to 'remake' herself in the image of the 'angelic' or erotic stereotype of Mary Fisher. Ruth appropriates power for her own ends, certainly, but what she uses this borrowed power to do is rather more ambivalent from feminist perspectives. She turns her back on the possibility of living in a female commune, or the comforts of a lesbian relationship, and instead devotes herself to winning back her husband. When her strategy succeeds, however, the power relations between Bobbo and Ruth have been reversed: 'I cause Bobbo as much misery as he ever caused me, and more. I try not to, but somehow it is not a matter of male and female, after all; it never was, merely of power. I have all, and he has none. As I was, he is now' (256).

Weldon's novel employs a chiasmic structure, in which the hierarchy which begins the novel is reversed in the course of the narrative. That the hierarchy itself is unchanged, merely the switching of genders within it, should alert us to the ways in which the novel is suspicious of narratives of radical transformation. There are significant implications for feminist struggle, however, in the process of Ruth's transformation. The first is implicit in the Frankenstein allusions throughout the novel. The fact that Bobbo names Ruth as a 'she devil' suggests that he creates her as a monster. She is his monstrous creation, and, like Frankenstein, wreaks vengeance on his world, destroying his wealth and his lover, and depriving him of his sanity and freedom. Weldon's novel functions as a kind of feminist moral fable, a warning against the patriarchal stereotyping of femininity as destructive and ultimately self-implosive. Ruth shifts between two powerful feminine archetypes in the novel, either the grotesque witch or the dangerous siren. The second implication of Ruth's transformation is related to the postmodern aspects of Weldon's novel. Ruth's capacity to alter her identity from domestic housewife to nurse, entrepreneur, nanny, charwoman, counsellor, lover, romantic novelist, and, through the ultimate masquerade of cosmetic surgery, 'an impossible male fantasy made flesh' (239), proves what her cosmetic surgeon asserts, that 'there is no such thing as the essential self' (234). Weldon seems to suggest in the novel that femininity is neither an essential identity, nor is it the polarised stereotypes constructed in patriarchal discourse, but is rather a continuum of performed identities. Ruth Patchett is, in other words, Riviere's 'womanliness as masquerade', the masque of femininity which conceals not an underlying essence, but an underlying absence (Riviere 1986, 35–44). This, Waugh argues, is the function of Weldon's parodic adoption of fantasy and Gothic conventions in the novel, for the 'subversive potential' of those genres 'for decentring liberal concepts of gender and identity' (Waugh 1989, 190). Weldon's novel serves to illustrate the complexities of feminist politics of representation, for it at once utilises the stabilising tendencies of first-person narrative (the autobiographical voice of Ruth Patchett, which validates her experience and identity as worthy of attention), and simultaneously destabilises the notion of authentic experience and identity, showing Ruth instead to be a series of performed roles and masques. Thus, Weldon establishes the grounds upon which women have been represented, and continue to be represented, and systematically opens up the process and politics of representation for interrogation.

The same playful, paradoxical structure is presented in Angela Carter's *Nights at the Circus* (1984). Carter's novel reconstructs the mythological archetype of winged, angelic woman, who acquires power through the mesmerising spectacle of her fantastic body. As such, it offers the reader a return to a seemingly fixed myth of femininity – angel, Nike, the Golden Bird – while at the same time it continually remarks upon the instability and contingency of this myth. 'Fevvers' wings create an eroticised hermeneutic enquiry: what is she?' Isobel Armstrong asks, 'Is she a bird or a woman? Or could she, given her strength and size, be a man? Is she a hoax?' (Armstrong 1994, 273) Fevvers transgresses conventional boundaries between reality and fantasy, the ordinary and the mythical, popular and high culture, so that she is at once the recreation of classical Greek myth and the voice of late nineteenth-century working-class femininity. She is simultaneously the orphan whore, and the coveted 'Golden Bird' of Yeatsian myth. Carter's novel strides towards the inclusion of the voice of working-class women, a rare phenomenon in twentieth-century women's writing, but paradoxically infuses this voice with the self-reflexive narratives of classical archetypes and mythical episodes. *Nights at the Circus*, in other words, fictionalises the coming-into-representation of silenced working-class women, while undermining with postmodern instability and self-reflexivity the representation of identity itself.

Like Weldon's novel, *Nights at the Circus* reverses the power relations which begin the novel, moving from the masculine rationalism of Walser's narrative which opens the novel, to the chaotic, picaresque narratives of Fevvers and Lizzie as the novel progresses. Carter focuses on a clash of discourses, between the magical and the scientific, the masculine feminine, in which Fevvers seduces Walser into her own narrative, and, as Sarah Bannock argues, 'the novel performs some sort of magic trick, within itself': 'At the beginning of the novel, Walser is metaphorically on top, writing Fevvers down; but by the end, she has taken the ascendancy. Fevvers achieves this feat by means of wooing and subverting the concepts of time, gravity, perspective' (Bannock 1997, 201). Walser, at the beginning of the novel, interviews Fevvers with a view to exposing her as a hoax, bringing the penetrating gaze of his rationalism to bear on the supposed enigma of the flying circus woman. By the end of the novel, however, Fevvers proposes to appropriate Walser as the scribal witness of the new woman:

'Think of him, not as a lover, but as a scribe, as an amanuensis,' she said to Lizzie. 'And not of my trajectory, alone, but of yours too, Lizzie; of your long history of exile and cunning which you've scarcely hinted to him, which will fill up ten times more of his notebooks than *my* story ever did. Think of him as the amanuensis of all those whose tales we've yet to tell him, the histories of those women who would otherwise go down nameless and forgotten, erased from history as if they had never been, so that he, too, will put his poor shoulder to the wheel and help to give the world a little turn into the new era that begins tomorrow. And once the old world has turned on its axle so that the new dawn can dawn, then, ah, then! all the women will have wings, the same as I. (Carter 1985, 285)

Fevvers's utopian faith in the dawn of new femininity, the turning of the world from patriarchy to liberty, is gently offset by the cynical caution of Lizzie: 'it's going to be a little more complicated than that ... this old witch sees storms ahead, my girl' (286). Fevvers is not simply the bearer of the new world, but a liminal space between the old and the new, between the whore, angel and monster myths of literary and cultural tradition and the imagined future in which 'all woman will have wings'. Fevvers's wings allow her to escape the nets of Walser's rationalist discourse, and generate a feminist aesthetics of flight.

Carter's novel seems, on this note, to be particularly in tune with contemporary feminist philosophies of power and resistance. In *The Laugh of the Medusa*, Hélène Cixous argues that woman is subversive because of her history of subjugation, and uses the metaphors of flight and laughter – two significant tropes in the figuration of Fevvers – to construct an image of woman as antithetical to and subversive of masculine rationalist discourse:

Flying [Voler – to fly, to steal] is woman's gesture – flying in language and making it fly. We have all learned the art of flying and its numerous techniques, for centuries we've been able to possess anything only by flying; we've lived in flight, stealing away, finding, when desired, narrow passageways, hidden crossovers ... . [Women] go by, fly the coop, take pleasure in jumbling the order of space, in disorienting it, in changing around the furniture, dislocating things and values, breaking them all up, emptying structures, and turning propriety upside down. (Cixous 1981, 263–4)

Nights at the Circus illustrates through a series of tableaux the attempt to contain and control women institutionally and discursively – the brothel, the museum, the circus, the panopticon prison. Fevvers represents the powerful subversion of these institutional and discursive means of control, in each case, heralding their disintegration or implosion. The brothel falls apart and is destroyed after Fevvers appears as 'winged victory' (the women burn down the house of their incarceration, a symbolic effect shared with Rhys and Weldon). Fevvers liberates her fellow inmates from Madame Schreck's grotesque museum, and causes Schreck's death. The circus disintegrates after Fevvers joins it. Her proximity to the panopticon prison, arguably, is responsible for the subversion of order which takes place there. The novel concludes with an image of the subversive impact of Fevvers' laughter which 'began to twist and shudder across the entire globe, as if a spontaneous response to the giant comedy that endlessly unfolded beneath it, until everything that lived and breathed, everywhere, was laughing' (295).

As in Cixous's conception of the subversive flight and laughter of woman, Carter's conclusion figures women in terms of dislocation, disorientation, destruction and the inversion of order. Fevvers is more than an instrument of destruction – she teaches love to Walser and the Strong Man and rescues Mignon from abuse – but she represents the disorder, the chaos, which the novel suggests necessarily precedes the dawn of the new woman. Carter's conception of Fevvers's struggle against masculine discourse is essentially dialogic, which is to say that Fevvers does not transcend or supersede patriarchy, but rather simultaneously is constructed within and 'flies by' it. Mary Russo suggests that Carter's model for Fevvers might be Juliette, the Marquis de Sade's heroine, 'who wraps herself in the flags of male tyranny to avoid victimization ... and yet who will renew the world' (Russo 1995, 165). Carter's novel is no less aware of the conditions of women's oppression in modern patriarchy than Lessing or Rhys, but it imagines the possibilities for subversion and resistance in rather more optimistic terms. Fevvers is shown to appropriate the power of masculine discourse for her own ends, and to emerge through the transformative space of narrative 'on top'. *Nights at the Circus* never fails, however, to register the ironic and self-parodic ways in which Fevvers's 'victory' might be co-opted back into patriarchal discourse, and so, in common with postmodern narratives, conceives of fantasy and utopian fictions as necessarily contingent strategies for resisting powerful discourses.

The equivocation between utopia and irony, between the symbolic and the real, between myth and history, is an important element in contemporary women's writing. Carter's winged heroine, for example, is both monstrous and sublime, male and female, fact and fiction, and so on. There seem to be endless ways in which Fevvers is a hybrid creature, in a novel which itself transgresses and mixes genres and fictional conventions all the time. Lidia Curti argues that this interest in hybridity and transgression has manifested itself in contemporary women's writing in particularly gothic, monstrous forms. 'Strange unfamiliar shapes, freakish bodies, disquieting forms and hybrid creatures have been creeping into women's narratives', Curti writes, 'putting in question the frontier between foulness and loveliness, the human and the animal, me and you, female and male' (Curti 1998, 107). One could argue that the emergence of a 'gothic feminism', with its monstrous bodies, fantasy forms and hybrid narratives, is an inevitable consequence of the increasing need after second-wave feminism to deconstruct and move beyond the binary structures familiar from patriarchal discourse. To put it more simply, if patriarchal discourse, in common with rationalist thought generally, structures the world according to a philosophy of 'either/or', gothic feminism proffers instead a pluralist philosophy of 'both/and'. Carter's novel, in common with Weldon's, pursues this interest in the hybrid form, in the trangressiveness of plurality, in its narrative forms as well as its figuration of monstrous bodies.

Jeanette Winterson's *Sexing the Cherry* (1989) explores the same theme, through the shifting, fragmentary stories of the 'Dog-Woman' and her adopted son, Jordan. These stories are set against the turbulent politics of seventeenth-century London, and, intermittently, late twentieth-century London. The Dog-Woman is a monstrous creature, capable of extraordinary feats of violence and destruction, mostly against Puritans, whom she despises for exalting the sin of denial over the sin of excess. She is capable too of great love, in adopting the infant whom she names Jordan after finding him floating in a basket in the Thames. The Dog-Woman plays fire to Jordan's water – she signifies the cleansing power of destruction while his maritime birth presages a life as shifting and boundless as the sea. This constitutes a reversal of conventional gender stereotypes, in the sense that the male signifies fluidity in Winterson's novel against the corporeal solidity and violence of the female, and this is reflected in the narrative styles of the Dog-Woman and Jordan. Jordan's narrative is dreamy, introspective and self-reflexive, while the Dog-Woman explains in a matter-of-fact style the everyday reality of life in the stinking streets of a rotting city. The Dog-Woman believes, in common with the emergent scientific rationalism of her time, that the world can be known through exhaustive scrutiny and travel, while Jordan is drawn to the vastness and emptiness of space and time, to the very unknowability of the world. The purpose of reversing gender stereotypes in the novel (itself an indication that Winterson is conversing with feminist analyses of gendered identities), is to confuse and disrupt the conventions of gender.

The title of the novel intimates its concern with gendering. Jordan attempts to graft two species of cherry together, upon which his mother, the Dog-Woman, exclaims 'Of what sex is that monster you are making?': 'I tried to explain to her that the tree would still be female although it had not been born from seed, but she said things had no gender and were a confusion to themselves' (Winterson 1989, 79). The pertinence of their conversation to his own situation is implicit – Jordan has, in one sense, 'not been born from seed', and so will either be female, according to his argument, or genderless, according to the Dog-Woman's. In either case, his identity has been 'grafted' together by his powerful mother, and his strength and independence in traversing his boundless ocean world testifies to the success of her hybrid creation. This, for Curti, is the significance of the novel's theme of 'grafting':

> It is about giving strength to the weak and about metamorphosis and transformation; it is also about postcoloniality and its condition of transplanting oneself elsewhere, or the elsewhere here; about de-spatialisation; about travels and love; about coming into existence without seed or parent; about artificial as well as natural creation. Finally it is about the hybridity of sexual identities. (Curti 1998, 130)

The hybridity of sexual identities, a common theme in Winterson's writings, is a marked departure from the androgyny celebrated by Woolf. Where androgyny obviates or makes irrelevant gender differences, hybridity foregrounds the process of transplantation, of transgression. Winterson weaves into her narrative the story of how strange fruits first came to England, such as the banana brought by the naturalist John Tradescant, and later, the pineapple brought by Jordan himself. These fruits figure in the novel as symbols of trans-plantation, suggesting the wider contexts of colonial 'discovery' and exploitation. Jordan's dream of travelling the seas and bringing to the King an exotic fruit is thus simultaneously a harmless, boyhood fantasy, and the extension of colonial ideologies. The grafting of Jordan's fantasies onto maps of the world, like the grafting of exotic species of fruits and plants into English gardens, signifies the mutabil-ity of identity, and destabilises the notion of fixed identity which underpins both colonial and patriarchal ideologies.

The significance of 'grafting' in *Sexing the Cherry*, then, is that it signals, in all of the forms it takes in the novel, the inevitable hybridity of identity. Just as the novel implies that England is not, and never was, self-identical, but rather, has always been intimately identified with other lands and peoples, so too, femininity is not an essential, immutable gender, but rather, it crosses over, blends with, inter-changes with, cancels out and exceeds masculinity. Winterson's novel counters, in other words, the essentialist division of identity into fixed gender categories, and supplants this with a model which imagines gender identities as diffuse, changeable, transgressive and boundless. So too, the novel begins by recognising that there is no 'common ground', no consensual space which we all inhabit:

> The Hopi, an Indian tribe, have a language as sophisticated as ours, but no tenses for past, present and future. The division does not exist. What does this say about time?
>
> Matter, that thing the most solid and the well-known, which you are holding in your hands and which makes up your body, is now known to be mostly empty space. Empty space and points of light. What does this say about the reality of the world? (Winterson 1989, 8)

In this sense, and in others, Winterson's novel confirms Terry Castle's depiction of lesbian fiction as that which unsettles the realist and rational conventions of masculine rationalist discourse: 'It dismantles the real, as it were, in a search for the not-yet-real, something unpre-dicted and unpredictable' (Castle 1993, 90). In recognising the muta-bility of gender identities, the possibilities for the subversion and transgression of traditional models of femininity and masculinity, *Sexing the Cherry* begins to imagine a utopian vision of hybrid genders, in a world in which peoples are de-territorialised, heterogenous, and infinitely interconnected. Such a vision begins to respond to the imperatives of postmodern, post-colonial feminisms: to reconnect the utopian projects of feminist politics with the demands of a world inevitably hybridised and incorrigibly plural.

Notes

1. See, for example, Elizabeth Wilson, *Only Halfway to Paradise: Women in Postwar Britain, 1945–1968* (London: Tavistock, 1980), 63: 'the "new" problem of the educated housewife masked the perennial problem of the female wage slave at the bottom of the economic ladder'.
2. See Alva Myrdal and Viola Klein, *Women's Two Roles: Home and Work* (London: Routledge & Kegan Paul, 1956); Judith Hubback, *Wives who went to College* (London: Heinemann, 1957); Vera Brittain, *Lady into Woman* (London: Andrew Dakers, 1953); Pearl Jephcott *et al.*, *Married Women Working* (London: Allen and Unwin, 1962).
3. The paper 'Feminism as femininity in the nineteen-fifties?' was written for the *Feminist Review* by Lucy Bland, Angela Coyle, Tricia Davis, Catherine Hall and Janice Winship, representing the thoughts and responses of a wider discussion group on feminist history. The paper acknowledges in an endnote that there are 1970s feminist assumptions influencing how they perceive feminist writing and politics of the 1950s, and that these assumptions need to be tested too.
4. There were Royal Commission reports on equal pay in 1946, on population in 1949, marriage and divorce in 1956, on sexuality in 1957 (Wolfenden), on children in 1960 (Ingleby), and the education of girls in 1963 (Newsom).

5 From Anger to *Blasted*: trauma and social representation in contemporary drama

'If you seek a tombstone, look about you; survey the peculiar nullity of our drama's prevalent genre, the Loamshire play. Its setting is a country house in what used to be called Loamshire but is now, as a heroic tribute to realism, sometimes called Berkshire. Except when somebody must sneeze, or be murdered, the sun invariably shines. The inhabitants belong to a social class derived partly from romantic novels and partly from the playwright's vision of the leisured life he will lead after the play is a success – this being the only effort of imagination he is called upon to make. Joys and sorrows are giggles and whimpers; the crash of denunciation dwindles into "Oh, stuff, Mummy!" and "Oh, really Daddy!". And so grim is the continuity of the thing that the foregoing paragraph might have been written at any time during the last thirty years.'

Kenneth Tynan (1954), reprinted in *Curtains* (83–4)

The theatrical landscape Tynan describes was transformed utterly on May 8th 1956, according to most literary histories of the postwar period, by the opening performance of John Osborne's *Look Back in Anger* at the Royal Court Theatre in Sloane Square, London. Osborne's play, indeed, sets up a dramatic contrast between the decorum and emotional restraint of its middle-class characters, Alison, Helena and Colonel Redfern, and the rebellious energy and articulate 'anger' of its working-class characters, Jimmy Porter and Cliff Lewis. Jimmy Porter, in particular, was heralded by Tynan, the influential theatre critic of *The Observer* newspaper, as the representative voice of a new generation: 'The Porters of our time deplore the tyranny of "good taste", and refuse to accept "emotional" as a term of abuse; they are classless and they are also leaderless' (Tynan 1956, 11). Tynan had spent considerable energy berating the lack of ambition and experiment in English theatre after the war, and Osborne's play was seized upon as the champion of dramatic innovation. As Osborne admitted in the early 1960s, however, *Look Back in Anger* was actually very conventional in form (Osborne 1961, 216). In fact, it differs little in form from the play to which it has been habitually contrasted, Terence Rattigan's *A Deep Blue Sea* (1952).

There are many reasons to be sceptical about the pivotal, or revolutionary, status attributed to Osborne's play.[1] Chief among these reasons is that *Look Back in Anger*, in hindsight, doesn't stand up to much analysis as a socialist, or progressive, piece of theatre. Jimmy Porter's violent outbursts tend to be directed against women, rather than the social or political order, and the criticisms he does make of the state, the empire and the church seem to be tinged with nostalgia for the securities these institutions were perceived to have offered in the past. Secondly, any analysis of the social composition of theatre audiences (Sinfield 1983, 173–97), or the class milieu of the actors, directors, writers and producers involved in putting *Look Back in Anger* on stage (McGrath 1996, 7–15), would reveal that no great revolution was effected in pragmatic terms by the play itself, and it certainly didn't represent the arrival of the working class or youth culture in English theatre, as Tynan claimed. Osborne's success, John McGrath argues, was instead to have achieved 'a method of translating some areas of non-middle-class life in Britain into a form of entertainment that could be sold to the middle classes' (McGrath 1996, 10). Moreover, the myth of Osborne's achievement has been constructed out of an equally forceful myth about the conservatism and aridity of 'pre-Osborne' theatre, whereas productions in the 1990s of J.B. Priestley's *An Inspector Calls*, T.S. Eliot's *The Family Reunion*, Noël Coward's *Private Lives*, and reconsiderations of the reputation and achievements of Terence Rattigan have tended to complicate the reductive image which Tynan depicts in the above epigraph. Something did change in British theatre in the 1950s, which encouraged the emergence of a new wave of dramatists who were both concerned to represent or imagine social and political change, and committed to experimenting with the theatrical forms available to them. But there are other 'landmarks' in postwar theatrical history, such as the production of Beckett's *Waiting for Godot* in 1955, or the visit of Brecht's Berliner Ensemble to England in late 1956, which might equally account for the new trends in British theatre. There are other narratives in postwar theatrical history, too, which might elevate other plays, such as the first London performances of Errol John's *Moon on a Rainbow Shawl* (1958), Shelagh Delaney's *A Taste of Honey* (1958), Brendan Behan's *The Quare Fellow* (1956), or Harold Pinter's *The Birthday Party* (1958). These plays, perhaps in equal measure with *Look Back in Anger*, changed the language, attitude, and cultural politics, of theatre in England.

We might question the reasons for the iconic status of *Look Back in Anger*, or the justice of its place in English theatrical history, but what is beyond doubt is its significance as a mythic event. Playwrights, critics, and cultural historians, too numerous to list here, have all attested to its importance, and cited it as an originary moment in the emergence of political theatre in postwar England. It is significant not for what it presents on stage, however, nor in the language or form with which it does so. Arguably, the attempted suicide in Rattigan's *The Deep Blue Sea* is more shocking to the audience than Jimmy's tirades in *Look Back in Anger*, the impact of Rattigan's silences and his characters' inhibitions more powerful than Jimmy's posturing. The importance of Osborne's play is that it divided audiences and critics, so that while Tynan professed doubt that he 'could love anyone who did not wish to see *Look Back in Anger*' (Tynan 1956, 11), Milton Shulman described the play as 'self-pitying snivel' (Taylor 1968, 41). Most early reviewers recognised talent and potential in Osborne's writing, but the character of Jimmy Porter was received in widely divergent ways, from those who saw him as a representative figure of disillusioned youth, to those like Stephen Williams of the *Evening News*, who memorably declared that Osborne had wasted his dramatic gifts 'on a character who could only be shaken into sense by being ducked in a horse pond or sentenced to a lifetime of cleaning latrines' (Taylor 1968, 43). Osborne had the desire to shock, which in turn, for a short time in the late 1950s and early 1960s, put theatre at the centre of popular media attention, and made it a contentious space of representation. With the impact of *Look Back in Anger*, English theatre was no longer about the well-made play, about formal experiment, or even about murders in country houses. Theatre was now about society, about the highly publicised and mythologised changes in English society and culture. Tynan claimed that the play was charting the emergence of a new youth culture, but there is little in the play to support this, apart from Jimmy's preferences for jazz and his occasional outbursts of youthful energy. Shelagh Delaney's *A Taste of Honey* is much closer to representing the problems and concerns of contemporary youth than Osborne's play. What mattered was that Osborne was seen to be provoking his audiences, attempting to shock them, and, in the process, adopting a new posture in the dynamics between playwright and audience. *Look Back in Anger* is a conventional, not to mention conservative, play, but it appeared in its original production as an *agent provocateur*, and provided a model for a theatre of shock, which would assault its audiences with defiant images of social and cultural difference. This chapter will examine several plays as exemplary of this attitude towards the audience, and will explore the dynamics of shock and provocation in contemporary theatre. It does so not in order to delineate a tradition, of which Osborne would appear as the founder, but rather, the chapter traces a series of distinct but interrelated moments in postwar theatre in which dramatists attempted to explode the implied complacency and conservatism of their audiences with the language and imagery of trauma and violence.

Myth and violence

When Ann Jellicoe's first play, *The Sport of My Mad Mother* (1958), was produced at the Royal Court, it was a commercial and critical failure.[2] It was withdrawn from the theatre's programme after fourteen appearances, and was largely damned by theatre critics. It was produced, however, in the spirit of experiment which pervaded the Royal Court in the wake of Osborne's success. *Look Back in Anger* had become such a commercial success that it enabled the Royal Court's artistic director, George Devine, to gamble with new plays, innovative forms, and young writers and directors. Jellicoe's play came to his attention after it came third in the 1957 *Observer Prize*, and he offered her the opportunity to direct her own play in its first performance. *The Sport of My Mad Mother* contains many of the ingredients which Osborne's play had reputedly pushed on to the agenda of mainstream theatre in the 1950s, such as contemporary youth culture, social change, and class differences. Jellicoe's play leads the audience away from the main road, down a back alley, to a hidden corner in which we find a gang of rootless, restless young people, who struggle to articulate any meaningful statement about their own lives. The life of the gang revolves around highly mythologised street battles with their Aldgate rivals, which are reported in varying degrees of fear and excitement. Jellicoe sets her play in a landscape of back alleys and deserted factory roads, strewn with the broken bottles and razors of gang warfare. In presenting on stage the dispossessed underbelly of the urban working class, Jellicoe was forging drama in the same spirit of making the theatre a space for social and cultural representation as Osborne had done two years earlier. This was the working class stripped of the lyricism of O'Casey, the political self-awareness of Corrie, or the articulate anger of Osborne. It should be stressed that Jellicoe's working class is no more 'authentic' for avoiding the pitfalls of her predecessors, but her play is a radical experiment in attempting to represent the inarticulate, to give symbolic expression to an underclass which was simultaneously out of sight and constantly represented as a threat.

The play opens with a musician, Steve, testing various instruments, and alluding self-consciously to the audience and to the theatrical space around them. As Jellicoe notes in the introduction she wrote to the play in 1964, the play attempts to 'reach the audience through rhythm, noise and music' (Jellicoe 1964, 5)[3], and this is what Steve tells the audience as he sets up his instruments at the side of the stage. Throughout the play, Steve frequently prefaces, accompanies or offsets the action on stage with music, while, more importantly, the action and speech of the characters themselves frequently take on rhythmic forms. Such devices are not designed to underline the musicality of working-class youth, although this might be one implication, but instead they aim to emphasise the orchestration of effects within the play's structure. Steve shifts between addressing the audience, to manipulating the characters on stage with music, to chatting to stage hands in between the acts of the play. He is both in and out of the play, thus drawing attention at various stages to the conventions of stagecraft and theatricality. So too, the characters speak in self-consciously musical ways at times, and perform various symbolic rituals and rhythmic chants, so that the play seems to elevate a choric notion of communication above rational discourse. Jellicoe transforms the everyday ritual of a young woman having her hair 'permed', for example, into a rhythmic, symbolic event, in which her friends chant the instructions to 'section, saturate, paper, wind' until it becomes an incantation, summoning upon the hair its magical metamorphosis of shape (44–9). There is comedy in Jellicoe's play alongside the dark, elemental forces of myth and violence.

The language of Jellicoe's characters is ritual, borrowed and imitated from its everyday forms in popular music, commercial advertisement and folklore, and repeated often as disturbing performances of mimicry and mockery. The impression generated by such performances is one of characters who are stripped of personality, who whip each other into hypnotic frenzy through the ritual recitation of meaningless phrases and words. Fak and Cone, for instance, two boys whose very names are emblems of alienation or depersonalisation, hypnotise each other merely by repeating the word 'Dolly', and then turn menacingly on Patty, reciting the word 'Shoo' until Patty screams (24–5). Although the play contains tense scenes of physical violence, in many ways it is the characters' use of a kind of verbal terrorism which gives the play its most chilling scenes. Jellicoe shares with Pinter, in this respect, a common interest in exploring a rich vein of dramatic and performative potential in the violence of language itself, which Pinter has tapped into in every play since and including *The Birthday Party*.

For Jellicoe's characters, language is a mask, a performance of verbalisation which reveals nothing of their identity or emotions. Language is the force which speaks through them, repeated, imitated, or borrowed from the social and cultural discourses in which they are enveloped. Nonetheless, this gives their ritual chants and incantations considerable symbolic power. The gang begin their attempt to terrorise the American character, Dean, by dressing in masks and blankets and chanting 'Please to remember / Please to remember / Please to remember / Please to remember the fifth of November' (51). Greta, the most menacing of all the characters, moves among the others as they perform this ritual, and, when Dean fails to unmask her, the stage directions indicate that he 'loses his psychological balance'. Identity is confused here, first among the gang members who dress to confuse, and then in Dean, who loses his own sense of identity as the game becomes more sinister. The familiar ritual of dressing up as 'the guy', commemorating Guy Fawkes's plot to blow up the Houses of Parliament, and reciting the plea to remember, is transformed by the gang into a terrifying instrument of intimidation. The ritual becomes a kind of pagan, anarchic dance, which strips Dean of his senses, and subdues him before the mythic power of Greta. Dean is reduced to screaming 'Mamma!' at the end of a long scene of verbal and physical intimidation, thus signifying his submission to Greta as a primordial mother figure. Michelene

Wandor suggests that Greta is a Lilith figure, the mythical first wife of
Adam who killed all of her babies every day only to give birth to new
ones, a figure of monstrous motherhood, at once the source of all
destruction as well as all creation (Wandor 1987, 46). She is also Kali,
of course, the Hindu goddess of death and destruction who is
worshipped as the divine mother, and who was worshipped and
honoured especially by the legendary 'thugs' of India, from which the
word's contemporary usage to describe a gang of violent youths
derives.

Greta functions as a powerful mythic force in the play, a potent
symbol of the dark, irrepressible force of motherhood, whose semiotic
language of gesture, motion, and chant destabilises the rational,
moralising pleas of Dean. Dean, who enters the gang as an outsider, is
Greta's antithesis, and is the only character who speaks with a rational, articulate voice. He, along with Steve towards the end of the play,
attempts to articulate questions of morality, responsibility and
humanity among the gang:

> DEAN: ... we men, we must try and become better, we must seek to
> become better and better, to help to create order, truth and love. It's
> so easy to slide into chaos – don't you see that? (82)

Greta dismisses his talk of 'order' as nonsense, however, proclaiming
instead the primal power of human reproduction:

> GRETA: Rails, rules, laws, guides, promises, terms, guarantees,
> conventions, traditions: into the pot with the whole bloody lot. Birth!
> Birth! That's the thing! Oh, I shall have hundreds of children, millions
> of hundreds and hundreds of millions. (Jellicoe 1964, 86)

The play ends, however, not with the bang of creation but with the
whimper of submission, as Greta is confined to looking on admiringly
at her baby, after being told by Steve to 'keep out of mischief – or else'
(87). The conclusion to the play draws a striking, if somewhat abrupt
contrast, then, between the symbolic and mythic potency of motherhood, and the manner in which motherhood is the primary means by
which women are subdued and contained in contemporary society.
This abrupt finale is itself only the culmination of another, more
sweeping transition in the plot of the play, from the gang warfare and
youth subculture with which the play begins, to the mythic clash

between male rational order and female creative power with which it concludes.

One could argue that such spectacular transitions of theme and focus make *The Sport of My Mad Mother* difficult to follow, and hence perhaps doomed to fail as a piece of mainstream theatre, but it is the play's ambition, and, I would argue, its achievement, to gather into the compelling force of its performance the violent maelstrom of a social underclass, gender war, territorial competition, tribal subcultures, and urban dehumanisation. That it does so in a form which attempts to wed linguistic rhythm with musical structures, and to offset verbal poverty with a poetry of gesture and motion, is testament enough to its aspiration as a piece of radical, experimental theatre. The play ends with Steve warning the audience to 'clear out': 'I'm blowing this place up. We'll have a bonfire: bring your own axes. All right everyone off! Off!' (87) This is a witty, boisterous move at the end of the play, for it puns on the idea that everyone has axes to grind in the theatre, and that the final ambition of the dramatist must be to burn the theatre to the ground.

Theatre and society

One theatre, in particular, played a central role in re-inventing English drama in the postwar period as a drama of shock and disturbance, and that is the Royal Court Theatre. If Osborne's *Look Back in Anger* was intended to provoke audiences and critics, as Osborne claimed, this also seemed to be the effect of John Arden's *Serjeant Musgrave's Dance* (1959), Osborne's *A Patriot for Me* (1965), and, perhaps the most shocking of all plays produced in postwar English theatre, Edward Bond's *Saved* (1965). One scene, in particular, is the source of much of the controversy in Bond's play, the notorious scene six, in which a gang of young men abuse, torture, and then brutally stone an infant to death in its pram. The latter two plays were, in fact, produced at the Royal Court under so-called 'club' conditions, in which the theatre had to be turned into a private club with the performances open to 'members only', in order to circumvent theatre censorship laws. Every drama script scheduled for performance had to be checked by the Lord Chamberlain's office against standards of decency and taste, which in practice in the 1950s and 1960s meant that theatre directors negotiated with the censor about the degree of nudity, 'bad' language, or violence which was permitted on stage. Effectively, playwrights and directors would attempt to anticipate what the censor would allow, but both the Royal Court under George Devine and the Theatre Royal under Joan Littlewood began in the late 1950s to test the Lord Chamberlain's resolve. This resulted, for instance, in Brendan Behan's *The Hostage*, produced at the Theatre Royal in 1958, being placed under police supervision by the Lord Chamberlain, when he suspected that some aspects of the play which he had expressly forbidden would slip back into the performances.[4]

Perhaps the most significant point to consider about Bond's *Saved* is that it is credited with having initiated the process which ended theatre censorship in England, for it provoked the censor, critics, and audiences into violent reactions, which have had a lasting, tangible effect on the fate of theatre in England. The play resulted in the Lord Chamberlain prosecuting the Royal Court theatre for presenting an unlicensed play, two years before the Lord Chamberlain's office was itself divested of its powers to control and check theatre productions by the Theatre Bill of 1968. Philip Roberts cites a report that the play was interrupted with verbal abuse from the audience, and that there were fights in the foyers at the interval and afterwards (Roberts 1986, 40). Critics were divided too, with many expressing outrage that such scenes could be shown on stage, while others tentatively suggested a defence of why a serious theatre must deal with themes of violence and abuse. It is testament to the Royal Court's commitment to the importance of contemporary drama dealing with social and moral themes that its directors, having failed to negotiate a compromise production between Bond and the Lord Chamberlain, proceeded to stage the play (and pointedly revived it in 1968 to celebrate the demise of theatre censorship). The issues which concern me here, however, are not the flaws and ignominies of theatre censorship, but rather, how Bond's play mobilises the language and imagery of violence and social deprivation in a sustained, almost unbearable assault on the audience. The reaction of the audience, critics, and the censor, is merely an illustration of how successful Bond and the Royal Court were in producing drama of truly shocking and disturbing effect.

Saved contains thirteen scenes, which span perhaps about three years. It is concerned, like Jellicoe's play, with a section of working-class society which struggles to represent itself, and in which violence, gesture, and non-communication intensify the experience of social, economic and cultural deprivation. Bond represents the inarticulacy of his characters by confining most lines of dialogue in the play to three or four words – this prevents the characters from expressing anything other than basic needs or desires, and prevents any sustained explanation of their motives or responses. The play begins with Pam bringing Len back to her family home for sex. It is clear from the beginning that sex has little or no connection with emotional attachment. When Len asks 'Wass yer name?', for example, Pam responds 'Yer ain' arf nosey' (Bond 1977, 21). This establishes a pattern of emotional detachment which is repeated, with tragic consequences, in the course of the play. The first scene contains some of the elements of situation comedy: Pam and Len are attempting to have sex on the sofa while being occasionally interrupted by Pam's father, who is preparing to go to work. This has comic potential, but it also strikes a note of moral anomie, for Len seems to be the only character who is half-heartedly concerned about being seen having sex with Pam by her own father. The social world which Bond depicts is one in which certain taboos are ignored or at the very least are being severely tested.

Pam's family, we discover as the play progresses, emblematises social dysfunction and the breakdown of social communication. Her parents, Harry and Mary, live in the same house but have not talked to each other in years. After the first scene, Len has moved into the house, but Pam has ceased to be interested in him, and forms a relationship with Len's friend, Fred, after the second scene. The relationship between Pam and Len becomes fractious and bitter thereafter, especially after Pam gives birth to their child, and then proceeds to neglect the baby. This forms the basis for the first disturbing scene in the play, scene four, in which Pam, Len, Harry and Mary are all in the living room, and all are oblivious to, or deliberately ignore, the increasingly strained cries of the baby from the bedroom, offstage. The characters are all aware of the cries of the child, but are too intent on passing the burden of responsibility on to each other to do anything to help. The scene sets up an important context for the truly disturbing actions in scene six, in which Len's friends, a gang of young men, encounter the baby, left alone and drugged with aspirins, in a pram in the park, and, after failing to get some response from the baby, proceed to assault it. They rock the pram violently at first, pull the baby's hair, pinch it, spit at it, punch it, rub a soiled nappy in the baby's face, and then throw burning matches and stones into the pram. These final acts prove fatal for the baby, in what the men refer to as 'the evenin's entertainment' (70). The horror is not quite finished when the men run off, however, for Pam returns and wheels the pram off, oblivious to the harm which has been inflicted on the child. This seems to be as much the focus of this scene as the actions of the men, for Pam commits her own act of violence against the baby when she fails even to notice it. This conclusion to the scene, Bond explained, was intended to deflate the 'classical cries of horror' which would follow the stoning of the baby, to prevent the audience from escaping into anger (Hay and Roberts 1978, 50).

Pam ignores the child with arguably the same sense of emotional numbness as has permitted the men to commit horrific acts of brutality in the name of 'entertainment'. *Saved* is focused not on the violence, but on the lack of any moral context or response to the violence. Despite the fact that Len has witnessed his friends killing his own child, he continues to befriend them. So too, even when Pam is aware that Fred is guilty of killing the baby, she continues to seek a relationship with him, long after he has ceased to be interested in her. The death of the infant seems to mark no significant turning point for the characters, nor does it compel them to reflect even on the motives for the violence. Instead, Fred and his fellow gang members feel sorry for themselves. Bond places the scene of infanticide at a relatively early stage in the play, however, so that we can watch the effects of the tragedy on all of the characters. No one expresses sorrow, remorse, or anger, nor even recognises that the death of the baby is tragic. Ignored in life, the child continues to be ignored in death. The purpose of Bond's play is not to invite us to feel rage against the men who have tortured and killed a baby, however, nor to encourage anger against Pam or Len for abandoning the child. Bond wants to place this act of obscene, grotesque murder, in an explanatory social and political context: 'the stoning to death of a baby in a London park is a typical English understatement. Compared to the "strategic" bombing of German towns it is a negligible atrocity, compared to the cultural and emotional deprivation of most of our children its consequences are insignificant' (Bond 1977, 310–11).

This is to say, in one sense, that these examples of violence and horror are interconnected, and there are ways in which the play itself suggests such interconnections. In our first encounter with the gang, for example, in scene three, we are told that Pete has already killed a child in a road accident:

PETE: What a carry on! 'E come runnin' round be'ind the bus. Only a nipper. Like a flash I thought right yer nasty bastard. Only ten or twelve. I jumps right down on me revver an' bang I got 'im on me off-side an' 'e shoots right out under this lorry comin' straight on. (Bond 1977, 38)

Pete feels no guilt about this incident either, for, as his friend, Mike, explains, 'accidents is legal', and the coroner apologises to him for the trouble caused by the inquest. In his own account of the 'accident', at least, Pete is responsible for the murder of this child, however. Pete learns here that some murders are legal, a point which Barry confirms in the same scene, when he recalls his experiences with the army, presumably in Korea or Malaya: 'I done blokes in … . In the jungle. Shootin' up the yeller-niggers. An' cut ''em up after with the ol' pig-sticker. Yeh.' (39). It is not clear from the language and posturing used by the young men in the play how we should treat these stories, whether we should believe them or not. What is certain is that they reveal a fascination with violence, and particularly with circum-stances in which murder is either permissible or possible without penalty. The gang in the park kill the baby ultimately not for any motive, but because, as Pete says, 'yer don't get a chance like this everyday.' (79). They tell themselves that the baby is like an animal with 'no feelin's', but this is merely to justify the pleasure which they derive from systematically abusing and killing it (77). Here, Bond's play treads a fine line between depicting the murder as the result of violent, evil instincts, and providing the explanatory contexts in which such violence might be understood as rooted in social and cultural forces. This is potentially a problem in the play, particularly, as Stephen Lacey argues, 'in the context in which the plays were origi-nally produced, being performed to a largely middle-class audience in the West End, where it became easy to blame, and thus dismiss, the characters themselves' (Lacey 1995, 149).

There is, in other words, a problem with presenting on stage scenes of such disturbing and shocking impact to audiences who may be predisposed to see the action in relation to a pre-determined set of moral responses, rather than the social and political implications suggested (but never clearly defined) in the play. The significant issue for Lacey here is that Bond deliberately neglects to give us an articu-late, 'Jimmy Porter'-like hero, who might explain the circumstances and contexts to the audience. As a result, the shock of the park scene is left unmediated, and is the subject of little subsequent reflection or consideration by the characters thereafter. We are offered no glimpse of life outside of the closeted, barely articulate world of Pam's house and the macho jostling of the gang. Audiences and critics might therefore be tempted into condemnation rather than understanding, outrage rather than reflection.

The key to placing the violence in the play within some sense of social context, however, is perhaps the most noteworthy point about the play, its language. The brevity of lines, the staccato dialogue, the incomplete questions, the constant interruption of conversations, and the whole array of emotions, responses and problems which go unexpressed, and seem inexpressible – all these problems with communication which recur throughout the play seem to suggest that the characters have no control over how to represent themselves to others. Verbal communication has two functions in the play, Jeanette Malkin argues, either as 'a form of attack ... to repel contact', or as a 'group-language' to indicate a common bond (Malkin 1992, 128). The former function is most visible in the scenes set in Pam's home, in which the fraught relationship between members of the household, particularly between Pam and Len, is articulated almost wholly through acts of verbal violence. The latter function is demonstrated in the scenes in the park between members of the gang, where they repeat and play off each other's lines, so that, as Malkin suggests, 'the gang speaks, like the poisonous Hydra, with one multi-tongued voice' (Malkin 1992, 129). The gang members seem to derive their identity from the common expressions which bind them, so that, even though Fred utters some cautions against harming the baby initially, he is dragged like all the others into a kind of rhythmic incitement to violence by the steady rise of aggressive language and chants. The aggressive taunts against the baby which begin the scene are played out in the sort of boisterous comedy which characterises the group relationship, but they slowly become more real, more vicious, as if each threat uttered in play conjures up before the gang the image of what they will do to it. Pete jokes at the beginning of the park scene that Barry will put the baby to sleep 'with a brick', and this fate becomes the inevitable consequence of their play-acting. No one member of the gang is in control, or seems to have motive or inclination to kill the child. In fact, their first interactions with the child tend towards the clichéd 'cooing' and tickling of the familiar encounter between stranger and infant. But the aggressive undertones of all of the gang's play-acting begins to take over, so that each joke and line they utter brings them closer and closer to their deadly deed. It is language which permits them to kill the child, not just in the sense that they are subject to the rhythmic course of verbal incitement, but also in the way in which they can dehumanise the baby through language. Throughout the play, the characters refer to the baby as 'it', making it nameless and genderless. In scene six, as the gang grow closer to killing the child, Colin says that it 'looks like a yeller-nigger' (Barry has already told us that he has killed 'yeller-niggers' in the jungle, legally, as a soldier) (78). Others call the baby 'a yid', and a 'stupid bastard', thereby mimicking the taunts used to legitimate murder in various modern atrocities. What seals its fate, however, and turns their play into torture is the inability of the child to respond, to communicate. Pam has put it to sleep with aspirins, and when the baby fails to respond to the initial jerks and jabs of the men, they proceed to treat it in more violent and reckless ways.

Bond's play does not attempt to lead us to sympathise with Fred and the gang members, nor with Pam or Len. It does attempt, however, to provide us with the means to understand the conditions which give rise to the senseless acts of violence which the play depicts, and which are rarely missing from our newspapers and television screens. 'Violence is not a function of human nature but of human societies', wrote Bond, a maxim which might stand as the theme of the play (17). Bond approaches this theme in the play, however, not through didactic means, but through a more risky strategy of assaulting the sensitivities of audiences, asking them to endure torturous scenes in the expectation that this will lead them necessarily to explore the rationale for such scenes. But Bond described the play in his author's note, written a year after the initial production, as 'almost irresponsibly optimistic' (309). This, he explains, is because, in its own minimal way, the play has a happy ending when Len indicates at the end of the play that he will stay with Pam, Harry and Mary. He does not even communicate this to them verbally, but by 'mucking in', fixing a chair, which suggests that he is doing something constructive for the house, and for his relationship with his co-inhabitants. This is a tentative new beginning, which is limited in its optimism by the fact that Len is no more aware of the reasons why he should stay or go, struggle on in his relationship with Pam or give up, than he was at the beginning of the play. But it suggests the possibility of hope, and perhaps leaves an invitation to the audience to consider why it is necessary or desirable to stay put, to try to make one's relationships with others more humane. *Saved* was banned by the Lord Chamberlain, but it is a daring play, which challenges us to try to understand the conditions in which the most horrific acts of abuse and violence take place. It risks the ire and disgust of its audiences, the probability that the systematic neglect and abuse depicted in the play will provoke moral outrage, rather than understanding. But it also offers important connections between violence and social conditions, between language and behaviour. The shock of violence on Bond's stage is indicative, then, not of an attempt to anger the Lord Chamberlain, but of a desperate attempt to mobilise the visceral and cathartic resources of a theatre of violence towards a more rigorous understanding of social and political conditions.

Trauma and representation

The risk of such an attempt is that audiences might experience the trauma of violence and obscenity, but might not necessarily feel compelled to examine their causal or contextual conditions. This certainly was the experience of some of the reviewers of the first production of *Saved*. 'I don't want to see the play again', wrote Jeremy Kingston in *Punch*, for example, expressing his revulsion from the effectiveness of Bond's presentation of violence and abuse.[5] J.W. Lambert in the *Sunday Times* argued that the play failed to produce either compassion or understanding, and functioned simply as 'a concocted opportunity for vicarious beastliness'. This was a play, for Lambert, which provided no contexts in which its obscene slice of life could be understood. 'I spent a lot of the first act shaking with claustrophobia and thinking I was going to be sick', recorded Penelope Gilliatt in *The Observer*, while the reviewer for the *Daily Express* wrote that the violence presented on stage was so 'entirely unmotivated and unexplained', and so 'obscene', that it 'cannot be touched on in print'. In some of these reviews, the trauma of having witnessed a staged representation of infanticide was the only reaction registered, as if the reviewers could not respond critically or reflectively on the experiences depicted. For some too, perhaps chiefly the Lord Chamberlain's office, Bond's play was attempting to present what should be unrepresentable, what was for them outside of the conventional boundaries of representation.

The relationship between trauma and representation, and the question of how the overwhelming experience of trauma can be processed in representational form, has been the concern of recent critical debates in the United States.[6] For Shoshana Felman and Cathy Caruth, in particular, it is the ineffability of trauma, its apparent incomprehensibility, which marks it out for critical attention as a category of experience removed from, or beyond, the representational technologies of modern culture. Trauma – whether the experience of torture, rape, incest, or other forms of abuse – has the potential to explode the categories of representation precisely because its effects take the form of secrecy or silence; it seems only to signify what is not possible to communicate or represent. Thus, Felman argues that the value of trauma studies is not that they reveal new knowledge of history or experience through the transmuted perspective of the trauma victim, but that they enable us to 'gain new insights into what not knowing means, to grasp the ways in which erasure is itself part of the functioning of our history' (Felman 1992, 253). Felman's example here is the holocaust, but arguably, other forms of trauma manifest themselves in the same kind of abyssal structure, in which the subject of trauma analysis seems always to be elusive, unspeakable, and impossible. Even psychoanalysis, which sets itself up as a quest to bring into representation what is beyond representation, only manages to do this, according to Linda Belau, not by critically exposing the mechanics and causes of trauma, but instead by repeating the traumatic experience in the present.[7] This makes psychoanalysis as much the scene of traumatic experience, as it is an attempt at interpretation, since the psychoanalytic encounter is where trauma is not just relived, but perhaps is experienced at its most intense, traumatic level.

The same argument, I would suggest, is feasible for the function of trauma in contemporary drama. Drama as an art form offers a privileged, dynamic engagement between an audience and the simulated experiences and symbolic situations presented on stage. Depending on its genre, the mode of performance, or, indeed, the expectations of the audience, drama can function merely as entertainment, or can have powerful emotional, didactic, rhetorical or psychological effects on an audience. In 'serious' theatre in England since the mid-1950s, however, realist, political drama has tended to dominate, and routinely engages audiences in debates, dilemmas, or demonstrations of particular social, cultural and political issues. This is to say that such theatre works to bring forth strong effects in its audiences, to push against complacency or apathy, either to overturn casual political assumptions, or to do what Osborne claimed was his intention in *Look Back in Anger*, to 'make people feel, to give them lessons in feeling' (Maschler 1957, 65). Seen in this context, Bond's *Saved* is an attempt to present the audience with traumatic experiences, chiefly the horrific murder of the baby, experiences which are intensified for the audience by the fact that subsequent scenes are silent on the trauma of witnessing such an event. Thus, Bond's play is not just a representation of trauma – it is a repetition and intensification of trauma, hence the symptoms of revulsion, disgust, fear, and rejection evident in the reviews. Trauma is not the subject of the play – it is the very form and defining experience of the play.

Bond was among the first to defend Sarah Kane's first play, *Blasted*, when it was first performed at the Royal Court Theatre in January 1995, against some of the same accusations which were levelled at *Saved* when it opened thirty years previously. *Blasted* is a more vicious, relentless play than *Saved*, where the depiction of violence and the use of trauma are concerned. It contains scenes of rape and sexual abuse, torture, violence, depravity, and the cannibalism of a dead baby. *Blasted*, one is tempted to suggest, is *Saved* without the optimism, without redemption or reprieve. It is set in an expensive hotel room in Leeds, apparently contemporary, until a soldier enters with a rifle halfway through the play, and it becomes clear that this is an England which resembles the internecine, sadistic warscape of Bosnia.

The first half of the play is concerned with a troubled, disturbing relationship between a middle-aged journalist, Ian, and a twenty-one-year-old woman, Cate, who suffers repeatedly from fainting fits and from recurrent mental illness. Ian carries a gun, and is constantly anxious for his security and desperate for sexual gratification. He forces Cate to masturbate him, and simulates sex with her as she lies unconscious, pointing a gun to her head all the time. Ian is repeatedly abusive to Cate, as he is abusive about 'wogs', 'Pakis', 'retards', 'lesbos', and women in general. Such offensive language and behaviour are deployed to delineate the character of Ian, whose constant oscillation between fear and aggression serves to situate him as the dialectical figure of victim and bully. This is exemplified in the second half of the play, when the soldier enters as Cate escapes. The soldier holds Ian captive and scared, tortures him, then rapes him, and then, in a scene bursting with mythical resonance, eats Ian's eyes out of their sockets before shooting himself. Ian is left scrabbling in the darkness, and, after Cate has returned with a dying infant, and leaves again in search of food, is seen in various stages of deprivation – masturbating, defecating, crying, weak with hunger, and then devouring the body of the dead baby. In the final scene of the play, Ian is buried alive in a hole in the floor, only his head visible, and Cate has returned with food, having probably been raped outside.

Blasted, in one respect, is a series of dark, spectacular tableaux, depicting the habitual but shocking scenes of modern violence and terror, from the casual abuse and 'domestic' violence of the first half of the play, to the routine, calculated torture and war of the second half. As is the case in Bond's *Saved*, Kane's characters are unable or unwilling to articulate the vicious, destructive motives which drive them to abuse. Cate is represented from the outset as childlike, sucking her thumb, smelling the flowers in the hotel room, and giggling at Ian's absurd actions. She communicates to Ian as much through gestures as language, and even then, her verbal expressions are short, frequently stammered, and often confused. Yet, she is not simply Ian's passive victim, either, for, after she has been raped, she begins to perform oral sex on him, only to bite down hard on his penis as he comes. Sex is associated throughout the play with violence and violation. Even as Ian comes, and Cate bites, he is uttering the words 'I am a killer'. Ian's abusive relationship with Cate, in other words, is as much about sadistic gratification as sexual gratification.

This tableau is mirrored in the second half of the play when the soldier rapes Ian, in a symbolic act of revenge for his own girlfriend who has been raped and killed by an enemy soldier:

> [The Soldier] *kisses* Ian *very tenderly on the lips.*
> *They stare at each other.*
> **Soldier** You smell like her. Same cigarettes.
> The Soldier *turns* Ian *over with one hand.*
> *He holds the revolver to Ian's head with the other.*
> *He pulls down* Ian's *trousers, undoes his own and rapes him –*
> *eyes closed and smelling* Ian's *hair.*
> The Soldier *is crying his heart out.*
> Ian's *face registers pain but he is silent.*
> *When the* Soldier *has finished he pulls up his trousers and pushes the*
> *revolver up* Ian's *anus.* (Kane 1996, 49)

Here, Kane's play establishes the repetitive, abyssal structure of trauma, in which the soldier relives the traumatic experience of his girlfriend's rape and murder by acting out the rape on Ian, which is simultaneously a simulation of sex with his girlfriend. The repetition of rape, from Cate to Ian to the soldier's girlfriend, serves firstly to remark upon the cyclical pattern of sexual and physical abuse. Recurrence, or re-enactment, is a definitive symptom of trauma, in which the only outlet for the expression of trauma is to relive the experience, or to become the perpetrator of the same traumatic experience on others. The soldier can only express his pain, therefore, when he is making Ian take the burden of his shame and sense of victimisation. There is only one part of the scene between the enemy soldier and his girlfriend which the soldier in *Blasted* does not perform; where the soldier should shoot Ian in the head to complete the simulation of his traumatic memory, instead he shoots himself in the head. This act, and the emotions which we see him express as he rapes Ian, figures the soldier in the role both of the rapist and the victim, the killer and the dead.

On one level, then, *Blasted* articulates the repetitive and ineffable structure of traumatic experience, and suggests that the silences, re-enactments, withdrawals, and evasions exhibited by all the characters denote the pervasive, overwhelming effects of trauma. Cate's fainting fits are thus as expressive of traumatic experience as Ian's anxious quest for violent sex, or the soldier's painful re-enactment of his girlfriend's rape and murder. What is lacking, of course, in this representation of trauma is any sense of understanding, or context. The debates surrounding Bond's *Saved* focused in particular on the issue of whether the play presented its violent scenes in sufficient social context to make it possible for audiences to assemble explanations for the violence, to understand the motivations or causes for such obscene acts of torture and murder. The experience of some reviewers quoted above, however, illustrates the concern that the play may have succeeded in passing on the trauma of such experiences, not any sense of context or social understanding. Kane's *Blasted*, however, is even less ambiguous on this issue. The only context for the violence presented in the play is violence. Trauma is a response to trauma – it is, apparently, its own language and context, which can be expressed only in the act of repetition. Bond's play offered some optimism about the recovery from trauma, symbolised in Len's attempt to mend the chair, and thus, his decision to stay and work out a habitable relationship with Pam and her parents. Kane's play, on the other hand, offers a dark cycle of violence and abuse, which is relieved only in the most impoverished, Beckettian sense at the end of the play when Cate feeds Ian as he pokes his head from out of his hole in the ground.

Blasted does not aim to provide understanding, however. It is not, in this sense, part of a theatre of representation. It attempts not to satisfy the audience with representations of experience, nor to enlighten the audience politically or socially, but to mobilise the audience through experience. Kane's play does not just depict trauma, but seeks to induce trauma in the audience, and thus to explode the limits of representation. Kane's method borrows from Artaud, rather than Brechtian realism, in supplanting the imitative concept of realist theatre with the negative theatricality of Artaud's 'theatre of cruelty'. Derrida explains Artaud's divergence from representational theatre:

> The theater of cruelty is not a *representation*. It is life itself, in the extent to which life is unrepresentable. Life is the nonrepresentable origin of representation. 'I have therefore said "cruelty" as I might have said "life"' [from Artaud's *Theatre and its Double*] ... Artaud wants to have done with the imitative concept of art ... Theatrical art should be the primordial and privileged site of this destruction of imitation: more than any other art, it has been marked by the labor of total representation in which the affirmation of life lets itself be doubled and emptied by negation. (Derrida 1978, 234)

Blasted refuses to allow what it represents to remain 'in front' of the audience, and this is true, I would suggest, of Bond's and Jellicoe's plays too. Each in turn mobilises a theatrical dynamic of shock and trauma, which seeks to close the gap between audience and representation, and to permeate the audience with the *experience* of theatre. Hence, Kane offers no privileged 'outside' of trauma from which to judge the traumatic experiences presented on stage. There is nothing withheld, in that sense, from the audience, in a theatrical encounter which Artaud describes as 'a frightful transfer of forces from body to body' (Derrida 1978, 250). This is, in essence, what is presented on Kane's stage, an endless transfer of forces, which is transferred from stage to audience too. Like Bond, Kane attempted to produce a theatre of shock, which would compel the audience into witnessing, and thus experiencing, trauma, in its incomprehensibility, its ineffability. Only in such moments of uncompromising representation is it possible to encounter the limits of representation. *Blasted*, in seeming to transgress the boundaries of acceptable theatrical representation, makes it possible to enact the traumatic presentation of life as we would like to forget it. Kane was championing a new role for theatre in England: theatre as the disruptive, tortuous memory of a broken society.

'Little stories'

Forty years after Kenneth Tynan described the English theatre as a place where 'the sun invariably shines', then, Sarah Kane was writing in a very different theatrical landscape, in which plays were more likely to be set in the grim, violent, urban underworld than in country houses, and in which the 'giggles and whimpers' had been replaced with brutal rapes and dark silences. Tynan had mocked the lazy, stifled entertainments which passed for theatre in the 1940s, and longed for a theatre strong enough to hold before its audience a trembling mirror of a changing, bewildered society. For Kane, however, it was necessary to move beyond the representational principle of such theatre, beyond what James Macdonald describes as 'the Royal Court play of the Seventies and Eighties, driven by a clear political agenda, kitted out with signposts indicating meaning, and generally featuring a hefty state-of-the-nation speech somewhere near the end' (Macdonald 1999, 9). *Blasted* makes no attempt to diagnose social ills, nor to offer the audience lessons in politics or ethics. Instead, it spews the sicknesses of modern society on to the stage, its own traumatic excess the dramatic testimony to a traumatised age.

A similar process is at work in Mark Ravenhill's *Shopping and Fucking*, produced at the Royal Court in September 1996. The focus of Ravenhill's play is a love triangle of Mark, Robbie and Lulu, who live in a bare, run-down flat, and survive on microwaved ready-meals, shoplifting, and drug-dealing. The play opens with Mark vomiting up the take-away food Robbie and Lulu are trying to make him eat; a symptom, as it turns out, of the sickness of addiction which is killing him. 'I'm fucked', Mark tells them, 'I can't control anything. My ... guts, my mind' (Ravenhill 1997, 2). This is a theme which runs throughout the play: characters are compelled into their actions, contained in their thoughts and desires, channelled into an inevitable series of events. This is reflected in the story that Lulu begs Mark to tell, of the moment at which the three characters came together:

> **Mark** It's summer. I'm in a supermarket. It's hot and I'm sweaty. Damp. And I'm watching this couple shopping. I'm watching you. And you're both smiling. You see me and you know sort of straight away that I'm going to have you. You know you don't have a choice. No control.
>
> Now this guy comes up to me. He's a fat man. Fat and hair and lycra and he says: See the pair by the yoghurt?
>
> Well, says fat guy, they're both mine. I own them. I own them but I don't want them – because you know something? – they're trash. Trash and I hate them. Wanna buy them?
>
> How much?
>
> Piece of trash like them. Let's say … twenty. Yeah, yours for twenty.
>
> So, I do the deal. I hand it over. And I fetch you. I don't have to say anything because you know. You've seen the transaction.
>
> And I take you both away and I take you to my house. And you see the house and when you see the house you know it. You understand? You know this place.
>
> And I've been keeping a room for you and I take you into this room. And there's food. And it's warm. And we live out our days fat and content and happy. (Ravenhill 1997, 3)

Mark tells Robbie and Lulu a story which comforts them, which functions as a kind of fairy tale in which their dreams of warmth, happiness and love come true. It is a fairy story adapted to the conventions and dispositions of the late capitalist society, however, in which the supermarket is the hub of social exchange, and in which 'the transaction' is the only truth. 'Having' is everything; so much so that Robbie and Lulu can dream only of being owned, of the joy of being possessed, had, used, and abused by the hands of another. This is a play about the rituals of exchange, possession, consumption and addiction which define the customs and mores of contemporary capitalist society. Robbie and Lulu have no choice, no control, because they are commodities to be bought and sold, like everything else. They have desires, but these desires are prescribed within the system of exchange and consumption. They desire what they are already being offered.

Mark leaves Robbie and Lulu in order to free himself of his addiction to 'scag', and discovers in the process that he must free himself of his addiction to emotional attachments with people too. When he returns he seeks relationships with people which are based purely on financial transactions. This is what he can trust above love, friendship, and care, the sicknesses of human dependence from which he has apparently suffered. Robbie and Lulu, in the meantime, search for ways to feed themselves by selling drugs, and, when this fails and they are threatened with gruesome torture by the drug-dealer, Brian, they sell sexual stimulation to clients over the phone. Brian describes the transactions he compels Robbie and Lulu to undertake as 'tests', and tells Lulu the story of the Disney film, *The Lion King*, to illustrate that these tests are rites of passage into the world of power and possession. Robbie and Lulu, it is implied, will only become 'kings', will only be able to command their own destiny, if they can learn to master the power to sell. The 'transaction' is again shown to be the basic foundation of all human relationships. Even the story of *The Lion King* which fascinates Brian is made to yield up this lesson of the symbolic exchange of power between father and son, of the symbolic ritual enacted in the process of exchanging money.

Mark, Robbie and Lulu discover, however, that life is never quite as simple as 'shopping and fucking'. Mark attempts to rid himself of emotional attachments by paying a rent boy, Gary, for sex, but this fails when Gary confides in Mark that he has been repeatedly and violently raped by his stepfather. Mark is thus drawn into a human bond of sympathy and care, which compels him to invite Gary to the flat with Robbie and Lulu. There Gary tells them of his secret fantasy, which resembles the story Mark has told earlier in the play, of being sold to a big man who brings him to a warm house. This forms the most disturbing scene in the play, when Robbie and Lulu offer to play out Gary's fantasy with him. Gary's fantasy moves from this comforting dream of being owned and used, to a traumatic re-enactment of his childhood abuse, and he demands first anal sex from Robbie and Mark, and then, after Mark has beaten and fucked Gary viciously, Gary demands that they fuck him with 'a knife ... or a screwdriver. Or something' (82). Gary's fantasy involves repeating the trauma of his childhood, and he screams abuse at Robbie when he refuses to play out the end of his fantasy, because, Gary tells them, 'when someone's paying, someone wants something and they're paying, then you do it' (83). The scene concludes with the suggestion that Mark is then willing to abuse and hurt Gary in the way that he desires. Ravenhill's play produces in this shocking scene a caustic demonstration of the ills of a society based on the unmitigated law of demand and desire, for in drawing together the stories of materialist with sadistic desire, the play exhibits the connections between desire and abuse, possession and exploitation, fantasy and humiliation.

Shopping and Fucking, like *Blasted* and *Saved*, concludes on something of an optimistic note. Mark is able to eat, and to hold down his food, as Robbie and Lulu take it in turns to feed him. The love triangle is restored, and Brian has allowed them to keep the money which they owed him, on the basis that they have learned that the deal, the transaction, is the only thing to be trusted. 'You understand this', Brian tells them, indicating the money, 'and you are civilized' (86). Brian is, in this sense, part of the apparatus in Ravenhill's play which articulates to the audience the causal connections between the actions on stage and a broader social context. He epitomizes the ethos of Thatcherist politics, part entrepreneurial spirit, part brutal gangster, who achieves his own dreams by violating the dreams of others. This, he explains, is all performed in the service of future generations, who will live in the comfort afforded them by the labour of others. Mark concludes with a smaller, more cynical vision of the future, in which 'the Earth has died. Died or we killed it' (87). These competing versions of the future cancel each other out, so that the play has no authoritative final vision of the reasons for the exploitation and hardship of contemporary society.

The conclusion to Ravenhill's play returns us to the moment, and the sentiments, of John Osborne's *Look Back in Anger*. In particular, it returns us to the most renowned soliloquy from that play, in which Jimmy Porter bemoans the absence of any 'good, brave causes', and reflects that 'if the big bang does come, and we all get killed off, it won't be in aid of the old-fashioned, grand design. It'll just be for the Brave New-nothing-very-much-thank-you' (Osborne 1957, 84–5). *Shopping and Fucking* offers its own soliloquy to the absence of any explanatory contexts or designs, in a similar vein to Osborne's play:

> **Robbie** I think ... I think we all need stories, we make up stories so that we can get by. And I think a long time ago there were big stories. Stories so big you could live your whole life in them. The Powerful Hands of the Gods and Fate. The Journey to Enlightenments. The March of Socialism. But they all died or the world grew up or grew senile or forgot them, so now we're all making up our own stories.

> Little stories. It comes out in different ways, But we've each got one.
> (Ravenhill 1997, 64)

There are no grand visions of what point poverty, suffering, and struggle serve in human existence, nor are there explanations for the ceaseless quest for money, possessions and gratification. Like Osborne,
Ravenhill's play suggests the absence of any coherent rationale, and
presents merely the scraping and scratching of contemporary existence. *Shopping and Fucking* seeks not to serve up depictions of the
underclass for the entertainment of middle-class audiences, but to
connect the structures of economic and cultural power with the
symptoms of trauma and exploitation in a society in which, the play
suggests, if you're not selling, you're sold, if you're not fucking, you're
fucked.

A theatre of shock

All five of the plays discussed here were produced first at the Royal
Court Theatre in London, and, as such, are testament to the central
role that theatre under its various managers and artistic directors has
played in the history of drama in postwar England. The arguments
above are offered not as the narrative of a history of the Royal Court
Theatre, however, nor are they meant to indicate the dominant trends
of postwar drama. Rather, they represent five distinct but interrelated
moments in a broader attempt to challenge and renegotiate the
modes of social representation in the mainstream theatres of
England. To this end, Jimmy Porter's anger was not, as it was much
vaunted at the time, directed towards the articulation of working-
class or youth culture, but was rather constructing a new, provocative
attitude towards middle-class audiences. In a variety of forms, and
with varying intensities of force, the plays of Jellicoe, Bond, Kane, and
Ravenhill have since attempted themselves to reconfigure the relationship between theatre and audience, and to bring the 'forgotten',
or repressed, memories of social dysfunction and violence into the
theatre. Such moments in theatre as Bond's *Saved* or Kane's *Blasted*
have sent shivers down the spines of their audiences, or sent them
reeling from the theatre in horror and disgust. That the reactions of
the reviewers registered anger at the plays or playwrights themselves
is a measure, perhaps, both of the effectiveness of such theatre, and

the ease with which these plays could be dismissed as vicarious and tawdry excuses for making a spectacle out of social disturbances. It was always a risky strategy for these playwrights and their directors, actors and managers to set out to shock and provoke their audiences, to cast the cold light of theatre on the unacknowledged darkness of contemporary 'civilisation'. The plays of Osborne, Jellicoe, Bond, Kane and Ravenhill participated in a theatre of shock, a theatre which constructed its vision of a broken society in the language and imagery of that society, in which violence and trauma took their rightful place in the vocabulary and armoury of a living theatre.

Notes

1. See Aleks Sierz, 'John Osborne and the Myth of Anger', *New Theatre Quarterly*, vol. XII, no. 46 (May 1996), 136–46.
2. See Philip Roberts, *The Royal Court Theatre and the Modern Stage* (Cambridge: Cambridge University Press, 1999), 63.
3. I have used the 1964 Faber edition in referring to the play, which is a revision of the original 1958 version. In the original the characters to whom I refer here as 'Steve' and 'Dean' were called 'Flim' and 'Caldaro' respectively.
4. See the Lord Chamberlain's correspondence files on Brendan Behan's *The Hostage*, in the British Library.
5. This and subsequent quotations from the reviews of Bond's play are taken from John Elsom (ed.), *Post-War Theatre Criticism* (London: Routledge & Kegan Paul, 1981), 174–80.
6. See in particular, Shoshana Felman and Dori Laub, *Testimony: Crises of Witnessing in Literature, Psychoanalysis, and History* (London: Routledge, 1992), Cathy Caruth (ed.) *Trauma: Explorations in Memory* (Baltimore: Johns Hopkins University Press, 1995), Cathy Caruth, *Unclaimed Experience: Trauma, Narrative, and History* (Baltimore: Johns Hopkins University Press, 1996).
7. See Linda Belau, 'Trauma and the Material Signifier', *Postmodern Culture*, vol. 11, no. 2 (January 2001): http://jefferson.village.virginia.edu/pmc/.

6 English Journeys: cultural geographies of contemporary England

'I came to the conclusion, such as it is, that the English are a surprising people. How tolerant they are, how extremely eccentric, and how variously they live in the insular villages, the cosy cathedral towns, the brutal wastes of the northern cities. And I thought that was about it, one way and another.'

Beryl Bainbridge, *English Journey, or, The Road to Milton Keynes* (158)

In the summer of 1983, Beryl Bainbridge joined a BBC television crew on a journey around England, which was partly homage, partly voyage of discovery. Bainbridge retraced the journey undertaken by J.B. Priestley fifty years earlier and narrated in *English Journey* (1933), and her own travel narrative, *English Journey, or, The Road to Milton Keynes* (1984), pays homage to Priestley, and, as its subtitle suggests, also to Orwell's *The Road to Wigan Pier* (1937). Bainbridge's journey is one of nostalgia for Englands past, and she takes with her not only the ghosts of Priestley and Orwell, but also the ghosts of England's former industrial, maritime, and cultural glories. She visits the abandoned mines, struggling shipyards, and deserted factories, and deplores the ubiquity of shopping malls, motorways, dole offices, and automated assembly lines.

What she discovers, in her journey through an England which had just re-elected Margaret Thatcher's Conservative party to government with a landslide majority, is that even the bleak depression of the 1930s can evoke nostalgia and a lost sense of security to a generation mired in post-industrial recession. Late in her journey, as it turns to autumn, she enters Jarrow, and describes its mutation from the depression of Priestley's time, to the hopelessness of the early 1980s:

When Priestley visited here he wrote that the whole town looked as if it had entered a bleak, penniless Sabbath. A stranger from a distant civilisation, he said, would have arrived at the conclusion that Jarrow had deeply offended some celestial emperor and was being punished for it. During that recession of fifty years ago it must have appeared as though life would continue to be lived in the same depressing way forever. The rich would get richer and the poor poorer. Nothing would alter. Who could have foreseen that the slow process of change would accelerate to an extent not experienced since the Industrial Revolution, wiping away buildings and traditions and values in the twinkling of an eye, and that the sum total of such momentous changes would amount in the end to no more than a modern version of that earlier, bleak Sabbath of a hole, with a shopping precinct and a dole-office called by another name, its memories housed in an air-raid shelter, the grandchildren of its penniless generation supported by the State? (Bainbridge 1997, 132–3)

Jarrow seems to undergo a second death in Bainbridge's narrative, the first the decimation of poverty and unemployment in the 1930s depression, the second the disappearance even of this bleak world, and its replacement with another, perhaps even more alienated world, in which the dole office makes its own grim, ironic comment on the consumerist delights of the shopping precinct. Although Bainbridge's journey takes her into the 'cosy Cathedral towns', the landscapes to which she is constantly drawn are ones of erasure, disappearance, decimation, the rotting, forsaken landscapes which bear the scars of once industrious communities.

So many of the towns she visits are memory-towns – Jarrow, Liverpool, Southampton, Bristol, Newcastle, Bournville, Bradford – places which seem only to have lived and breathed in the distant past. 'There should be a rule against change', Bainbridge remarks glibly, 'Memories have to live somewhere' (27). England seems figured in her account as the site of memory, its present form merely a shadow of the global empire still visible in its dockyard ruins. The malaise of contemporary England, discernible in every facet of the landscape and architecture she visits, seeps even into Bainbridge's own narrative. Priestley's narrative aspires to the form of a quest, seeking (and finding) 'the inner glowing tradition of the English spirit', and celebrating the ingenuity and richness of English history (Priestley 1934, 417). 'We stagger beneath our inheritance', wrote Priestley in his conclusion, but Bainbridge's journey seems to drag and pale beneath the weight of history. Her narrative goes forth to encounter disappointment, waste, and hopelessness, her conclusion meagre in its summation of a people who live 'variously'.

Bainbridge confesses that the backward look of her narrative is, in large part, attributable to a strong sense of nostalgia inherited from her parents (Bainbridge 1997, 7). She endeavours, therefore, with some degree of irony, to counter this bias by finishing her journey in a place with no memory – the new town of Milton Keynes. Here she cannot lament the passing of buildings, traditions and values, but is compelled to report on a utopian dream of postwar urban planning, 'a cathedral dedicated to the worship of the credit card, a place where people could come and pay their respects to the consumer-society' (155). Milton Keynes promised not to honour tradition, but to raise its inhabitants into the future. It is a space of prophecy, a landscape dreaming of the yet-to-be Englands of speed, prosperity, and social harmony. If so, Bainbridge mocks at its prophetic powers, for she finds its housing estates empty, its shopping arcades derelict, and an architectural planner who tells her that Milton Keynes has failed because 'no one had foreseen a recession and unemployment' (156). In short, Milton Keynes seems silently, ironically, to vindicate Bainbridge's nostalgia, her ever-present sense of historical tradition. The dereliction of its utopian spaces seems to mock the vacuous dream of consumption and mobility which shaped its design.

If Bainbridge journeys in search of England, then, as J.B. Priestley, George Orwell, H.V. Morton and John Betjeman did for an earlier generation, she finds a vanishing, ineffable England, which slips constantly back into the past, or into failed dreams of an impossible future. *English Journey* is an attempt to read the relationship between geography and culture, to trace the ways in which the landscapes and social spaces of contemporary England are constitutive of England's cultural identities. The subject of this chapter is this relationship between writing, space, and culture. The chapter argues that literature in postwar England participates in the construction of new cultural and historical geographies of England, and interrogates the relationship between spatial experience and cultural behaviour. The journey traced in Bainbridge's narrative, I argue here, is exemplary of a recurring trope in cultural representations of contemporary England and Englishness, that such writings take the form, by accident or design, of anecdotal forays into an unknowable, unrepresentable labyrinth. Bainbridge's *English Journey* begins as an imaginative quest, but it becomes instead, as in her failure to navigate Milton Keynes, an encounter with an ineffable, impenetrable England.

English idylls

The scheme to build new towns in the Greater London area, beginning with Stevenage, and which would eventually include Milton Keynes, was announced in March 1946 by the Minister of Town and Country Planning, Lewis Silkin. As David Matless shows, it was not long before local opposition groups in Stevenage had dubbed the new development 'Silkengrad', itself a revealing insight into contemporary anxieties about postwar planning measures, and the symbolic significance of the landscape (or townscape, for that matter) as the repository of 'traditional' English values.[1] The old town had roots as a market town in the fifteenth century, and thus symbolised to its defenders the palimpsestic space of Englishness. The proposed new town threatened to wipe the slate clean, to abandon the heavily inscribed and scarred text of tradition for the blank, disinfected spaces of postwar modernity. Between 1945 and 1960, the landscape of England increasingly became the subject of attempts to rewrite the nation. Motorways tore through the dense patchwork of farms and villages, dreaming of a land of autonomous, interconnected cities. New towns seemed at their conception to assume that nothing existed in the spaces where they were to be built, that the new towns would produce their own space, a miraculous act of self-invention. In the Festival of Britain in 1951, the conventional symbol of Englishness, the rooted, thickly historical tree, was replaced with the apparently rootless, floating 'Skylon', a model of the new modernity of England. In the aftermath of the war, I would suggest, the meanings of Englishness were contested through public conflicts about its cultural spaces, its landscape, topography, and architecture, conflicts which are highly visible in the literary texts of the period.

The symbolism of the new town is the focus of Angus Wilson's *Late Call* (1964), which tells the story of Sylvia Calvert, the retiring manageress of a hotel, who is encouraged with her husband to live with their son, Harold, and his children in the fictional new town of Carshall. Harold, recently widowed, is something of a crusader for what he sees as the cause of new towns, and proud of his 'pioneer' venture into 'the first district of Carshall to be completed after the Town Centre ... the first to have its own shopping centre and community hall. And we were the first residents' (Wilson 1968, 42). Harold depicts the new town as a new beginning, a revolution in social organisation which heralds the end of inequality and division, and which promises the liberal dream of social integration and harmony. The new town is, as Harold's father boasts, 'one of England's showpieces' (59), designed to demonstrate that England could be as modern and fresh as America.

The novel sets up contrasts between the new town and older forms of social organisation. The first contrast, which Harold in particular evokes as the ugly antithesis to the liberal ideal of Carshall, is the industrial cities and towns of the Midlands. To underline this contrast, Harold directs a production of John Osborne's *Look Back in Anger* for his fellow citizens, explaining what he sees as the principal function of the play: 'Osborne's hit off exactly the sort of old-fashioned, industrialized, unneighbourly jungle-world Midland town that the New Towns are going to replace. The very sordidness of it all may make Carshallites count their blessings a bit' (125). Osborne's play becomes, in Harold's interpretation, a mouthpiece against the old order, and a herald of the socially-engineered utopia promised in the wide avenues, multi-storey shopping malls, and spacious housing of the new town. Jimmy Porter's decayed, cramped surroundings in his attic flat are, for Harold, the source of his anger and anti-establishment views, and what Harold reads as the moral of Osborne's play is that space determines happiness. Carshall is thus emblematic of a conflict between Victorian England, with its dark factories and claustrophobic slums, and postwar England, in which the reinvention of the English town and landscape will generate the new social and cultural conditions of a utopian future.

The utopian promise of Carshall is represented with considerable irony in the novel, however, not least through the perspective of Sylvia. The ironic depiction of Carshall is made possible through a second contrast between the new town and a prior model of community. The second contrast, which comes increasingly to trouble Sylvia, is the hard rural world of her upbringing, in which she has been told by her mother that 'God put 'er here to work for others' (30). This rural world is the one over which Carshall has been built, of course, so that Harold's depiction of himself and his family as pioneers, as the first residents, seeks unwittingly to erase the memory of the places and communities of Sylvia's upbringing. If the problem with postwar England as Harold perceives it is that 'the whole country seems to be dying of a surfeit of nostalgia' (42), that its towns are museums to dead industries, its architecture nothing but monuments to the vitality of the past, the new town offers to bulldoze the past to make room for a bright new future. Sylvia finds it less than convincing, however.

The new town offers to bring the space of the countryside into the urbanity of the town, to provide 'natural' landscape as theme park within the civic space, to give all of its citizens an opportunity to recreate the picturesque in their own private gardens and public parks. It thus signals an attempt to abolish the chasm between country and city, between landscape and architecture, between nature and design, and to co-opt the ideologies of the English rural idyll for the project of postwar modernity. Harold, in his oppressive enthusiasm for the new town, depicts this as the successful integration of town and country, but Sylvia finds Carshall a poor parody of the country, its sycamore trees 'leafless', 'dried up and sad', its parkways offering pathetic 'narrow, well-trod, ant-infested way[s] as some substitute for the ranging, unbounded choice of the solitude of the countryside' (194). Instead of integration with the country, Carshall seems instead to proffer nothing but endless forms of self-referentiality, as Sylvia discovers when she sets out to discover the countryside:

> Yet, once sought, the endless 'Midlands', that lay open before her in such terrible enticement from her bedroom window, proved hard to find. The New Town, though it merged into the country, was yet cut off from it by a system of lanes and roads that turned back on themselves and eventually returned to Town Centre, as inevitably, by contrast, the paths in a maze lead away from its core. Often and again she would follow the lanes that, leaving behind the last primary school's bold colours and even the white pavilions of the last sports ground, passed on between fields of tender young wheat and stretched ahead, it seemed, to an endless rolling patchwork of fields – when suddenly there would appear a familiar green sign white-lettered: 'Footpath to Melling' or 'Footpath to Carshall' or 'Footpath to Darner's Green'. (Wilson 1968, 198–9)

In quest of an elusive, and highly symbolic image of the endless, enchanted countryside, Sylvia is constantly returned to the autographic space of the town, which signifies itself at every turn. If

Sylvia's underlying anxiety is that Carshall has produced its own space by erasing the memory of the landscape it was built upon, the ability of the town to enclose itself as a self-signifying system seems to suggest an even more worrying reproductive capacity. Carshall at once seems both to gesture to its place in the surrounding countryside, and to contain that countryside within itself, so that even the rolling wheat fields, which appear to be outside the town's limits, are merely the illusion of a rural 'outside'. The countryside becomes bound up in the urban sign system; it is experienced as an 'effect' of the town, a thought which occurs to Sylvia when Harold points out the landscapes of the Midlands to her 'as though he had put them there' (69).

Harold begins to have his own anxieties about the reproductive appetites of the town, and organises a campaign to save an outlying meadow threatened by urban expansion. Sylvia's interest in the rural is understood to derive from much more personal, psychological foundations than Harold's however. The novel begins in 1911 with a depiction of Sylvia as a child in her rural home. Her later determination to rediscover the countryside of her youth stems from a troubled interrogation of her life as a badly made jumper, loose, shapeless and muddled: 'Perhaps to weave all the threads together again, she needed to return to the country world of her childhood – but even this idea seemed more something she had once been told than any personal conviction' (200). Even when Sylvia does discover the paths which take her outside of Carshall, into what she thinks of as the boundless countryside, she discovers there merely a monotonous, unrevealing experience of space. She walks for hours through the landscape without noticing anything remarkable, or, sometimes, notices vetches, poppies, rows of wheat, coarse thistle, but such sights 'merely passed in blank visual succession, leaving no trace in her memory' (201). Sylvia attempts to find understanding in the landscape, but she regards the landscape initially through the urban, voyeuristic mode of the picturesque. It is only when she is compelled to connect with the country as country – when she humanely snaps the neck of a badly wounded rabbit, for example – that she begins to recognise the pull of her past life, and the necessity of finding some way of making sense of her past.

This becomes possible through a fateful event in which she saves the life of a young girl in a thunderstorm by judiciously calling her away from a tree which is immediately struck by lightning thereafter.

The coincidental act of salvation brings her into contact with the girl's family, farmers who live on the outskirts of Carshall, and it is through Sylvia's growing intimacy with this family, and her articulation of her own experiences as a country girl that she begins to put the past in perspective. She emerges from under the shadows of her mother's domination, and her husband's demands, and in the climax to the novel, when she has just been widowed, determines to live her own life. In her new found confidence, Sylvia articulates not only her own problems and anxieties, but manages to radiate understanding and warmth to Harold's family too, healing the squabbles generated by Harold's vain pursuit of a spurious ideal of socially-engineered harmony.

It is not her renewed encounter with rural space which finally solves Sylvia's sense of disquiet and anxiety, therefore, so much as an experience of reconnecting with her own sense of place in a community. The idealised urban space of Carshall offers an illusion of harmonious living, which turns out to be false. Sylvia discovers in Carshall the unsettling experience of urban space described by Henri Lefebvre in *The Production of Space*: 'the architectural and urbanistic space of modernity tends precisely towards this homogeneous state of affairs, towards a place of confusion and fusion between geometrical and visual which inspires a kind of physical discomfort' (Lefebvre 1991, 200). Carshall is figured in the novel as the disorienting landscape onto which Sylvia's psychological and emotional desires for self-realisation are displaced. So too, Sylvia's pursuit of a rural idyll is fallacious, for it projects onto the rural the hidden fears and desires of her self-identity, promising to find in the picturesque the image of her own coherence. If Sylvia's quest for self-coherence is analogous to the autochthonic dream of the new town, *Late Call* suggests the need for both to situate themselves within the dense network of social relations and functions which make up the imagined spaces of self-identity.

The new town in Wilson's *Late Call* functions not as a specific place, but as a symbolic space of postwar modernity in England. It is presented as an imaginative site of conflicting models of possibility and identity, which serves to juxtapose the liberal, progressive ideology of the 'brave new world' and 'the new Jerusalem', current in left-wing politics in the immediate aftermath of the war, with the rhetoric of conservation and figurative return to past greatness, which continued to find political expression in England in the 1950s and early

1960s.[2] Wilson's novel engages not just with the political contexts of a changing landscape, but with the landscape as a political form itself, as a symbolic space in which political discourses shape social structures and seek to play out ideological struggles for social and cultural power. The same process of engaging with the landscape as a symbolic marker of social and political change is evident in H.E. Bates's popular pastoral novel, *The Darling Buds of May* (1958).

The Darling Buds of May, the first of Bates' novels about the Larkin family, is a self-consciously idyllic representation of rural life. The first hot sun of the year, and the jamboree of blooms, fruits and feasts, sets the scene for an edenic vision of the English countryside. It is a novel of excess – of food, sex, sun, and laughter – which conforms to the traditional pastoral evocation of the rural as the site of plenitude and voluptuous abandon. There is no sin in this idealised world. Pop and Ma Larkin are unmarried, their eldest daughter is believed to be pregnant by an unknown father, Pop kisses another woman, but each of these apparently immoral acts is accepted within the permissive, indulgent bounds of their society. So too, in keeping with the pastoral tradition, the novel depicts the Larkins enjoying limitless happiness and endless wealth, without disclosing the plausible, material sources of their wealth. They live from the labour of picking fruit, harvesting crops, and trading in whatever commodities or scrap materials come their way, in a manner which suggests the working habits of the labouring rural poor. But their lifestyle seems to exceed their means, as is apparent to the tax inspector, Cedric Charlton, who is quickly integrated into the Larkin family. The Larkin household contains all the conveniences of modern home technology, including two televisions, while Pop Larkin acquires a Rolls-Royce car to drive his family around the countryside in luxury, and barters with the local aristocrat for his estate.

In typical pastoral fashion, then, *The Darling Buds of May* evades the material reality of rural labour in favour of a picturesque world of bountiful feasts and rude health. It does so, in part, in order to dispel the image of social incohesion, suggesting instead that all who partake of the joys of the rural paradise depicted are rich. The Larkins's lifestyle is opulent, in some respects, in the feasts they can provide for themselves and their neighbours, or in the lavish displays of familial congeniality, but their material surroundings are also *imbued* with paradisiacal significance by them:

'Gawd A'mighty, Ma, you know we got a beautiful place here. Paradise ...'. Standing in the evening sunlight, gazing across the pile of junk, the nettles, the rusting hovels, and the scratching, dusty hens, Pop sighed loudly and with such content that the sound seemed to travel with perfect definition across the surrounding fields of butter-cups and may, gathering its echo at last from the mingled sounds of the remaining geese, the voices of cuckoos calling as they flew across the meadows and the small, passionate, invisible nightingales. 'Perfick,' Pop said. 'You couldn't wish for nothing more perfick nowhere.' (Bates 1991, 25)

Junk, nettles and hovels do not a paradise make, in themselves, but this is to ignore the imaginative and symbolic construction of pastoral representation, the defining effect of which, according to William Empson is 'to imply a beautiful relation between rich and poor' (Empson 1950, 11–12). John Lucas amplifies Empson's point to argue that the pastoral form necessarily 'implies a vision of social relationships, harmoniously structured, hierarchically ordered, and succoured by full creativity' (Lucas 1990, 4). The point is not that the Larkin family abide in a comfortable haven in a beautiful landscape, but that they perceive themselves to be entirely in harmony with the prevailing social hierarchy, and would not wish to change places with anyone else.

It is a characteristic of the pastoral form that the humble or power-less actively renounce the dream of becoming wealthy or powerful, that they find in their own ostensibly poor surroundings all of the wealth and happiness they require. The shepherd thus signals the perfection of his own life by refusing to aspire to positions of higher social or political prestige. *The Darling Buds of May* replicates some-thing of this trope in its representation of social relations and struc-tures. Ma takes interest in the lives of the aristocracy on a television documentary (31), for example, but she is depicted later as the happy sovereign of her own blissful kingdom as she rides in Pop's newly acquired Rolls Royce. The Rolls Royce functions symbolically, in other words, as a token of the inestimable wealth of the imagined paradise of the Larkin household. Likewise, Mr Charlton mistakes Mariette Larkin for the niece of an aristocrat, but it is much more significant and appropriate to the novel's pastoral function that she is not:

> Mr Charlton made a startling, embarrassed confession.
> 'I thought – well, I was actually told you were someone else in point of fact – that you were a niece of Lady Planson-Forbes – you know, at Carrington Hall –'
> Mariette began laughing, in ringing tones, very much like her father.
> 'Now you've just found I wasn't.'
> 'Well, yes –'
> 'You feel it makes any difference?'
> 'Well, in point of fact –'
> 'I'm just the same, aren't I?' She smiled and he found his eyes level with her bare, olive shoulder. 'I'm just me. The same girl. Just me. Just the same.' (Bates 1991, 24)

That Mariette is not the niece of an aristocrat, and 'just' a country girl of unremarkable origin, is necessary to the political function of the novel as pastoral vision, since it suggests that nobility of birth is no prerequisite for nobility of beauty, mind or character. It suggests the reversibility of the social hierarchy, in one sense, but it also presents as harmonious the social relations between rich and poor, so that the poor might be mistaken for the rich, and vice versa. This is conveyed by other means in the novel, too, in the characters of the Brigadier and Miss Pilchester, who, although they come from upper-class backgrounds, are now depicted as living in poverty and hardship, and surviving partly as a result of the charitable, generous disposition of the Larkins. In the case of Miss Pilchester, the inversion of her status is marked by the domestic space she inhabits: 'that terrible, cramped, untidy, woolly, television-less little bolt-hole' (88).

Bates's novel, in this sense, weaves the then current theme of social mobility into the pastoral form, so that the rich and powerful are economically as well as symbolically exchanging places with the poor and powerless. Pop Larkin has overtaken the Brigadier in wealth and stature, for example, although he has no title, rank, inheritance, nor membership of elite clubs, nor network of highly-placed acquaintances. He has acquired sufficient power to be able to provide the Brigadier with the use of a meadow on which to hold the community gymkhana, and to be invited to inject new blood into the local hunting set by becoming the 'master of fox hounds'. At the same time, however, Larkin is dependent upon an invisible structure of casual farm labour and informal trading, while appearing to be the master of his own fate and welfare. The absence of an economic hierarchy – the landlords and rich farmers on whom Larkin presumably depends for his casual labour – obscures the material conditions of the Larkins's blissful life in the country, but the novel presents sufficient indication of the social structure to track the changes in status and mobility within it.

This cross-fertilisation of genres, the pastoral with postwar social realism, combines the material with the symbolic to offer an intriguing implication. If earlier versions of pastoral function by playing with an imaginary reversal of symbolic value in a rigid social hierarchy, so as to present, for example, a shepherd as more blissful and comfortable than a queen, *The Darling Buds of May* delineates a semi-imaginary, semi-plausible situation in which a family of labouring farmers are depicted as acquiring both the symbolic and material wealth befitting those of higher social status. Bates's novel functions, therefore, by inverting both the material and the symbolic, by merging the pastoral vision of social harmony with the conservative political reading of English society in the 1950s as evolving towards a generalised, classless affluence in which material prosperity was available to all.

This is to go some way to confirming Louis Montrose's reading of pastoral as centrally and especially concerned with 'the symbolic mediation of social relationships', relationships which are, he argues, 'intrinsically, relationships of power' (Montrose 1980, 153). In evoking the idealised cultural landscapes of pastoral tradition, *The Darling Buds of May* is not simply offering a nostalgic or edenic image of rural, summer living, but is participating actively in the negotiation of social structures and relations. Bates's novel depicts the slide into obscurity of the prewar elites of landed gentry and commissioned officers, and reflects the postwar trust in the promise of an emergent class of affluent workers and the prospect of permeable social divisions. As such, the novel fosters the illusion of material and symbolic transformation of social structures, so that the poor and the aristocracy might exchange places, so that the ideal of effortless, bountiful living, lax morality, and liberty from the law is made to appear almost tangible. The idyllic landscape that *The Darling Buds of May* depicts then, is primarily neither material nor imaginary, but profoundly and relentlessly political. It is deployed and evoked as a space in which questions of social identity, cultural authority, and political power are brought into focus, and in which political discourses of Englishness find symbolic expression. The pastoral form of the novel appears effortless in its casual evocation of a rural idyll, but perhaps what is most remarkable about *The Darling Buds of May* is how effectively it strives to transmit its implied vision of an emergent, affluent society, embedded in a familiar cultural landscape steeped in the symbolic associations of Englishness.

Landscape and culture

The representation of landscape in literary texts, in common with all representations of landscape (indeed, landscape is never anything but representation), is related to and embedded in social and political structures. Even the most elementary issues of describing, naming, or delineating a landscape inevitably intersect with the political implications of territory, language, cultural appropriation, social divisions, and historical association. This is the case not just in political representations of landscape, but in landscape as a political form of representation itself, by which I mean the landscape not as something given or pre-existent, but brought into being through the self-conscious constructions of men and women living on the earth. 'World is what men and women in their living together make', writes J. Hillis Miller, 'for example in cutting paths through a forest or across a heath. Such paths are decisive fissures setting boundaries … . Paths give the world edges and measures' (Miller 1995, 14).

To think of such features as paths, dykes, bridges, fields, roads, and boundaries, or the demarcation of the limits of a forest or a plain, as the writing of landscape (*topo-graphein* – the writing of place), as the effects of human representations of the earth as dwelling place, is to begin to recognise literature as an extension of that process of creating the landscape. As Miller argues in his discussion of the novels of Thomas Hardy, 'novels themselves aid in making the landscapes that they apparently presuppose as already made and finished' (16). In the previous section of the chapter, I focused on representations of the landscape as the symbolic marker of social and political change. In this section, my attention shifts to two exemplary works of topographical poetry, Basil Bunting's *Briggflatts* (1965) and Geoffrey Hill's *Mercian Hymns* (1971), and in particular to the dialogic, intergenerative relationship between landscape and culture offered in those poems.

Briggflatts consists of five sections and a coda, which imitate the structure of a musical composition in their deployment of what Peter Makin calls 'sonata-like patterns of subject-matter and of rhythm-phrase' (Makin 1992, 152). The poem weaves several strands of narrative together: the story of abandoned love, which begins in the first movement with the boy and girl who accompany the stone mason on his journey; the mythological tale of the bull who rapes Pasiphae; the historical narrative of the murder of Eric Bloodaxe at Stainmore; the legend of Alexander the Great reaching the edge of the world; the *Bildungsroman* narrative of the poet-artist emerging into troubled, guilt-ridden maturity; and the story of the slowworm, which functions variously in the poem as a figure of natural, cyclical process, as a phallic symbol, as a model of stable identity, and as an exemplar for the poet for how he might embrace the local, unheroic life of his home. Bunting constructs these narratives elliptically, so that the plot seems to proceed as much by implication as by revelation. This formal patterning of narratives places Bunting oddly in relation to the neo-modernism for which he became renowned in the 1960s, for *Briggflatts* combines the formal, musical complexity of modernist poetry with narratives that are relatively apparent and coherent. Like the modernist poems of W.B. Yeats and T.S. Eliot, however, Bunting's poem situates itself within a dense network of mythic and historical frameworks (principally those connected with Northumbria), and it is this attention to its own 'location' – in space and time – that I think makes *Briggflatts* such an important poem.

Briggflatts locates itself, first of all, in its subtitle as 'an autobiography'. It does 'write the self' in the sense that it traces through not just the isolatable, individual life story of the poet, but also through the physical, linguistic, geographical, historical, and cultural elements which make up a complex, interconnected subjectivity. It is then, as Bunting avers in his 'Afterthoughts', 'not a record of fact' (Bunting 1966, 43), but instead it acknowledges that 'self' comprises an elaborate arrangement of personas, effects and relations. This is perhaps most apparent in the ways in which the poem melds alternate personas together: the boy in the first movement of the poem, for example, merges into the 'Copper-wire moustache, / sea-reflecting eyes / and Baltic plainsong speech' (13) of the Vikings at Stainmore; the first person narrators of the central section of the poem slide from the self-effacing voice of one of Alexander's men into the portentous declaration 'I am neither snake nor lizard, / I am the slowworm' (28). *Briggflatts* is thus a poem in which voices shift location, and in which identity is encountered in mutable, fluid shapes. The self is constructed through language: it is named into existence, just as in the second stanza of the poem we are told of the mason who strikes into the marble 'till the stone spells a name / naming none, / a man abolished' (11).

From the beginning, Bunting's poem demystifies the self, so that it is exposed as a figurative projection of presence set against the more concrete, durable forces of landscape and history. The self is depicted as a vessel through which the historical and regional particularities of language pass. We are told of the boy in the first movement of the poem: 'Fierce blood throbs in his tongue, / lean words.' (13). Those lean, hard words, the 'Baltic plainsong speech' of Northumbria's Viking ancestry, permeate the poem, and give it its distinctive cadences and rhythms of sound. For example, listening to the sound of the cart wheels turning, the children in the first movement hear 'harness mutter to shaft, / felloe to axle squeak, / rut thud the rim, / crushed grit.' (12). These lines, like many in the poem, encapsulate the cultural history of the language, with their smattering of Norse, Germanic, and French sounds, and the emphasis on short-lined, lean verse gives the impression of a hard, plain-speaking culture. Just as the poem inscribes a regional identity through the sounds of its language, it also maps out a journey through the topography of Northumbria, encompassing Garsdale, Stainmore, Hawes, the rivers Till and Tweed, and dales, Teviotdale and Wensleydale. It situates this region along a Viking axis of power, running from Norway to Orkney, through Northumbria to Dublin. This east-west axis of power is offered as a sub-textual counter-narrative to the history of 'English' dominance in Northumbria, which commenced with the slaying of Eric Bloodaxe at Stainmore. The Norse influence is particularly acute in Northumbria, and this enables Bunting to construct through the language and topography a distinctive cultural identity and ancestry for the region. The words which the boy might speak in describing his surroundings in the present-day vestiges of the Northumbria region connect him culturally, almost psychically, with his historical antecedents at Stainmore, Lindisfarne, or Teesdale.

This is articulated not in the form of a racial consciousness or essential identity, but in the form of historical and cultural forces continuing to exercise their presence in the lives and expressions of Northumbrians. Bunting's understanding of history is not of mythic fates and predetermined destinies, but of currents of possibility, which run true to channels shaped by time and happenstance. Hence, the questions which conclude the poem, pondering the possibilities which might have set other courses:

> Where we are who knows
> of kings who sup
> while day fails? Who,
> swinging his axe
> to fell kings, guesses
> where we go? (Bunting 1966, 41)

There is the acknowledgement here that 'we' are on the same journey, and that 'our' journey has been jostled into course by decisive, bloody actions, actions which are determined but never understood. The contrivance of kings is just so many 'guesses'. Bunting knows to be true the small, simple movements of human action – the swinging axe, the hammer, wheel and water which make the axe head, the ship's keel which raises 'cold cliffs where tides / knot fringes of weed' (18). These are the motions and energies which inscribe human endeavour on the world, but some more complex, ineffable pattern is sewn by such actions. This could be the subject of the poem's melancholic tone, a sense of resignation to the inevitable processes of historical change, which have carried Northumbria from its ancient renown for learning and art (recalled in allusions to Aneurin, Taliesin, Columba, Aidan and Cuthbert, and to Lindisfarne, of course), to its current subservience to the demands of those Bunting derisively calls 'southrons'. But the poem might also be marking here the mutability of history, of identity, for the question of 'where we are' and 'where we go', while the 'day fails' on the current kings, is left unresolved. If much of the poem establishes through language and topography that Northumbria is still audible and traceable, its concluding verse maintains the sense that it has not yet run its course.

This is to suggest that what appears to be an historical allusion to what might have happened had Eric Bloodaxe remained 'king of Northumbria' instead of being dethroned by the southern English could be read as a more contemporary political or cultural question about the possibilities yet to be encountered in the narratives of Northumbrian identity. This might seem to make *Briggflatts* a more parochial poem than its neo-modernist form would imply. As Keith Tuma argues, however, *Briggflatts* sets its 'Northumbrian core ... in a field of international influences and traditions, confronting the parochialism of the English center with continuities beyond its view' (Tuma 1998, 168). Bunting thus implies a view of Northumbria which makes the 'English center' look parochial. Tuma's reading of the poem as participating in the construction of a regional, post-imperial response to the postwar crisis in Englishness is broadly right, I think, in stressing that the poem utilises a sense of Northumbria's cultural heritage as a means of dissenting from the intensely metropolitan concentration of postwar English culture. Faced with the declining economic and cultural significance of the region, Bunting attempts to shore up a sense of the endurance of Northumbria as a cultural entity, but does so by tracing the sedimentary layers of Northumbrian art and history in relation to wider geo-historical contexts. This is not the archaeological approach familiar from Heaney, for example, of digging into the primeval mud, but is perhaps better described by the role adopted by the poet at the opening of the poem, that of a choreographer or conductor of diverse dances and melodies through time:

> Brag, sweet tenor bull,
> descant on Rawthey's madrigal,
> each pebble its part
> for the fells' late spring.
> Dance tiptoe, bull,
> black against may.
> Ridiculous and lovely
> chase hurdling shadows
> morning into noon. (Bunting 1966, 11)

The poet here orchestrates and arranges the 'ridiculous and lovely' into the dance, gathering his materials, 'each pebble its part', into the diverse, interweaving narratives which comprise Northumbria. His materials are 'shadows', however; only the ghosts remain of those diligent, artful monks on Lindisfarne, the conspiratorial whispers of those assassins at Stainmore, the scratched stone inscription of the 'man abolished'. Bunting's art is constructed of the ephemeral, symbolised in the movement of the dance, not the monumental, earth-clad remains of Heaney's poetry, for example. The allusions to history, to the barely discernible traces of Northumbria's ancient past, are moulded not from fossils, but from figures of motion, energy, and return. *Briggflatts* mobilises the figure of the journey, of movement and transit, to intimate the difficult, restless fate of a culture which is not yet, or no longer, 'an acknowledged land' (32). *Briggflatts* lays bare its European cultural dreams – the culture of Scarlatti, Monteverdi, Schoenberg, the landscapes of Italy, the myths of Greece – but celebrates those fleeting shadows of hope for the 'fields we do not know' (41). Northumbria remains an unknown land, even, Bunting suggests, to its own inhabitants, and so *Briggflatts* undertakes a journey to discover the meanings and resonances of Northumbria.

The problem for the poet in *Briggflatts* is that Northumbria, like the mason's stone in the second stanza, names nothing. It is discernible only in its ghosts, shadows, and traces, or as the discarded husk or shell, an image repeated several times in the poem. It is, for the poet, an abandoned home, a home to which he feels compelled to return, literally and imaginatively, drawn by the pull of 'a strong song' (41). Bunting's task is to construct a fictive Northumbria, an imaginative construct, which emerges as a distinctive cultural pattern from the webs of meaning and allusion spun in the poem. This is the method which Bunting admired in the *Codex Lindisfarnis*, particularly its 'carpet pages', in which an apparent confusion of ornament and innumerable detail forms, with careful attention, into a central pattern – the Christian symbol of the cross, in the examples Bunting considers (Makin 2000, 1–18). *Briggflatts* presents such a confusion of narratives and motifs, a frenetic welter of symbols, sounds and images, from which emerges the outline of a journey homeward. The return to home depicted in the poem is, however, filled with a sense of loss and transience. The compulsion to return home is borne of nostalgia, but the poem recognises that memories of the past, however idyllic, make for unreliable foundations: 'Today's posts are piles to drive into the quaggy past / on which impermanent palaces balance' (31). So too, *Briggflatts* recognises the paradoxical inevitability and impossibility of return, the compulsion to revisit an irretrievable home.

The sea voyages which surface repeatedly in the poem serve to illustrate this recognition. The sea epitomises mutability, inscrutability, for while the land yields up its millennia of inscriptions, 'Wind writes in foam on the sea' (18). The sea refuses to remember, and even takes the lives of those 'who sang' (19), but the sea is readable, navigable, by means of the stars. Here again, the poem illustrates impermanence, for even though each star, through 'a sextant's bubble present and firm/ places a surveyor's stone or steadies a tiller', it is already 'beyond chronological compass' (38). 'The star you steer by is gone', the poem tells us, alluding not just to our state of transience, not just to the constant signs of mortality and loss which surround us, but also, more specifically, to the compass points of Northumbrian history which are distant bright lights, and yet might still steady the tiller in defining its course.

The journey homeward is plotted in the poem through a complex web of navigational aids, drawn from language, topography, astronomy, botany, history, artistic and cultural heritage, myth, and music. Northumbria is such an evasive, diffident entity that it can only be located by overlaying successive, alternate grids of reference, and out of such grids, out of its compound of connections and interweavings, emerges the poem's patterning of a landscape and culture hidden in the conventional perceptual focus of metropolitan England. *Briggflatts* is, in this sense, not an archaeological poem, but a remarkable feat of prosopopoeia, of breathing expressive vitality into the ghosts of an ancient, long-submerged culture. Bunting is not content to 'number the dead and rejoice', like Aneurin (31); instead, *Briggflatts* hears the voices and recovers the traces of the past, imagining the past as distant stars, long dead, yet still 'beckoning boats to the fishing' (37). By the light of these stars, Bunting delineates the intricate patterns of a specific landscape and culture, and, as he would later describe the task of Northumbrian art, he sets his theme 'with infinite care in just the right place ... and leave[s] it there for the reader to discover for himself' (Makin 2000, 18).

Bunting's poem is one of the most influential works of the spatial or topographical imagination in postwar English poetry, but it is important to emphasise its implied sense of distance from metropolitan English culture. Northumbria in Bunting's vision is an historical and cultural location displaced or submerged by the colonising tendencies of Englishness. There are many similarities between *Briggflatts* and Geoffrey Hill's *Mercian Hymns*, but the relationship with a mainstream English culture is where they most crucially diverge. Hill's poem, like Bunting's, returns to an ancient political territory, Mercia in Hill's case, and presents the reputed figure of King Offa, who, like Bloodaxe in *Briggflatts*, is an ambivalent 'hero', and appears to be interchangeable with the contemporary protagonist of the poem. Hill delineates an historical landscape, less complex than Bunting's, but equally vibrant with the signs of its continuous regeneration. Hill interpenetrates the narratives of mythology and history with the stories and images of his own childhood, just as *Briggflatts* styles itself 'an autobiography'. There are formal parallels too: while *Briggflatts* is structured in the form of symphonic movements, *Mercian Hymns* takes the shape of the canticles or collects of church music, imitating the liturgical prose of the collects, and the rhythmic forms of Anglican hymns. But this is part of what distinguishes Hill from Bunting, too, for Bunting's poem sets its regional subject within the wider sphere of European cultural contexts, while Hill seems closer to and more comfortably accommodated within a conservative understanding of English culture.

This is certainly the argument of one of Hill's most vocal and outspoken critics, Tom Paulin, who initiated a controversial debate in the *London Review of Books* in April 1985, when he argued that Hill's poetry was the product of a deeply conservative imagination peddling a reactionary Anglo-Catholicism, and an authoritarian veneration for lost kingdom and declining power. Perhaps most controversially, Paulin draws attention to the possible correspondences between *Mercian Hymns* and the notorious speech made by Enoch Powell at the Midland Hotel in Birmingham in April 1968. Hill began to write *Mercian Hymns* in the Midlands around the time of this speech, Paulin recalls, an alarmist, racist speech which warned of the threat to English ways of life posed by the mass immigration of black and Asian people. Powell famously drew his speech to a close with the analogy, 'Like the Roman, I seem to see "the River Tiber foaming with much blood"', which appears both to prophesy and to encourage racist violence (Smithies and Fiddick 1969, 43). Hymn XVIII of Hill's poem finds the protagonist 'set in motion the furtherance of his journey. / To watch the Tiber foaming out much blood' (Hill 1985, 122). The construction seems to be too close to be anything other than deliberate reference, and Paulin gives credit to the critic Peter Robinson for 'tracing Offa's spoor back to the Midland Hotel', although he complains that Robinson 'baulks at drawing any conclusions from this conjunction of Black Country powers' (Paulin 1993, 283). Ironically, Paulin also baulks at drawing conclusions from this disturbing correspondence between Powell's racist rhetoric and Hill's poem, preferring to leave for his readers the implication that Hill shares Powell's brand of apartheid nationalism.

Paulin's suggestion (and we should be wary of the provocative, goading manner in which the suggestion is made) is that Hill's poetry delineates the rudiments of an obnoxious English nationalism, grafted, in the case of *Mercian Hymns*, from the stuff of myth, history, topography, ecclesiastical tradition and community ritual. Paulin is partly reacting against the conservatism of the form of the poem, that it utilises the traditional form of Anglican hymns, which Hill admired for their combination of human response and historical continuity:

> The responses are to be understood both as recurring within the limited time-span of a particular Anglican evensong, following the established pattern of the rubric, and as recurring over an implied and indefinite number of years, recurring Sunday by Sunday, season by season, year after year. It is by such means that 'channels' are created; by the joint working of abrasion and continuity. (Hill, quoted in Milne 1998, 94–5)

The same structure of instant emanation within an implied sense of historical recurrence, of the integer within the matrix, or even the individual within Eliotic tradition, pervades the poem. The poem suggests that the historical person of King Offa is also a mythic figure who recurs through the history of Mercia, or the west Midlands, so that the poet-protagonist is the modern manifestation of this figure, and his everyday actions as a child are exaggerated into the mythic proportions of a legendary king. Offa is both a real, dead king, and a recurring trope of aggression and authority through English history. Mercia, likewise, is an ancient, long redundant political territory, but it also functions in the poem as the imaginative projection of an enduring, powerful England, strong in trade and commanding in its authority. Hill returns constantly to this paradoxical structure, so that King Offa is both 'alive and dead' (131), the protagonist's childhood both 'rich and desolate' (109), Offa's funeral attended by both 'Welsh mercenaries' and 'Merovingian car-dealers' (131). This is a device used similarly in *Briggflatts*, which enables the poet to represent continuity, temporal recurrence, or what Hill describes as 'channels' through time. Through such channels, Hill implies, 'we' are connected with Offa and Mercia of eighth-century history, and it is this 'exclusive, ethnically biased' 'we' of which Paulin is so suspicious (Paulin 1993, 283).

The Mercia of Hill's poem is not confined by the topographical features identified in the poem, between the rivers Teme and Trent (125), with its scattered references to Iron Bridge, Holy Cross,

Malvern, and the capital of a nearly-united England, Tamworth. The
poet's childhood is associated with these places, with this sense of a
regional or parochial identity, but Offa is also *Rex Anglorum*, king of
England. Mercia conquered England in Offa's time, and Offa was duly
recognised and legitimated as its king. Thus Offa, like Arthur in
Tennyson's *Idylls of the King*, is the historical antecedent through
which England as a political and cultural entity is brought into existence. Hill constitutes this correlation between Mercia and England
further by siting the poetic evocation of Mercia within the established,
ritual form of Anglican devotional worship, and connects the corona-
tion and reign of Offa with the symbolism of Christ, the saviour,
martyr, and crusader:

> Where best to stand? Easter sunrays catch the ob-
> lique face of Adam scrumping through leaves; pale
> spree of evangelists and, there, a cross Christ
> mumming child Adam out of Hell. (Hill 1985, 128)

The poet stands before the stained-glass depictions of Adam's sin,
here cleverly described as 'scrumping', and Christ's crucifixion,
imagined as a cross mother ('mumming') saving her child from
danger. Offa, like Christ, is the resurrection, and is repeatedly resurrected in the poem. Hill's theme is the continual fall and resurrection
of England, its constant process of destruction and regeneration.
Offa is also the 'starting-cry of a race' (106), and the origins of
modern capitalist England, for his legacy is to have reformed the
system of coinage, and to have initiated England's renown for trading
prowess in his commercial treaty with Charlemagne. Coins recur
through the poem, culminating in the final image of Offa vanishing:
'he left behind coins, for his lodging, and traces of / red mud' (134).
Offa's achievement, then, is to have created the legend of England as
a trading nation, the nation of shopkeepers, and the poem imagines
the current embodiment of Offa as a business tycoon, 'dismissing
reports and men', and threatening 'malefactors with ash from his
noon cigar' (118). The coin is Offa's imprint on English culture,
stamped with the graffiti of his own greatness, '*Offa Rex*', and a
symbol of his authority: 'Exactness of design was to deter imitation;
muti- / lation if that failed' (115). Hill shows Offa to be symbolic of
defining tendencies of English nationalism, its system of kingship
and state authority, its Anglican traditions, its commercial prowess.

Paulin's reaction against Hill's nationalism might be articulated in provocative terms, but it is by no means an obscure or devious approach to the poem.

This view, however, does not yet take account of the poem's own doubtful and playful voices, which continually emerge to undercut and deflate Offa's arrogance and pomposity. This is evident from the beginning of the poem:

> King of the perennial holly-groves, the riven sand-
> stone: overlord of the M5: architect of the his-
> toric rampart and ditch, the citadel at Tamworth,
> the summer hermitage in Holy Cross: guardian of
> the Welsh Bridge and the Iron Bridge: contractor
> to the desirable new estates: saltmaster: money-
> changer: commissioner for oaths: martyrologist:
> the friend of Charlemagne.

> 'I liked that,' said Offa, 'sing it again.' (Hill 1985, 105)

The opening of *Mercian Hymns* mimics the style of royal invocation, a chant to summon to mind the achievements and greatness of the king. Offa is 'king', 'overlord', 'guardian', and 'the friend of Charlemagne', but his power is comically deflated when he is described as 'commissioner for oaths', a familiar notice to be seen adorning any local solicitor's office. He is 'architect' of ramparts, defensive ditches, and citadels, testaments to his magnificence, but he is also 'contractor' to housing estates, a less noble calling, and 'overlord of the M5', the motorway running along the Welsh border. This first hymn could be read for more serious suggestions, that the M5 is somehow the modern equivalent of 'Offa's Dyke', that housing estates are the citadels of our time, but the mimicry of portentous language implies a comic function. This is implied further in Offa's rather less pretentious reply. The name 'Offa' is satirised itself in the second hymn, where it is suggested that the name might currently refer to 'a pet name, a common name. Best selling brand, curt graf-fito', or any number of other, less majestic subjects (106). The same device of comic undercutting is evident in Hymn IX, where the speaker tells us of Offa's burial, and comments to Offa: 'I unburden the saga of your burial, my dear. You had/ lived long enough to see things "nicely settled"' (113). Here again, the heroic implications of a saga of burial are deflated by the platitudinous observation that he had settled his affairs nicely before dying.

The point about such humour in *Mercian Hymns* is that it is difficult to determine what is being deflated or undercut by it. Is the portentous, authoritarian Hill sneering at the mundanity of the secular, modern England of democracy and housing estates? Or is there a more genial, self-parodic Hill, raising the mythology of King Offa of Mercia only to laugh at its pretensions? The satirical strategies of the poem make it difficult to determine exactly which Hill we should see at work here. Hill seems to occupy an ambivalent location in this historic landscape, either nostalgic for the achievements and power of Englands past, or contemptuous of the smug, narcissistic authority of such Englands. Everything about the poem depends upon how we locate Hill's mocking voice within it, even how we view the interpenetration of autobiography and history in the poem. In the authoritarian, conservative view of Hill, King Offa is the mythic figure who is reincarnated in the palsied body of modern England, resurrected in the body of the poet as a child at play in the quarry, where he flays his friend Ceolred for his ineptitude (111). In a less serious view of Hill, the children are merely playing at being Offa and Ceolred, and such myths are easily derided as childish games. Offa is either a deeply ingrained, mystical embodiment of a racial Englishness which is ever-present through history, or is a childish fiction of power, the stuff of idle fantasy which is hard to take seriously when set against the modern industrial landscape. Offa is either the symbolic architect of the origins of the English state and nation, or is merely a comic caricature. *Mercian Hymns* is ambivalent in how it locates itself in relation to Mercia and King Offa, and thus the politics of its location are more difficult to read than Paulin's view allows.

There is, however, a further twist to the legacy of Offa than either Hill or Paulin could countenance in their writings. In recent years, this scarcely understood Mercian king has become central to an ongoing debate about the nature of Englishness, as a number of Islamic commentators have argued that Offa converted to Islam during his reign over England.[3] The evidence for this conversion comes from the Arabic inscriptions on Offa's coins, which have been interpreted as quotations from the Qur'ân. 'There is no god but Allah; He has no associate', it reads in the centre of one side, while the reverse quotes from the Qur'ân IX, 33: 'He it is who hath sent His messenger with the guidance and the Religion of Truth, that He may cause it to prevail over all religion, however much the idolaters may be averse'. I am ill-equipped to make any contribution as to the veracity of these claims and their refutations, but amidst contemporary Powellite debates about the degree to which the Islam faith is congruent with Englishness, the possibility that Offa might prove to be the ancestor of a diversely oriented, multi-cultural, multi-faith England is a salutary reminder of the polymorphous legacies of history.

Urban cartographies

The relationship between culture and landscape, as Marshall Berman has argued, achieves particular intensity, and enters a new, dynamic and powerful phase, in the quintessentially modern space of the city (Berman 1983). The city is at once the ultimate statement of modernity, and the architectural machine through which the economic and social structures of modernity are brought into existence. It is a paradoxical space, which, as Berman shows, has generated the prevailing pastoral and anti-pastoral discourses of the modern era. The city is the triumph of culture over nature, the supreme expression of human mastery over the dark, elemental forces of nature, and yet it is also an embodiment of the dark, elemental forces of our own urban nightmares. Its architecture boasts the civic ambition and political power of the city, but it is also the screen upon which modern culture projects its dystopian visions of violence, chaos and social disintegration. The city is the vortex of modern culture, the magnetic centre, against which the rural is merely defined as tributary, servile farmland, or as recreational space for the urban worker.

If the city is conceived as the monumental boast of modernity, it is also understood fundamentally as a construct. It is 'made' not born, and as such, is subject to constant vision and revision, construction and reconstruction, siting and re-siting. It is a malleable space, which exists principally in the mind, as an imagined, planned or mapped space. It is a text, comprising the imposition of geometry upon the vagaries of landscape, and the conglomeration of names and signs with a navigable network of routes and passages. It is made possible as an experience, as a conception, only by the influence of the cartographical and imaginative aids which are capable of bringing its existence as text into coherence. Literary texts help to give imaginative coherence to the city, to bring the city into consciousness as a navigable, readable space. The city played its part too, of course, in giving new, dynamic shape to literature, to make possible the new literary forms of the novel, and, in terms of style, the narrative modes of social realism, modernism and postmodernism. 'Technically, the city is an ideal mechanism, especially for the novelist', writes Burton Pike: 'it enables him to bring together in a plausible network extremely diverse characters, situations, and actions' (Pike 1981, 8). The novelist simultaneously presumes and creates the density of social relations we find in the city space, and enables us to read the city. We read the network which makes up the city through the interaction of its characters, through their encounters and movements, and thus we come to know what Pike calls the 'word-city', the complex interplay between textuality and lived environment which shapes the urban experience.

The novel is peculiarly suited to accommodating the varying degrees of magnification and miniaturisation required to encounter the modern city from its chance, minute encounters, to its colossal, seemingly incomprehensible totality. It is technically suited to presenting the experiences of historical change, cultural diversity, spatial distance, social structure, and random incident. This is the claim, for example, of Norman Collins's novel of urban experience, *London Belongs to Me* (1945). In his preface, Collins draws attention to the sheer vast mundanity of London: 'If you start walking westwards in the early morning from somewhere down in Wapping or the Isle of Dogs by evening you will still be on the march, still in the midst of shabby little houses – only somewhere over by Hammersmith by then' (Collins 1945, 8). Collins's novel magnifies the lives and occurrences of one of those shabby little houses to explore the city's paradoxical coagulation of design and coincidence, mundane routine and dramatic spectacle. This is Collins's view of London, as a social space which generates unpredictable, dramatic energies and events, but which is characterised by its uneventfulness:

> [It's] had a remarkably quiet history, London. Nothing very spectacular. Nothing exceptionally heroic. Not until 1940, that is. Except for the Great Fire and the Black Death and the execution of a King, not very much has ever happened there. It has just gone on prosperously and independently through the centuries – wattle one century, timber the next, then brick, then stone, then brick again, then concrete. Building new foundations on old ruins. And sprawling out

> across the fields when there haven't been enough ruins to go around. (Collins 1945, 7)

Collins's novel, like Michael Moorcock's *Mother London* (1988), Barbara Vine's *King Solomon's Carpet* (1991), or Victor Headley's *Yardie* (1992), explores the labyrinthine, sprawling, unheroic topography of London through the small events and contingent happenings of its many minor characters. The city is never background in such novels, but is the largest character of all, its shifting, ineffable presence shaping (and shaped by) every encounter. The contradictory presence of the city in contemporary English fiction is the subject of this final section of the chapter.

Sam Selvon interrogates this cultural geographical space of the city in *The Lonely Londoners* (1956). In this post-imperial novel, which depicts the 'reverse colonisation' of West Indian migrants arriving in England, 'London' remains a symbol of power, and functions as the defining centre of the world. The novel acknowledges the symbolic capital of London, the very place names of which – Piccadilly Circus, Charing Cross, Waterloo – serve as metonyms for the city's cultural power. *The Lonely Londoners* functions as a vehicle of this power in its representations of London:

> Jesus Christ, when he say 'Charing Cross', when he realise that is he, Sir Galahad, who going there, near that place that everybody in the world know about (it even have the name in the dictionary) he feel like a new man. It didn't matter about the woman he going to meet, just to say he was going there made him feel big and important, and even if he was just going to coast a lime, to stand up and watch the white people, still, it would have been something. (Selvon 1985, 84)

Sir Galahad, the nickname of Henry Oliver, intrepid explorer of London's cultural nuclei as well as its dark tenements and alleys, experiences London as an awe-struck outsider, filled with the sense of romance and importance of a 'big city'. The importance of place names lies in the way in which they delineate the political and cultural power of the city. In the course of the novel, renowned places in London such as 'Charing Cross', 'Piccadilly Circus', 'Trafalgar Square', 'Waterloo', 'Marble Arch' and 'Oxford Street' are cited no less than one hundred and seven times.

The wonder that is evident in Galahad's sentiments, and in the novel's obvious preoccupation with the eminence of London's place names, is characteristic of a form of reverence associated with the outsider, one who is always in the position of joyous trepidation at the cultural power of the metropolis. A distance is placed between the city and the outsider by this awe, a distance which separates Galahad and the immigrants from 'the white people', those who are oblivious to the power of London because they share in its power over others. *The Lonely Londoners* depicts this process whereby the social space of the city overwhelms the migrants, to such an extent that they lose their individuality, their identities, before the awesome, incomprehensible vastness of the city. London threatens to devour Selvon's immigrants, to subsume them, and this is depicted at a number of points in the novel as the exhilarating fear of losing one's identity in the city-labyrinth. For Donatella Mazzoleni, this paradoxical experience is the definitive symbolic rite of metropolitan living:

> To immerse oneself. To be swallowed up. The space around us becomes gigantic, the body shrinks. To lose one's identity in the 'ant-heap' of the crowd. These are metropolitan experiences, in which are intertwined and reactivated memories, inextricably knotted into symbiosis at deep, pre-individual levels of life – those which precede birth. (Mazzoleni 1993, 298)

For Mazzoleni, the experience of the loss or submergence of identity in the urban space is akin to life within the womb, a form of living without identity where the 'I' and the social space are indistinguishable. Moses, the central character of the novel, articulates this pervasive sense of being overwhelmed by the city in the figure of the crowd:

> he could see the black faces bobbing up and down in the millions of white, strained faces, everybody hustling along the Strand, the spades jostling in the crowd, bewildered, hopeless. (Selvon 1985, 142)

That the spades are 'bobbing up and down' suggests an image of drowning, being swamped by the millions of people, the vastness of the city, and that they are 'hustling' and 'jostling' conveys a sense of struggling against this submergence. Selvon's novel articulates the ambivalence of the migrants' experiences of London, for much as the city threatens to overwhelm them, they make themselves at home within it, and insert their own narratives and cultural inscriptions into the 'sign systems' of the city. Galahad may be overawed by the city, and consequently marked as an outsider, but he also struggles to appropriate the city for himself, surrounding himself in the hustle of central London in order to make it his own.

For Moses this process has resulted in London becoming 'like nothing', of no real significance, but this is where Moses is less successful than Galahad in resisting the power of London. For Moses the city has become an extra layer of his body, which, although it allows him to protect the boys to a certain extent and to feel the burden of their consciousness as a group, also traps him within a space to which he is more or less oblivious. Galahad, alternatively, has learned in his innocence how to 'feel like a king living in London' (85). Not only does he feel himself to be 'big and important' in London, but he also feels like a 'new man'. Within this city, where Galahad is constantly in the process of both being submerged and emerging, there is the possibility that identity can be formed again, but also that London can be formed again. This is the crux of the relationship between social space and identity in the novel. The immigrants are able, with varying degrees of success, to move London from a position of relative intransigence to a position of relative flexibility. Moses recalls that in the beginning 'it ain't have so many places the boys could go to' (120). The identity of the immigrants delimits the social space that they are assigned by the metropolis, but this imposition of space slowly becomes weaker with the interaction of the characters. There is initially a clear correlation of power to social space in the novel. The influx of new waves of cultural 'others' into the city is checked with the proliferation of signs in the city which attempt to delimit, control, and repress the movement of the immigrants. A space is marked out, albeit dispersed across the city, where immigrants can go ('Keep the Water White'). The space of the city is reconfigured in racial terms – the very arrival of the immigrants necessitates new maps, new cultural geographies of the city.

The Lonely Londoners depicts 'London', then, as a culturally and socially encrypted topography, but also as a plastic, malleable space:

> The changing of the seasons, the cold slicing winds, the falling leaves, sunlight on green grass, snow on the land, London particular. Oh what it is and where it is and why it is, no one knows, but to have said: 'I walked on Waterloo Bridge', 'I rendezvoused at Charing Cross', 'Piccadilly Circus is my playground', to say these things, to have lived

these things, to have lived in the great city of London, centre of the world. To one day lean against the wind walking up the Bayswater Road (destination unknown), to see the leaves swirl and dance and spin on the pavement (sight unseeing), to write a casual letter home beginning: 'Last night, in Trafalgar Square ...' (Selvon 1985, 137)

Selvon combines here the materiality of the city, evoked through its place names, and its immateriality, the impossibility of knowing material London because of the blurring effected by change. Here, change is represented again by atmospheric conditions – wind, leaves, sunlight, snow, turning the city into a space that 'no one knows'. The place names serve to locate the scene of the novel properly, identifying and marking a physical space, but the experience of this space serves to deterritorialise the city. It no longer operates as an imposed design on the individual, or as a device for containing and policing cultural 'others', but rather is now experienced and lived subjectively, even arbitrarily. The city is now lived 'unknown' by a subject 'unseeing', a mode of living the city that is an undoing. Moses and the boys 'undo' the city as a space of containment, by living in the city in its own terms, that which Henri Lefebvre describes as 'assembly, simultaneity, encounter' (Lefebvre 1996, 166).

Selvon's characters cut their own routes through the city, mapping out a Caribbean London which runs from Bayswater to Piccadilly, down to Waterloo. So, Waterloo station becomes a home from home for the boys, and even for Moses it 'is that sort of place you have a soft feeling' (26). It is the point at which they arrive in London, at which they meet the boundary of the city. As the character Tolroy discovers, when he fails to recognise his mother stepping off the train, this boundary has an estranging effect on the immigrants, as if localising the cultural shock of migration into this liminal space of arrival and departure. But if Waterloo marks the formidable strangeness of the city for Selvon's characters, it is also a gathering point for them, for it represents to those immigrants in London a ligature with the Caribbean. This is part of the process whereby Selvon's characters convert the alienating space of the metropolis into the accommodating places of belonging. So, Bayswater becomes 'the Water', and most poignantly, the character 'Big City' misnames the city – 'Pentonvilla, Musket Hill, Claphand Common', making 'London particular' for him. The boys then, attach their own meanings and sense of significance to the physical space of the city, making it clear that this is a representational space as much as a physical space. This internalisation and deterritorialisation of the city opens it up to the possibility of art, since London internalised belongs to figurative and not literal language. London in Selvon's novel is a textual, imagined space, a city of words, which is nonetheless (or perhaps all the more) rootedly material and affective terrain.

Literary texts lend themselves especially well to the work of cultural geography, for, as Sara Blair has argued, 'they testify with particular acuity to the relations between space and place and the conditions under which both are made' (Blair 1998, 557). They explore the meanings of space, the investment of notions of home and belonging, alienation and empowerment, metropolitan and marginal in the rudiments of lived space. This is to say that in fictive texts, space is always advertising its own textualisation, just as texts are spatial manifestations of the word. Space is a determinant of action and behaviour in fictive texts – it is part of the representational economy of the text. In the sense that all literary texts are embedded in space and produce narratives and subjects within figurative social and geographical spaces, an account of the cultural geographical work of the text is thus fundamental to the task of situating the text critically. The function of spatial practices in literary texts is part of this work, but it is also the case that literary texts are adept, in Blair's terms, at 'charting the "strange effects" of space – its simultaneity, its encryptions, its dynamism and repressions' (Blair 1998, 556).

The topographical space of London, as it is charted in Iain Sinclair's *Lud Heat* (1975), is densely marked with such strange effects. Sinclair sets out to explore what he calls the 'dead hamlets' of London, tracing the geometrical patterns and symbolic spaces of the city. He acknowledges the incomprehensible vastness of the city's cultural, historical and symbolic meanings: 'the scenographic view is too complex to unravel here, the information too dense; we can only touch on a fraction of the possible relations' (Sinclair 1995, 16). Sinclair's text, part prose, part poetry, is a hybrid fusion of urban geography, occult divination, architectural history, fictional autobiography, quest narrative, textual explication, and dream exploration, which charts the mysterious concentrations of symbolic and mystical power in the cultural geography of historical London. In particular, Sinclair explores the imaginative geography delineated by the interconnections between Nicholas Hawksmoor's eighteenth-century churches and other symbolic sites of cultural power:

These churches guard or mark, rest upon, two major sources of occult power: The British Museum and Greenwich Observatory. The locked cellar of words, the labyrinth of all recorded knowledge, the repository of stolen fires and symbols, excavated god-forms – and measurement, star-knowledge, time calculations, Maze Hill, the bank of light that faces the Isle of Dogs. (Sinclair 1995, 15)

For Sinclair, the topography of contemporary London is no accident, no jumbled concatenation of arbitrary and incongruent buildings and roads. To some, the city might seem an indecipherable palimpsest of centuries of building and rebuilding, but Sinclair slowly unfolds the mysterious coincidences by which patterns of meaning and symbolic significance emerge. The eight Hawksmoor churches lie between the British Museum and the Greenwich Observatory, between book and geometry set, word and number, memory and observation, history and geography. In both sites, space and time are condensed, or achieve particular intensity, for the Museum collects the 'stolen fires and symbols' of the empire, and makes the past available to the present, while the Observatory marks the zero degree of longitude, the beginning of east-west spatial measurement, and the 'mean time' from which time measurement is derived. This is to chart London's imperial as well as occult history.

The churches, moreover, form patterns between them when drawn on a map. 'We can produce the symbol of Set, instrument of castration or tool for making cuneiform signs. To maim or to mark' (16). Sinclair is pulled towards these inscriptions which the geometric patterns between such symbolic sites seem to mark out on maps of London. They suggest no accidental design, but some mystical, predetermined form to which, unwittingly, the planners and builders and dreamers are constantly drawn. Sinclair too feels the call of such mysterious voices, and wonders at their meaning. The narrative unfolds a process not of revelation, but of divination, of being led by the dowsing rod of temporal and spatial coincidence. The siting and design of the churches unlocks a series of resonances with the pyramidal chambers of Egypt, the Roman burial grounds in east London, the Arthurian connections with Glastonbury, the occult visions of Blake, Stevenson and Yeats, the thick veins of immigration running into these east London dens. Sinclair acknowledges the heterogenous grids and maps even of this historical, palimpsestic space of the city:

> The churches are only one system of energies, or unit of connection, within the city; the old hospitals, the Inns of Court, the markets, the prisons, the religious houses are the others. They have their disciples, aware of the older relations. (Sinclair 1995, 17–20)

These systems have their own magnetic power, their own 'disciples', which do not detract from the lodestar bearing of Sinclair's quest.

Sinclair traces in his narrative the invisible lines of power running through London's streets and buildings, which account for the sporadic eruptions of mysterious, inexplicable incidents – of murder, sacrifice, madness. Sinclair explains these incidents as the recurrent appearance of that 'imprecise itch of ritual observance' (24), something coursing in the veins of the city which finds expression in bizarre, seemingly incomprehensible acts. It is clear, however, that the occult spatialisation of the city is not just accountable for the fires which gutted St Anne's in 1850, St George's in 1941, or the rituals which attend the burial of a murderer. Sinclair ponders too how the displaced, homeless poor of the modern city are drawn to the same iconographic sites of dispossession, of marginalisation, as their medieval forebears. Their habitation of the gravestones and benches of east London parks is described as 'the opening shot of a lepers' pilgrimage':

> There is a further possible reading to the vagrant invasion of these vestry-protected lands – that they have come to consult the oracle that can no longer be discovered, made their cross-country journeys by well-worn migration tracks, to extinguish ego in the bladed flame; that they have been prematurely released, by catastrophe and shock, from the incubation cubicles beneath the church – half resolved dream victims, half-cured – they babble of the vision which they carry as identity. (Sinclair 1995, 21)

Unwittingly, the modern city exiles its poor, its unwanted, out to the same symbolic sites of exclusion, where they 'babble' the visionary, 'mad' discourse of the occult. This is the invisible city, the city which repeats its own ritual tides of incursion and excursion, which is haunted by the returning ghosts of its cyclical, dark history. 'There are always two cities at work', writes Richard Lehan: 'one visible, the other invisible; one of the surface, the other underground or hidden; one a realm of mastery and control, the other of mystery and turmoil' (Lehan 1998, 273).

For Sinclair, of course, this is true, but the two are inseparable, interconnected in unfathomably infinite ways. Sinclair pursues the geometric shapes emerging from his continually unfolding imaginative geography of London to the central, connecting point of the 'set', the 'epicentre of energies' (137). He finds that the shrine of this city-wide spiritual geometry is none other than the 'Northern Sewage Outflow', the meeting point of the sacred and the profane, which is also a ford over the river Lea, the exact spot of demarcation between English and Danish territory in the ninth century, and the conjoining of Roman Road and the Old Ford Road. The building which occupies this site, a wartime machine-gun bunker, turns out too to have its symbolic resonances:

> He circumnavigates the building, anti-clockwise, pushing through the wire growth. It is a six-sided enclosure, relating to so many other high-energy structures: the original Spittle fields ... his dream, the old map of the city, hexagonal field on the hill rim ... the fence that traps the Cerne Abbas Hercules giant ... the sheep-pen that Turner locates in his sketch of Llanthony Abbey ... the stock exchange booths in the bear pit. Feels for it, understands that it has meaning: does not know what that meaning is. (Sinclair 1995, 141)

For Sinclair there is something profoundly mysterious about the repetition of geometric patterns throughout the history of the city, which seem to defy, for example, the boast of a capitalist modernity symbolised by the stock exchange, by depicting its forms as merely the imitation of some more primeval, ritual structure. In the library afterwards he discovers that this site is yet another excavated burial site, yet another ligature between the living and the dead. For Sinclair, as for the Romans, the east London he charts is still 'a necropolis for the dead' (27), a haunted place which goes on shaping and pulling the city into its own time-bound, 'ground-held' forces of meaning and ritual. The city in *Lud Heat* is a construct, an elaborate textual fabrication, the product of so much inscription and imaginative projection, but it is not to be dismissed so lightly as *mere* textuality, for it weighs heavily in the primordial mud upon which it is built. The London of *Lud Heat* is a deep-rooted social conglomeration, yet it is also a profoundly mysterious, ghostly space, which gives powerful expression to the resilient anti-modernity of the city by compressing time into an affective, poetic space of imagined community with the dead.

According to Gaston Bachelard, space becomes meaningful through its inscription within a mnemonic or poetic economy.[4] Sinclair traces the structures of memory invested in the social and cultural space of London, and not just the visible markers of memory, but the hidden, haunting traces of repressed or elusive Londons. The relationship between social space and memory in *Lud Heat* suggests a powerful psychic geography of the city, one which reveals itself into long-forgotten patterns only to the kind of divining ante-*flâneur* that Sinclair depicts. Rushdie's London in *The Satanic Verses* (1988) is an altogether more amnesiac and polymorphous space. London in Rushdie's novel is the city of migrants, the capital of 'Vilayet' ('foreign country'), upon which Gibreel and Saladin fall as supernatural beings when their plane is blown up in mid-air by hijackers. Gibreel believes he has been sent to save what he calls 'Proper London, capital of Vilayet, laid out for his benefit in exhaustive detail, the whole bang shoot. He would redeem this city: Geographer's London, all the way from A to Z' (Rushdie 1998, 322). This is an exhaustively represented city, an over-determined and over-inscribed cultural geography, which is yet improperly known. Saladin likewise falls to earth dreaming of 'Proper London':

> Bigben Nelsonscolumn Lordstavern Bloodytower Queen. But as he floated out over the great metropolis he felt himself beginning to lose height, and no matter how hard he struggled kicked swam-in-air he continued to spiral slowly downwards to earth, then faster, then faster still, until he was screaming headfirst down towards the city, Saintpauls, Puddinglane, Threadneedlestreet, zeroing in on London like a bomb. (Rushdie 1998, 39)

Saladin has his own imaginative geography of London, a city of Lords and Queens, towers and columns, domes and needles. It is a city not so much of memory as imagination, since the elision of spaces between words – Bigben Nelsonscolumn – suggests an easy, but imaginary familiarity with the 'place', London. This is to say that once again we are dealing with a fictive London, London as a floating signifier, as a dream of a 'great metropolis', which exists, in a sense, as a *metronym*. If the fall is also birth – Saladin is rushing earthwards in the foetal position – Saladin is born into the metropolis, the mother-city. Migration is thus equated with re-birth, and not just for Saladin, but for London too, since Saladin will zero London 'like a bomb', and will, as Gibreel also sets out to do, 'make this land anew' (353).

In his journeys through London, Saladin discovers that it is not the solid, nameable, knowable place of his dreams, not the 'Geographer's London', but is instead 'that most protean and chameleon of cities ... that hellish maze ... that labyrinth without a solution' (201). The city is a shape-shifter, a satanic figure of constant restless movement and metamorphoses, which slithers into a new form every day. Even in its names, it is variously identified as 'Proper London', 'capital of Vilayet', Ellowen Deeowen, Alleluia. This is the living city, the city that is beyond the comprehension or design of a single source of power, the city as an unmanageable monster: 'the city in its corruption refused to submit to the dominion of the cartographers, changing shape at will and without warning' (327). Cartography invents borders and barriers, produces guards and immigration officials, turns space into territory, and territory into a system of inclusion and exclusion, home and foreign. Rushdie pits against this science the figure of the migrant as Satan, borrowing from Daniel Defoe for his epigraph: 'Satan, being thus confined to a vagabond, wandering, unsettled condition, is without any certain abode'. The migrant is 'without any certain abode', but so too, London is shown to be part of that 'wandering, unsettled condition', itself a place of ceaseless motion and transformation. It is a city, as the fifth chapter of the book suggests, 'visible but unseen'.

It is this invisibility, this elusiveness of the city, which makes it available for imaginative transformation, however. Saladin and Gibreel fall into London with a quest to reinvent it, to make it into a new, pliable and energetic city, to give it clarity, to 'heat' it up. The metereological metaphors emerge again. London, just as in Selvon's novel, is fog-bound, wet, slippery, invisible and constantly metamorphosing at the whim of the weather. This, for Saladin and Gibreel, is finally 'the trouble with the English':

> the trouble with the English was their ... *In a word*, Gibreel solemnly pronounced, *their weather.*
> Gibreel Farishta floating on his cloud formed the opinion that the moral fuzziness of the English was metereologically induced ... .
> 'City', he cried, and his voice rolled over the metropolis like thunder, 'I am going to tropicalize you'. (Rushdie 1998, 354)

The city, for Rushdie, is never a hard landscape of fact, never the epicentral power base of an empire, but the constantly shape-shifting, liquid city of the imagination. *The Satanic Verses*, like much contemporary fiction of the city, presents a malleable, ineffable and infinitely imaginable city, available to be troped and tropicalised over and over again. London is a centre only in its capacity for drawing into itself the stories and images of its diverse, migrant population, and in giving expression to the effects of diaspora, dislocation, cultural hybridity and diffusion. The new cultural geographies of England, at least in their literary forms, never cease to imagine how the relationship between culture and space, or culture and landscape, can be reconceived, and thus they never cease to play their part in constructing the landscapes of the imagined communities of the future.

Notes

1. See David Matless, *Landscape and Englishness* (London: Reaktion, 1998), 204–8.
2. See Peter Hennessey, *Never Again: Britain, 1945–1951* (London: Jonathan Cape, 1992); Kenneth Morgan, *Labour in Power, 1945–1951* (Oxford: Oxford University Press, 1984); Brian Brivati and Harriet Jones (eds), *What Difference Did the War Make?* (London: Leicester University Press, 1995); Paul Addison, *Now the War is Over: A Social History of Britain, 1945–51* (London: Jonathan Cape, 1985); Jim Fyrth (ed.), *Labour's Promised Land? Culture and Society in Labour Britain, 1945–51* (London: Lawrence & Wishart, 1995); Kevin Jefferys, *Retreat from New Jerusalem: British Politics, 1951–64* (London and Basingstoke: Macmillan, 1997); Vernon Bogdanor and Robert Skidelsky (eds), *The Age of Affluence, 1951–64* (Oxford: Oxford University Press, 1970).
3. See in particular the following websites, the first two of which support the argument that Offa converted to Islam, the last of which refutes this:
    http://users.erols.com/zenithco/offa.html
    http://www.islamic-awareness.org/History/Islam/offa.html
    http://www.answering-islam.org/Hoaxes/offa.html
4. See Gaston Bachelard, *The Poetics of Space* (Boston, Mass.: Beacon, 1969).

Conclusion

And above all, it is *your* civilization, it is *you*. However much you hate it or laugh at it, you will never be happy away from it for any length of time. The suet puddings and the red pillar-boxes have entered into your soul. Good or evil, it is yours, you belong to it, and this side of the grave you will never get away from the marks that it has given you. George Orwell, 'England Your England' (64–5)

> These days whenever I stay away too long,
> anything I happen to clap eyes on,
> (that red telephone box) somehow makes me
> miss here more than anything I can name.
>
> My heart performs a jazzy drum solo
> when the crow's feet on the 747
> scrape down at Heathrow. H.M. Customs …
> I resign to the usual inquisition,
> […]
> my passport photo's too open faced,
> haircut wrong (an afro) for the decade;
> the stamp, British Citizen not bold enough
> for my liking and too much for theirs.
> Fred D'Aguiar, 'Home', *British Subjects* (14)

'more than anything I can name'

In the year 2000, amidst all the anxiety and excitement of the millennium celebrations, an anthology of writing was published which exemplifies the complexity of the relationship between literature and nation, or literature and community in contemporary England. *IC3*, edited by Courttia Newland and Kadija Sesay, collects new poetry, fiction and essays by a wide spectrum of black writers in Britain, including David Dabydeen, Jackie Kay, Buchi Emecheta, E.A.

Markham, Benjamin Zephaniah, Merle Collins and Linton Kwesi Johnson (Newland and Sesay 2000). It is an invaluable, if troubled, anthology, which bears witness to the vitality and diversity of black writing in Britain, while at the same time, registers the difficulties of 'belonging' in a country in which the politics of nationhood frequently crystallise around a silent elision of race and nation.

This is particularly the case where the term 'English' is concerned, for, as Enoch Powell insisted in 1968, one can become a British citizen by being born there, but 'The West Indian or Asian does not, by being born in England become an Englishman' (Smithies and Fiddick 1969, 77). Britishness has long been a free-floating signifier of a mass of imperial, national and regional confusions and complications of identity, but Englishness is somehow a sense of belonging much more rooted, specific, and exclusive. Powell, of course, should not be mistaken for the authority on this matter, but it is the Powellite conception of the relationship between race and nation which has dictated the Thatcherist, and hence, to a certain extent, the Blairite, approach to issues of immigration, citizenship, and nationality. To understand the meanings of England and Englishness since 1945 is, at least in part, to chart the shift of focus in postwar English political rhetoric from glorifying the 'extended family' of empire to blaming 'the coloured invasion' for England's national decline.[1] If empire sought to ground Englishness as the symbolic cultural centre of modern civilisation, the meanings of 'Englishness' after the war have more frequently been made visible by the rearguard actions to fend off the 'invasions' of its shores by 'immigrants' or 'asylum seekers'. The ambivalent status of black people in England, as expressed in D'Aguiar's poem, 'Home', in which blackness is constantly tested and challenged at the threshold, liminal spaces of the nation, means that race becomes the unspoken, defining marker of national identity and culture.

The epigraphs I have chosen for this conclusion suggest a narrative, or more likely a series of narratives, about ideas of Englishness and national belonging. Between Orwell and D'Aguiar lie much history, much social change, and many different conceptions of England, and of England as 'home'. Orwell, in 1941, gave expression to an England of the 'common people', a left-wing appropriation of the nation as the core expression of solidarity and popular sentiment, but in what sense does the England of 'suet puddings and red pillar-boxes' differ from the England of 'that red telephone box' of D'Aguiar's poem? Is

Orwell's 'home' also the home of D'Aguiar? Is Orwell's concept of Englishness an expansive, dialogic one, capable of finding meaning among the multiple allegiances and cross-cultural identifications of a diverse immigrant population? Or, is Orwell's conception of Englishness the checklist of cultural allegiances that D'Aguiar has to satisfy before he is permitted re-entry to his 'home'? Do Orwell's 'common people' become the 'ordinary English people' of Powell's speeches who are frequently cited as afraid that 'in this country in fifteen or twenty years time the black man will have the whip-hand over the white man'? (Smithies and Fiddick 1969, 36) Is it possible that Lord Tebbit's 'cricket test',[2] or the more recent white paper proposing citizenship tests on English language and culture for arriving immigrants,[3] or the routine interrogation of black men and women at the gates of Heathrow or Dover, can be traced back to the quiet, insular Englands of Orwell, Priestley or Betjeman?

This is unfair to Orwell, who would most likely have responded to the changing social and cultural conditions of postwar England in markedly differently ways to Powell or Thatcher, but it is to begin to question the underlying political and cultural assumptions of modern discourses of Englishness. Orwell was not unaware of the degree to which definitions of Englishness function to produce exclusion and alienation as much as feelings of inclusion and belonging – the war-time context of his essay should at least alert us to the polarising tendencies of war on conceptions of nationality. We might situate Orwell, in this sense, within the contexts of left-wing appropriations of popular nationalist sentiments, which Paul Gilroy analyses in *There Ain't No Black in the Union Jack*. Gilroy argues that 'socialists from Orwell to [E.P.] Thompson have tried to find the answer to their marginalisation in the creation of a popular patriotism', but insofar as expressions of English national belonging rely upon blurring the distinction between race and nation, Gilroy finds socialists such as Orwell, Thompson and Raymond Williams appearing to endorse the assumptions of 'the new racism' (Gilroy 1987, 69).

Reading D'Aguiar's 'Home' in relation to Orwell's essay invites us to ask these questions about the politics of Englishness. D'Aguiar states his sense of belonging emphatically, as a feeling of longing for the 'here' of being in England 'more than anything I can name'. This echoes Orwell's insistence that 'you will never be happy away from [England] for any length of time'. Orwell's sense of Englishness was constructed in opposition to the nationalism evident in Germany and

Italy; his England polices its shores and skies on the watch for enemy invasions. D'Aguiar's poem, of course, recognises that he, the black Englishman is England's other. It is he who represents to the customs officials the threatened erosion of national identity and culture, and against whom the patrols, checkpoints and interrogations are put in place. It is him for whom that mark of 'British Citizen' is repeatedly a site of contest, suspicion and contradiction. The poem repeats the scene which recurs with telling frequency in black British writing, the scene of interrogation on arrival or re-entry. It happens to Selvon's Moses at the end of *Moses Migrating* (1983), to Victor Headley's 'D.' in *Yardie* (1992), to Rushdie's Saladin Chamcha in *The Satanic Verses* (1988). This scene marks the ambivalent construction of Englishness as a set of internal borders and frontiers, by which race is the unspoken currency of national identity. If the nation's sense of itself crystallises around hidden assumptions about race, then, as Gilroy argues, this has inevitable consequences for how the nation encounters racial difference through such institutions as the law, the police, the media, and education (Gilroy 1987, 72–113).

This has been the most vocal issue throughout the 1990s in terms of race, which focused on the controversies arising from the murder of Stephen Lawrence in Eltham, London in 1993, and the subsequent attempts to identify and convict his murderers, and to scrutinise the indifference and incompetence of police investigations of the murder. The Macpherson inquiry into the police response to Stephen Lawrence's murder found in 1999 that the police force in London was institutionally racist. The implications of this report are wide-ranging, and echo Gilroy's analysis more than a decade earlier. Can we separate Englishness from these institutions, or are those institutions expressions of the elision of nation and race, of Englishness and whiteness, which Gilroy finds commonplace? If we wish to reflect and celebrate the cultural diversity and hybridity of contemporary culture in England, should we abandon the term 'English' altogether in order to find the 'here' which is 'more than anything I can name'? Or can we find an elasticity in our notions of belonging and community which allows us to recognise the complexity and multiplicity of cultural allegiances and identifications?

I put these thoughts in the form of questions because that seems to be their only legitimate form in a society in which racially-motivated murders and maimings are still common, in which race riots are recent experiences (2001), in which governments still pander to some half-baked conception that an understated racism informing public policies on immigration, policing and welfare will win votes, and in which political asylum-seekers are detained, debased, marked out for public humiliation with special vouchers, and treated with contempt and suspicion. Benjamin Zephaniah's contribution to the *IC3* anthology, 'The One Minutes of Silence', is not content with the silences with which we mark the deaths of more victims of racism, and so the poem begins to ask questions instead:

> When I am standing still in the still silence
> I always wonder if there is something
> About the deaths of
> Marcia Laws
> Oscar Okoye
> Or
> Joy Gardner
> That can wake this sleepy nation.
> Are they too hot for cool Britannia? (Zephaniah/Newland and Sesay
> 2000, 141)

This poem too is an English elegy. Zephaniah's poem ponders if 'cool Britannia' is simply the same indifferent, casually racist nation as old England. There are many marks of hope in the rich volume of stories, poems, and commentaries which make up *IC3*, however. Questions are better than silence, and violence. Writing is a form of belonging, a way of constituting identity, and taking possession of cultural authority and responsibility. In this sense, *IC3* begins the task, as so many other writers in postwar and contemporary England have done, of making a difference, of imagining the language and culture of a new belonging. The contributors to *IC3* do so, of course, under the title that bears the scars of a difficult and ambivalent history. Courttia Newland explains in his preface that the title 'IC3' is the police identity code for black (and 'refers to Africans, Asians, West Indians, Americans and sometimes even Chinese'), and 'is the only collective term that relates to our situation here as residents'. There is, in other words, no positive identifier of the forms of belonging and affiliation appropriate to black people living in England. The title of the collection thus alludes to the long history of displaced names, of having to make do with or provisionally adopt the slave-name, the slang names of one's oppressors and taunters, the label of one's otherness, as a strategic starting point, from which to envisage the new homes of our inclusion, of our heterogeneity. 'How about us creating a name for ourselves, describing ourselves?' asks Newland.

This, I want to conclude, is the question around which this study has taken shape. The first three chapters of this book explored historical and elegiac representations of England and Englishness in postwar writing. I have tried to examine the cultural politics of late twentieth-century writings on history, nostalgia, a vanishing or threatened England, and cultural change. The prevailing tendency of the writings explored in those three chapters, perhaps, is to testify to the passing of a certain notion of England, and the emergence of something new, as yet unnameable and unmappable. The last three chapters of the book have made some journeys into the literature which attempts to give expression to 'new' narratives or forms of representation, to the ways in which we might register and chart the terrain of a new belonging. These chapters offer an inevitably partial and incomplete view of a rich, diverse and complex literature. Literature offers no model for rescuing England from its current crises and anxieties. But it does, from time to time, enable us to articulate the forms of our oppression, the limits of our understanding, and the imaginative potential for change. It does this by making itself available to us as a technology for representation, as a mode of cultural authority. In one sense, this should alert us to the potential of literary texts to reflect what we might think of as authorised narratives or representations, coming as they do from within prevailing social, cultural and political conditions. On the other hand, the hope of this book, and one of its enabling assumptions, is that literature is also available as a voice for the silenced, and as an imaginative space for dissidence, critique, and reinvention.

Notes

1. A shift which Wendy Webster sees represented in the attitudes and opinions of Enoch Powell. See *Imagining Home: Gender, 'Race' and National Identity, 1945–64* (London: University College London Press, 1998), 183–5.
2. In the late 1980s, Norman Tebbit proposed a test of British citizenship for West Indian immigrants and those of West Indian descent, known as the 'cricket test', which depended upon which team West Indians in

Britain would support when the West Indies played against England in cricket matches.

3. The Home Secretary, David Blunkett, produced a white paper, 'Secure Borders, Safe Haven', on February 8 2002 proposing such measures as a compulsory oath of allegiance and a citizenship test for arriving immigrants. The paper was drafted as a response to the argument that Britain had procedures for dealing with immigrants but no coherent immigration policy.

Chronology

Births and deaths	Principal publications	Cultural and scientific events	Historical and political events
1945			
	Green, *Loving*; Waugh, *Brideshead Revisited*; Mitford, *The Pursuit of Love*; Larkin, *The North Ship*; Betjeman, *New Bats in Old Belfries*; Taylor, *At Mrs Lippincote's*; Orwell, *Animal Farm*; Collins, *London Belongs to Me*	Brittain, *Peter Grimes*	First atomic bombs dropped on Nagasaki and Hiroshima; end of Second World War; Labour form new govt under Clement Attlee
1946 H.G. Wells d. (b.1866) Howard Barker b. Julian Barnes b. Jim Crace b.	Linklater, *Private Angelo*; Taylor, *Palladian*; Larkin, *Jill*; D. Thomas, *Deaths and Entrances*	Russell, *History of Western Philosophy*; Arts Council founded	National Health Act; Bank of England nationalised
1947 Salman Rushdie b.	Hamilton, *The Slaves of Solitude*; I. Compton Burnett, *Manservant and Maidservant*	First supersonic flight	India becomes independent; Marshall Aid for European recovery; coal industry nationalised
1948 David Edgar b. Ian McEwan b.	Greene, *The Heart of the Matter*; Fry,	F.R. Leavis, *The Great Tradition*;	End of British rule in Palestine; British

Births and deaths	Principal publications	Cultural and scientific events	Historical and political events
	The Lady's Not for Burning; Waugh, The Loved One; Rattigan, The Browning Version	T.S. Eliot, Notes Towards a Definition of Culture	Nationality Bill; railways nationalised; NHS founded
1949 Peter Ackroyd b. Martin Amis b. Michele Roberts b. Graham Swift b.	Bowen, The Heat of the Day; Mitford, Love in a Cold Climate; Orwell, Nineteen Eighty-Four; Eliot, The Cocktail Party		NATO formed; iron and steel industries nationalised
1950 George Orwell d. (b.1903) G.B. Shaw d. (b.1856) Grace Nichols b. Timothy Mo b.	Cooper, Scenes from Provincial Life; Greene, The Third Man; Pym, Some Tame Gazelle; White, The Lost Traveller; Waugh, Helena; Lessing, The Grass is Singing		War in Korea; Labour returned to govt, with small majority
1951	Manning, School for Love; Larkin, Poems	Atomic energy produces electricity; Festival of Britain	Burgess and Maclean defect to USSR; Conservatives form govt under Winston Churchill
1952 Linton Kwesi Johnson b. Andrew Motion b.	Christie, The Mousetrap; D. Thomas, Collected Poems; Lessing, Martha Quest; Wilson, Hemlock and After; Rattigan, The Deep Blue Sea	Britain produces its own atomic bomb; first contraceptive tablets made	King George VI dies

Births and deaths	Principal publications	Cultural and scientific events	Historical and political events
1953 Dylan Thomas d. (b.1914) Timothy Mo b.	Hartley, *The Go-Between*; Lehmann, *The Echoing Grove*; Wain, *Hurry on Down*; Ian Fleming, *Casino Royale*	Hillary and Tenzing climb Everest	Coronation of Queen Elizabeth II
1954 Kazuo Ishiguro b. Hanif Kureishi b.	D. Thomas, *Under Milk Wood*; K. Amis, *Lucky Jim*; Golding, *Lord of the Flies*; Lessing, *A Proper Marriage*; Lamming, *The Emigrants*		End of food rationing
1955	Beckett, *Waiting for Godot*; R.S. Thomas, *Song at the Year's Turning*; Bowen, *A World of Love*; Greene, *The Quiet American*; Rattigan, *Separate Tables*; Larkin, *The Less Deceived*		Treaty for European Union; equal pay for women in civil service; Churchill retires; Anthony Eden becomes PM; Conservatives returned as govt; state of emergency in Cyprus
1956	John Osborne, *Look Back in Anger*; Sam Selvon, *The Lonely Londoners*; Lewis, *The Chronicles of Narnia*; Wilson, *Anglo-Saxon Attitudes*; Behan, *The Quare Fellow*; Conquest (ed.), *New Lines*; Tolkien, *The Lord of the Rings*	Transatlantic telephone service started; Colin Wilson, *The Outsider* (phil.); Crosland, *The Future of Socialism* (pol.)	Suez crisis; USSR crush insurrection in Hungary

Births and deaths	Principal publications	Cultural and scientific events	Historical and political events
1957 Jean Binta Breeze b.	Ted Hughes, *Hawk in the Rain*; Braine, *Room at the Top*; MacInnes, *City of Spades*; Taylor, *Angel*; Waugh, *The Ordeal of Gilbert Penfold*; Naipaul, *The Mystic Masseur*; Osborne, *The Entertainer*; Murdoch, *The Sandcastle*; Larkin, *A Girl in Winter*	Hoggart, *The Uses of Literacy* (soc.); Wolfenden Report on sexuality; Maschler (ed.), *Declaration*;	Eden resigns as PM; Harold Macmillan becomes PM; Britain tests its first nuclear bomb; European Economic Community is formed; Ghana becomes independent
1958 Caryl Phillips b. Rose Macauley d. (b.1881)	Bates, *The Darling Buds of May*; Murdoch, *The Bell*; Delaney, *A Taste of Honey*; Jellicoe, *The Sport of My Mad Mother*; Sillitoe, *Saturday Night and Sunday Morning*; Behan, *The Hostage*; Pinter, *The Birthday Party*; Betjeman, *Collected Poems*; Macauley, *The World My Wilderness*; Scott, *The Alien Sky*	Galbraith, *The Affluent Society* (soc.); first stereo recordings; CND founded; Raymond Williams, *Culture and Society*	Race riots in Nottingham and Notting Hill; state of emergency in Aden
1959 Jeanette Winterson b. Ben Okri b.	Bradbury, *Eating People is Wrong*; Wesker, *Roots*; P.H. Johnson, *The Unspeakable Skipton*; Lee, *Cider*	First section of M1 motorway opened; C.P. Snow, *Two Cultures, New Departures* begins	Aldermaston demonstration against nuclear weapons; Conservatives returned as govt;

Births and deaths	Principal publications	Cultural and scientific events	Historical and political events
	with Rosie; MacInnes, *Absolute Beginners*; Peake, *Gormenghast Trilogy*; Sillitoe, *The Loneliness of the Long Distance Runner*; Waterhouse, *Billy Liar*; Arden, *Serjeant Musgrave's Dance*		state of emergency in Kenya
1960			
	Pinter, *The Caretaker*; L.R. Banks, *The L-Shaped Room*; Lessing, *In Pursuit of the English*; Barstow, *A Kind of Loving*; Durrell, *The Alexandria Quartet*; Harris, *The Palace of the Peacock*; Storey, *This Sporting Life*; Plath, *The Collossus*	*New Left Review* begins; heart pacemaker invented; *Coronation Street* begins; *The Lady Chatterley* trial	CND demonstrations in Trafalgar Square; demonstrations in Trafalgar Square against South Africa's apartheid regime
1961			
	Gunn, *My Sad Captains*; Waugh, *Sword of Honour Trilogy*; Spark, *The Prime of Miss Jean Brodie*; Osborne, *Luther*; Fisher, *City*	DNA structure detected; *Private Eye* begins	Commonwealth Immigrants Bill; South Africa leaves the Commonwealth
1962 Patrick Hamilton d. (b.1904)	Burgess, *A Clockwork Orange*; Lessing, *The Golden Notebook*; Alvarez (ed.), *The New Poetry*	Sampson, *The Anatomy of Britain*	Jamaica, Trinidad and Uganda become independent; end of national service

Births and deaths	Principal publications	Cultural and scientific events	Historical and political events
1963			
Sylvia Plath d. (b.1932) C.S. Lewis d. (b.1898) Aldous Huxley d. (b.1894)	Naipaul, *Mr Stone and the Knights Companion*; B.S. Johnson, *Travelling People*; Plath, *The Bell Jar*; Theatre Workshop, *Oh, What a Lovely War*; Dunn, *Up the Junction*	Brittain, *War Requiem*; Robbins Report on Higher Education	Kennedy assassinated in the US; Nuclear Test Ban Treaty signed; CND demonstrations in Trafalgar Square; Macmillan resigns as PM; Alec Douglas-Home becomes PM; Kenya becomes independent
1964			
Ian Fleming d. (b.1908) Brendan Behan d. (b.1923)	Larkin, *The Whitsun Weddings*; Wilson, *Late Call*; Selvon, *The Housing Lark*; Orton, *Entertaining Mr Sloane*	Marcuse, *One Dimensional Man* (pol.)	Labour forms govt under Harold Wilson
1965			
T.S. Eliot d. (b.1888) W. Somerset Maugham d. (b.1874)	Plath, *Ariel*; Manning, *The Balkan Trilogy*; Bond, *Saved*; Drabble, *The Millstone*	The Beatles awarded MBE	Race Relations Bill; abolition of the death penalty; CND demonstrations in Trafalgar Square against Vietnam war; Rhodesia declares independence
1966			
Evelyn Waugh d. (b.1903)	Orton, *Loot*; Fowles, *The Magus*; Rhys, *Wide Sargasso Sea*; Greene, *The Comedians*; Stoppard, *Rosencrantz and Guildenstern are Dead*; Bunting, *Briggflatts*	England wins World Cup; *Cathy Come Home* televised	Labour returned as govt; Guyana becomes independent; the Colonial Office is merged into the Commonwealth Office

Births and deaths	Principal publications	Cultural and scientific events	Historical and political events
1967			
Joe Orton d. (b.1933) John Masefield d. (b.1878) Siegfried Sassoon d. (b.1886)	Carter, *The Magic Toyshop*; Wilson, *No Laughing Matter*; Pinter, *The Homecoming*; Henri, Gough, Patten, *The Mersey Sound*; Naipaul, *The Mimic Men*; Dunn, *Poor Cow*; Jennings, *Collected Works*	First heart transplant; widespread use of the contraceptive pill	Abortion legalised; homosexuality decriminalised
1968			
Mervyn Peake d. (b.1911)	Hines, *A Kestrel for a Knave*; Bond, *Early Morning*	Theatre censorship ends; C. Day Lewis succeeds John Masefield as Poet Laureate	Commonwealth Immigration Bill; Race Relations Bill; Enoch Powell's Birmingham speech; May Uprising in Paris; anti-Vietnam war demonstrations in London; the Commonwealth Office merged into Foreign Office
1969			
Ivy Compton-Burnett d. (b.1884)	Fowles, *The French Lieutenant's Woman*; Greene, *Travels with my Aunt*; Lessing, *Children of Violence*; Rubens, *The Elected Member*; Horovitz (ed.), *Children of Albion*	US astronauts walk on the moon; human eggs fertilised *in vitro*; Booker prize started	Northern Ireland 'troubles' begin; largest miners' strike since 1944
1970			
E.M. Forster d. (b.1879)	Hughes, *Crow*; Snow, *Strangers and Brothers*	Computer 'floppy' disks invented; The Beatles disband;	Equal Pay Bill; Conservatives form govt under Edward

Births and deaths	Principal publications	Cultural and scientific events	Historical and political events
		formation of the Women's Liberation Movement	Heath; voting age reduced to 18
1971			
	Hill, *Mercian Hymns*; Naipaul, *In a Free State*; Taylor, *Mrs Palfrey at the Claremont*; Bond, *Lear*	Greenpeace founded; decimalisation of sterling currency	Immigration Bill
1972 C. Day Lewis d. (b.1904) L.P. Hartley d. (b.1895)	Stoppard, *Jumpers*; Drabble, *The Needle's Eye*; Carter, *The Infernal Desire Machines of Doctor Hoffman*; Berger, *G.*	John Betjeman succeeds C. Day Lewis as Poet Laureate	Miners' strike leads to state of emergency; Northern Ireland placed under Westminster rule
1973 Elizabeth Bowen d. (b.1899) Noel Coward d. (b.1899) J.R.R. Tolkien d. (b.1892) W.H. Auden d. (b.1907) Henry Green d. (b.1905) B.S. Johnson d. (b.1933) Nancy Mitford d. (b.1904)	Shaffer, *Equus*; Murdoch, *The Black Prince*; Greene, *The Honorary Consul*; M. Amis, *The Rachel Papers*		Britain enters the European Economic Community; oil and energy crisis; fishing disputes begin 'the cod war' with Iceland; NHS reorganised
1974 H.E. Bates d. (b.1905) Cyril Connolly d. (b.1903) Walter Greenwood d. (b.1903) Eric Linklater d.	Larkin, *High Windows*; Lessing, *The Memoirs of a Survivor*; Burgess, *The Enderby Novels*; Murdoch, *The*	First evidence of erosion of the ozone layer	First election results in no majority; a Labour govt forms under Harold Wilson; a second election

Births and deaths	Principal publications	Cultural and scientific events	Historical and political events
(b.1899)	*Sacred and Profane Love Machine*		confirms Labour govt
1975 P.G. Wodehouse d. (b.1881) Elizabeth Taylor d. (b.1912)	Griffiths, *Comedians*; Bradbury, *The History Man*; Jhabvala, *Heat and Dust*; Lodge, *Changing Places*; Powell, *A Dance to the Music of Time*; Scott, *The Raj Quartet*; Sinclair, *Lud Heat*; Rushdie, *Grimus*; Selvon, *Moses Ascending*; M. Amis, *Dead Babies*	Extraction of oil from the North Sea	Sex Discrimination Bill; inflation reaches 25%
1976 Agatha Christie d. (b.1890) Colin MacInnes d. (b.1914)	Edgar, *Destiny*; Storey, *Saville*; Lehmann, *A Sea-Grape Tree*; Tennant, *Hotel de Dream*	Concorde begins passenger service; National Theatre completed	Race Relations Act; Wilson retires as PM; James Callaghan becomes PM; riots in Notting Hill
1977 Terence Rattigan d. (b.1911)	Scott, *Staying On*; Stoppard, *Professional Foul*; Carter, *The Passion of New Eve*	First AIDS deaths recognised in New York; punk becomes popular; Tom Nairn, *The Break-Up of Britain*; Virago Press publishes first book	Anti-racist riots in Lewisham
1978 Paul Scott d. (b.1920)	Hare, *Plenty*; McEwan, *The Cement Garden*; Murdoch, *The Sea,*	The first 'test-tube' baby	

Births and deaths	Principal publications	Cultural and scientific events	Historical and political events
	The Sea; Weldon, *Praxis*; Tennant, *The Bad Sister*; Hill, *Tenebrae*		
1979 Jean Rhys d. (b.1894)	Tennant, *Wild Nights*; Golding, *Darkness Visible*; Raine, *A Martian Sends a Postcard Home*; Naipaul, *A Bend in the River*	Medical profession confirms that smoking causes cancer	Workers' strikes and bad weather conditions make up the 'Winter of discontent'; anti-racist protestor, Blair Peach, is killed at a National Front rally; Conservatives form govt under Margaret Thatcher
1980 Barbara Pym d. (b.1913) Olivia Manning d. (b.1908) C.P. Snow d. (b.1905) Antonia White d. (b.1980)	Manning, *The Levant Trilogy*; Burgess, *Earthly Powers*; Golding; *Rites of Passage*; Brenton, *The Romans in Britain*; Swift, *The Sweet-Shop Owner*; L.K. Johnson, *Inglan is a Bitch*	E.P. Thompson and Dan Smith, *Protest and Survive*	Zimbabwe becomes independent; riots in Bristol; British Airways and British Aerospace privatised; worst recession in 50 years
1981 Pamela Hansford Johnson d. (b.1912)	Rushdie, *Midnight's Children*; D.M. Thomas, *The White Hotel*; Swift, *Shuttlecock*; Fisher, *Poems 1955–80*	IBM launches the personal computer	British Nationality Bill; riots in London, Liverpool and Manchester; CND demonstrations in London
1982	Barker, *Union Street*; Churchill,	Compact disk players introduced	War against Argentina in the

Births and deaths	Principal publications	Cultural and scientific events	Historical and political events
	Top Girls; Gray, Lanark; Mo, Sour Sweet; Morrison and Motion (eds), Contemporary British Poetry		Falkland Islands; women demonstrate against nuclear weapons at Greenham Common
1983			
	Weldon, The Life and Loves of a She Devil; Swift, Waterland; Selvon, Moses Migrating; Rushdie, Shame		Conservatives returned as govt; US cruise missiles deployed in Britain
1984 John Betjeman d. (b.1906) J.B. Priestley d. (b.1894)	Carter, Nights at the Circus; K. Amis, Stanley and the Women; Lodge, Small World; Raine, Rich; M. Amis, Money; Ballard, Empire of the Sun; I. Banks, The Wasp Factory; Barnes, Flaubert's Parrot; Roberts, The Wild Girl	Ted Hughes succeeds John Betjeman as Poet Laureate; first successes of gene cloning	Miners' strike and police violence creates deep divisions; British Telecom privatised; IRA attempt to assassinate Thatcher in Brighton
1985 Philip Larkin d. (b.1922) Robert Graves d. (b.1895) Basil Bunting d. (b.1900)	Ackroyd, Hawksmoor; Brenton and Hare, Pravda; Winterson, Oranges are not the only fruit; Harrison, v.; Hill, Collected Poems; Phillips, The Final Passage	Eastenders begins; Live Aid pop concerts for famine relief in Ethiopia	Riots in London and Birmingham; public buses are privatised
1986 Christopher Isherwood d. (b.1904)	K. Amis, The Old Devils; Crace,	Laptop computers introduced	British Gas is privatised

Births and deaths	Principal publications	Cultural and scientific events	Historical and political events
John Braine d. (b.1922)	*Continent*; Barker, *The Century's Daughter*; Ishiguro, *An Artist of the Floating World*		
1987			
	Ackroyd, *Chatterton*; Churchill, *Serious Money*; Drabble, *The Radiant Way*; Lively, *Moon Tiger*; McEwan, *The Child in Time*; Winterson, *The Passion*; Chatwin, *The Songlines*	Gilroy, *There Ain't No Black in the Union Jack*	Conservatives returned as govt; storms cause massive destruction; stock market crash
1988			
	Larkin, *Collected Poems*; Chatwin, *Utz*; Rushdie, *The Satanic Verses*; Lodge, *Nice Work*; Warner, *The Lost Father*; Crace, *The Gift of Stones*; Moorcock, *Mother London*; Swift, *Out of this World*; Allnutt *et al.* (eds), *the new british poetry*; Hollinghurst, *The Swimming-Pool Library*	Hawking, *A Brief History of Time*	Social security system reformed; education system reformed
1989 Samuel Beckett d. (b.1906) Daphne Du Maurier d. (b.1907) Stella Gibbons d. (b.1902)	M. Amis, *London Fields*; Ackroyd, *First Light*; Ishiguro, *The Remains of the Day*; Winterson, *Sexing the Cherry*	Fatwa issued against Salman Rushdie; national curriculum introduced in schools; ruins of Shakespeare's	Revolutions in Eastern Europe; the end of the Cold War

Births and deaths	Principal publications	Cultural and scientific events	Historical and political events
Bruce Chatwin d. (b.1940)		theatres discovered in London; rave parties become popular	
1990 Lawrence Durrell d. (b.1912) Rosamund Lehmann d. (b.1901)	Byatt, *Possession*; Kureishi, *The Buddha of Suburbia*; Bainbridge, *An Awfully Big Adventure*	Human gene experimentation	Thatcher resigns as PM; John Major becomes PM; Germany reunified
1991 G. Greene d. (b.1904) Angus Wilson d. (b.1913)	M. Amis, *Time's Arrow*; Carter, *Wise Children*; Phillips, *Cambridge*; Sinclair, *Downriver*; Okri, *The Famished Road*; Mo, *The Redundancy of Courage*	Fukuyama, *The End of History*	War against Iraq in the Gulf; Britain opts out of European single currency
1992 Angela Carter d. (b.1940)	Gunn, *The Man with Night Sweats*; Unsworth, *Sacred Hunger*; Harrison, *The Common Chorus*; Crace, *Arcadia*; Hornby, *Fever Pitch*; Headley, *Yardie*; Roberts, *Daughters of the House*	Polytechnics given university status	Conservatives returned as govt; Europe creates the single market; govt forced to devalue sterling currency
1993 William Golding d. (b.1911) Anthony Burgess d. (b.1917)	Phillips, *Crossing the River*; Hulse, Kennedy and Morley (eds), *The New Poetry*;	Stephen Lawrence murdered	

Births and deaths	Principal publications	Cultural and scientific events	Historical and political events
	T. Johnson, *Hysteria*; D'Aguiar, *British Subjects*		
1994 Sam Selvon d. (b.1923) John Wain d. (b.1925) John Osborne d. (b.1929)	Gunesekera, *Reef*; Hollinghurst, *The Folding Star*; Coe, *What a Carve Up*; T. Johnson, *Dead Funny*; D'Aguiar, *The Longest Memory*; Ackroyd, *Dan Leno and the Limehouse Golem*; Sinclair, *Radon Daughters*	The National Lottery commenced; the Church of England ordained its first priests	Northern Ireland Peace Process began
1995 Kingsley Amis d. (b.1922)	Barker, *Regeneration Trilogy*; Rushdie, *The Moor's Last Sigh*; Kane, *Blasted*; M. Amis, *The Information*	The Channel Tunnel opened	
1996	Swift, *Last Orders*; Bainbridge, *Every Man for Himself*; Ravenhill, *Shopping and Fucking*; Pinter, *Ashes to Ashes*		
1997	Crace, *Quarantine*; Sinclair, *Lights Out for the Territory*; Phillips, *The Nature of Blood*; McEwan, *Enduring Love*		Labour form govt under Tony Blair; Hong Kong reverts to Chinese authority; Princess Diana killed in car crash; referenda on devolution of Scotland and Wales

Births and deaths	Principal publications	Cultural and scientific events	Historical and political events
1998 Ted Hughes d. (b.1930)	McEwan, *Amsterdam*; King, *England Away*; Barnes, *England, England*; Barker, *Another World*; Hughes, *Birthday Letters*; Motion, *Selected Poems 1976–1997*	Andrew Motion succeeds Ted Hughes as Poet Laureate	
1999	Armitage, *Killing Time*; Ackroyd, *The Plato Papers*; Bragg, *the Soldier's Return*; Rushdie, *The Ground Beneath Her Feet*	Solar eclipse	Macpherson Report; Racist bombs in London; the Scottish Parliament and Welsh Assembly open
2000	Smith, *White Teeth*; Newland and Sesay, *IC3*; Kneale, *English Passengers*; D'Aguiar, *Bloodlines*	Millennium celebrations feature 'The Dome' in Greenwich	

Key Concepts and Contexts

Culture

Definitions of 'culture' vary widely, of course, from the notion of a 'highbrow' or elite set of aesthetic tastes and practices, associated perhaps with opera, ballet, and poetry, to the more expansive, inclusive notion of the ways in which we live, work and enjoy ourselves. The latter idea not only suggests that football matches, television game shows, and bingo halls are part of 'culture', but also that culture includes what we eat, wear, drink, how we relate to others at home, at work, or in public, and all other aspects of our daily routines and habits. In the early part of the postwar period, the BBC, the Arts Council and Penguin publishers might be identified particularly with the attempt to educate the masses in 'high' culture. On the other hand, we might see the emergence of 'cultural studies' as an academic discipline, which, for example, treats literature as one form of cultural expression among many, as an attempt to analyse popular forms of entertainment and expression as indicative of 'our' culture. George Orwell's 'England Your England' might be considered an early cultural studies treatment of culture in England, in that it identifies the ordinary hobbies and leisure pursuits of working people as indicative of their culture. A key issue in the postwar period, then, is to identify how culture has changed, and what differences to 'our' culture the emergence of new global technologies and media, the increased cultural diversity and hybridity of English society, and the introduction of sweeping social reforms have made.

Education

Education in postwar England has been dominated by two concerns in particular: access and selection. The 1944 'Butler' Education Act ensured that all children would have access to secondary education from the age of eleven to fifteen. In general, this meant pupils took the 'eleven-plus' examination, which determined whether they would proceed to grammar schools for a more academic education or secondary modern schools for a more technical and vocational education. Wealthy families could still send their children to fee-paying 'public' schools, such as Eton and Harrow. Some critics of this three-tier system have argued that it serves to stream children into social classes, and that it enables an unequal distribution of investment. 'Comprehensive' schools emerged in the 1960s to provide some solution to the inequities of the system, but have remained controversial ever since. In the 1990s, educational reform tended to mean the establishment of standards agencies with the power to close 'failing' schools. Recruitment to the teaching profession, and retention of staff in the profession, became a major political issue in the 1990s. In higher education, the immediate aftermath of the war witnessed an expansion in the numbers of people going to university, although access was still heavily weighted towards the upper classes. Grants for maintenance and fees were awarded to those students with requisite academic ability to attend university. A more substantial expansion of higher education was achieved in the 1960s, with many colleges and teacher-training colleges gaining status, and colleges of technology became polytechnics with degree-awarding powers. New universities were also created. This was repeated again in the late 1980s, when polytechnics were allowed to become 'full' universities, with research degree awarding powers. The expansion of higher education in the 1990s reflects the need for an educated labour market, but, like many of the public services, underinvestment led to problems in supporting mass higher education. Maintenance grants were withdrawn, and a loans system was established. Government funding and support for universities became dependent upon teaching and research quality inspections.

Feminism

The war meant that many women were undertaking what had conventionally been regarded as 'men's jobs' prior to 1939. In practice, this meant that it was generally recognised after the war that women had the capacity to do any job, but increasingly in the 1950s this took the shape of an ideology which saw women's happiness and fulfilment better achieved in the home. Some have argued that this ideology emerged to push women back into the home so that men could return to their 'traditional' jobs. Others have argued that this ideology suited the new consumerism of the 1950s, in which capitalism needed women to have the 'leisure time' to be shoppers and consumers. The response of feminist writers and intellectuals to this ideology was varied, but many supported the view that, although women were equal to men, they were also better suited to domestic and child-rearing roles. This was increasingly challenged by the women's liberation movement to emerge in the 1960s and 1970s, which developed powerful critiques of the ways in which men, and masculine ideologies, dominated social and political structures. A thorough analysis of the social construction of gender and sexuality emerged from such critiques. The 1980s confirmed many of the arguments of the new wave of feminism. A woman occupied the highest political office in the country, but society remained as rigidly sexist and male-dominated as before. This meant that feminist political movements had to demand more than equal political rights, and work towards more sweeping social and cultural changes.

Literary production

Paper shortages were the immediate concern of the publishing industry in the aftermath of war, but this soon ceased to be a problem. The single most important change in publishing and reading literature since 1945 is the 'paperback revolution'. Although it started as early as 1935 with Penguin publishers, the publication of a wide range of literature in cheap, paperback editions took off from the late 1940s onwards. This, combined with an increasingly literate population achieved as a result of the expanding education system, has created a mass market for literary fiction. The expansion of university education has also created a sizeable market for literature in general, including some poetry collections, with some popular commercial successes for collections such as John Betjeman's *Collected Poems* (1958) and Ted Hughes's *Birthday Letters* (1998). The popularity of 'English' at secondary and tertiary education levels, however, has also meant that many 'set texts' are commercially successful. It is important not to overemphasise the commercial viability of literature, however. The paperback revolution did not just mean that everyone could read the 'classics'. The distinction between 'popular' and 'serious' or 'quality' fiction remains much in evidence, and 'popular', often formulaic, fiction far outstrips 'serious' fiction in sales. For most publishers, literary writing is subsidised in some form or other by the commercial successes of more popular titles. The tendency in the publishing industry through the 1980s and 1990s is that smaller, less viable publishing houses have become parts of larger, multi-national corporations. It is not yet clear whether or not the heavily commercial emphasis of such corporations will diminish the diversity and quality of literature published.

Postmodernism

On one level, 'postmodernism' refers to the period after modernism, roughly since the late 1950s. In this conception, the postmodern refers to the eclectic mix of styles and cultures in the postwar, post-imperial, postindustrial societies of Europe and North America, which Fredric Jameson argues is indicative of 'late capitalism' (Jameson 1991). This understanding of the term argues that certain stylistic features such as self-reflexivity, pastiche, and bricolage are particularly common in literature and art works of the contemporary period. In literature, we might say, for example, that Salman Rushdie, John Fowles and Martin Amis use some of these stylistic features in their writings, and this is related to the global mix of cultures which we experience on a daily basis. On another level, however, 'postmodernism' refers to a philosophical condition, in which reality is understood as the effect of signification and language. This post-structuralist form of postmodernism is deeply anti-humanist, and attempts to understand the world as a discursive or linguistic construct. Accordingly, it tends to privilege writing and art which advertises its own reflexivity, which is self-consciously 'inter-textual', or which is parodic of older styles or texts. Unlike the first definition of postmodernism, the post-structuralist view finds postmodern characteristics in art and writing of any period. Thus, Laurence Sterne's *Tristram Shandy* or Shakespeare's *Twelfth Night* might be postmodern.

Society

In the last years of the war, the national government began to plan for sweeping social changes in education, health and social welfare reform. This is largely believed to be the result of a recognition that the masses of men and women involved in the war would not tolerate a return to the divided society of the 1930s. Educational reforms made it possible for working-class children to acquire a secondary education, and to have the opportunity to rise up the social ladder through education. The introduction of the National Health Service, free and universal, in the late 1940s determined that even health treatment was no longer dependent on a person's ability to pay. The social welfare system was also reformed, so that the elderly, unemployed, poor, disabled and sick could access pensions, allowances and financial support funds. Housing was also a major area of government innovation, and the governments of the 1940s, 1950s and 1960s funded a huge increase in affordable rented housing. These social welfare provisions were supported by successive governments between 1945 and the 1970s, and formed part of what is known as the 'social consensus', whereby government saw its role as supporting those unable fully to support themselves. In the 1970s, and increasingly under the Conservative governments of the 1980s and 1990s these social welfare reforms were reversed or diluted, as Conservatives argued that such provisions made people dependent upon the state rather than self-motivated. The funding of public services and the provision of social welfare remains a key political question in British politics at the beginning of the twenty-first century.

Annotated Bibliography

Alexander, Flora. *Contemporary Women Novelists.* London: Edward Arnold, 1989.

A useful, broad-ranging study of contemporary women's fiction, which begins with an analysis of the feminist politics of the 1960s and 1970s before examining the work of Pat Barker, Angela Carter, Margaret Drabble, A.S. Byatt, Fay Weldon and Anita Brookner.

Appleyard, Brian. *The Pleasures of Peace: Art and Imagination in Post-war Britain.* London: Faber & Faber, 1989.

An insightful and detailed study of the arts in postwar Britain, which gives an impressive overview of the relationship between literature, criticism, art, sculpture, architecture and other forms of creative endeavour. Appleyard identifies some less obvious trends and themes in postwar writing, such as the influence of Graham Greene on the Angry Young Men.

Chambers, Colin and Prior, Mike. *Playwrights' Progress: Patterns of Postwar British Drama.* Oxford: Amber Lane, 1987.

This book provides a useful overview of postwar drama. It is divided into two parts, the first of which considers themes of class, gender, national identity and social change in relation to a wide range of drama. The second part contains chapters on playwrights Osborne, Wesker, Arden, D'Arcy, Bond, Brenton, Hare and Churchill.

Connor, Steven. *The English Novel in History 1950–1995.* London: Routledge, 1996.

An excellent study of the novel since 1950, which provides a lucid explanation of the relationship between literary texts and historical contexts, and analyses some of the historical themes and concerns of postwar fiction.

Corcoran, Neil. *English Poetry since 1940.* Harlow: Longman, 1993.

A valuable critical introduction to poetry since 1940, which is divided into considerations of the late modernism of the 1940s, the neo-romanticism of the late 1940s, the Movement in the 1950s, the neo-modernism and counter-cultural poetry of the 1960s, women's poetry, Northern Irish poetry, and a diverse range of contemporary poetry. Chapters are brief, but Corcoran provides useful critical analyses of a wide range of poetry.

Davies, Alastair and Sinfield, Alan eds. *British Culture of the Postwar: an introduction to literature and society 1945–1999*. London: Routledge, 2000.

A collection of essays which combines discussion of general themes and trends with consideration of particular authors. Essays are grouped around four themes: imperial and post-imperial Britain; welfare state and free market; Britain, Europe and Americanisation; and class, consumption and cultural institutions. There are essays on cinema, the ICA, the influence of Auden, drama, and on authors, Pat Barker, Penelope Lively, Salman Rushdie, Angus Wilson and Alan Hollinghurst.

Gąsiorek, Andrzej. *Post-War British Fiction: Realism and After*. London: Edward Arnold, 1995.

Gąsiorek's argument is that postwar writing has blurred the distinctions between realism and modernism, and this book examines many instances of fictions which are not so easily labelled. The book includes discussion of writers Ivy Compton-Burnett, Henry Green, V.S. Naipaul, George Lamming, John Berger, Doris Lessing, Angus Wilson, John Fowles, Angela Carter, Sara Maitland, Graham Swift, Salman Rushdie and Julian Barnes. These writers provide ample evidence for Gąsiorek of the necessity of re-thinking critical concepts of realism and experimentalism in fiction.

Hewison, Robert. *Culture and Consensus: England, art and politics since 1940*. London: Methuen, 1995.

Hewison is the best cultural historian of the postwar period, and has written extensively about the period in *Under Siege, In Anger, Too Much*, and *The Heritage Society*. *Culture and Consensus* is an attempt to synthesise the broader concerns of his work into one book, which is divided into chapters on each decade. An informative and persuasive view of the period is offered here.

Hobsbawm, Eric. *Age of Extremes: The Short Twentieth Century 1914–1991*. London: Michael Joseph, 1994.

A cogent and lively narrative of twentieth-century history, which is useful for providing an historical overview.

Joannou, Maroula. *Contemporary women's writing: From* The Golden Notebook *to* The Color Purple. Manchester: Manchester University Press, 2000.

One of the best and most lucid studies of contemporary women's writing, which takes the twenty-year span, 1962–1982, between the two novels of its subtitle as a set of artificial parameters within which to examine the relationship between women's writing and women's lives. The study is informed throughout by a lively engagement with the politics of women's liberation.

Middleton, Peter and Woods, Tim. *Literatures of Memory: History, time and space in postwar writing*. Manchester: Manchester University Press, 2000.

An ambitious and challenging study of postwar literature, which examines themes of history, memory, time, realism and cultural geography. Part 1 begins with post-modern concerns with the representation of the past, and includes four chapters on more general issues of recent historical fiction. Part 2 follows generic concerns with chapters on theatre, poetry, science fiction, and urban fiction.

Parker, Peter ed. *The Reader's Companion to the Twentieth Century Novel*. London and Oxford: Fourth Estate/Helicon, 1994.
—— ed. (1995). *The Reader's Companion to Twentieth Century Writers*. London and Oxford: Fourth Estate/Helicon, 1995.

Invaluable reference books. The companion to the novel is organised chronologically and provides descriptions of the plot and contexts of a huge range of novels. The companion to writers is organised alphabetically.

Scanlan, Margaret. *Traces of Another Time: History and Politics in Postwar British Fiction*. Princeton: Princeton University Press, 1990.

Scanlan's book examines postwar literary representations of 'the public past', meaning empire, the Cold War, the nuclear threat, and political conflict. This takes the form of chapters on the 'troubles' in Northern Ireland, 'spies and other aliens' in Murdoch and Philby, and 'apocalypse' in Scott, Lessing, and Burgess. Scanlan is also arguing here for a particular understanding of the historical novel in the postwar period.

Sinfield, Alan ed. *Society and Literature 1945–1970*. London: Methuen, 1983.

A collection of authoritative essays on various aspects of postwar writing. Sinfield explains the historicist methodologies of the collection in the introduction. The essays which follow tackle 'Literature, politics and society', 'The challenge of sexuality', 'Varieties of religion', followed by essays on literary production, theatre and its audiences, poetry, and novels.

——. *Literature, Politics and Culture in Postwar Britain*. Oxford: Blackwell, 1989; revised edition: London: Athlone Press, 1997.

The best study to date of postwar literature, which examines the social, cultural and political histories of Britain since 1945 through its literary and intellectual texts. Sinfield provides here a revisionist, materialist account of life in Britain since 1945, which develops in opposition to the cultural politics of Thatcherism. The revised edition includes a preface which examines the shifting cultural trends of the 1990s.

Taylor, D.J. *After the War: The Novel and England since 1945*. London: Flamingo, 1994.

The chief value of Taylor's book is its extensive coverage of novels written in England since 1945. The book's almost encyclopaedic breadth of reference derives from Taylor's experience of reviewing thirty or forty novels a year. This experience also takes its toll in the book, however, because Taylor doesn't believe that contemporary fiction compares favourably with previous periods in English literary history, notably the Victorians.

Waugh, Patricia. *Harvest of the Sixties: English Literature and its Background 1960 to 1990*. Oxford: Oxford University Press, 1995.

As its title implies, Waugh's book considers the 1960s as a defining period for contemporary literature, and examines the legacy of the 1960s on subsequent writing. Waugh provides an authoritative and lucid introduction to the political and cultural contexts of post-1960 literature, and focuses attention in her discussion of literary texts on themes of metaphysics, rationality, national identity, and the end of social consensus.

Bibliography

Ackroyd, Peter. *The Plato Papers* [1999]. London: Vintage, 2000.

Addison, Paul. *Now the War is Over: A Social History of Britain, 1945–51*. London: Jonathan Cape, 1985.

Alexander, Flora. *Contemporary women novelists*. London: Edward Arnold, 1989.

Alibhai-Brown, Yasmin. *Who Do We Think We Are? Imagining the New Britain*. London: Penguin, 2000.

Amis, Martin. *London Fields* [1989]. London: Penguin, 1990.

Anderson, Benedict. *Imagined Communities: Reflections on the Origin and Spread of Nationalism*. London: Verso, 1991.

Appleyard, Brian. *The Pleasures of Peace: Art and Imagination in Postwar Britain*. London: Faber & Faber, 1989.

Armitage, Simon. *Killing Time*. London: Faber & Faber, 1999.

Armstrong, Isobel. 'Woolf by the Lake, Woolf at the Circus: Carter and Tradition', *Flesh and the Mirror: Essays on the Art of Angela Carter*, ed. Lorna Sage. London: Virago, 1994, 257–78.

Bachelard, Gaston. *The Poetics of Space*. Boston, Mass.: Beacon, 1969.

Bainbridge, Beryl. *English Journey, or, The Road to Milton Keynes* [1984]. New York: Carroll & Graf Publishers, 1997.

Baker, Niamh. *Happily Ever After? Women's Fiction in Postwar Britain, 1945–1960*. New York: St Martin's Press, 1989.

Banks, Lynne Reid. *The L-Shaped Room* [1960]. Harmondsworth: Penguin, 1962.

Bannock, Sarah. 'Auto/biographical souvenirs in *Nights at the Circus*', *The Infernal Desires of Angela Carter*, ed. Joseph Bristow and Trev Lynn Broughton. Harlow: Addison Wesley Longman, 1997, 198–215.

Barker, Pat. *The Century's Daughter* [1986]. London: Virago, 1986.

—— . *Regeneration* [1991]. London: Penguin, 1992.

—— . *The Eye in the Door* [1993]. London: Penguin, 1994.

—— . *The Ghost Road* [1995]. London: Penguin, 1996.

Barker, Simon. 'Images of the sixteenth and seventeenth centuries as a history of the present', *Confronting the Crisis*, ed. Francis Barker *et al.* Essex: University of Essex, 1984, 15–26.

Barnes, Julian. *England, England*. London: Jonathan Cape, 1998.

Bates, H.E. *The Darling Buds of May* [1958], in *The Pop Larkin Chronicles*. London: Penguin, 1991.

Baucom, Ian. *Out of Place: Englishness, Empire and the Locations of Identity*. Princeton, NJ: Princeton University Press, 1999.

Belau, Linda. 'Trauma and the Material Signifier', *Postmodern Culture*, vol. 11, no. 2 (January 2001). http://jefferson.village.virginia.edu/pmc/

Bell, Ian ed. *Peripheral Visions: Images of Nationhood in Contemporary British Fiction*. Cardiff: University of Wales Press, 1995.

Belsey, Catherine. *Critical Practice*. London: Methuen, 1980.

Bergonzi, Bernard. *Wartime and Aftermath: English Literature and its Background, 1939–1960*. Oxford: Oxford University Press, 1993.

Berman, Marshall. *All That is Solid Melts into Air: The Experience of Modernity*. London: Verso, 1983.

Betjeman, John. *Collected Poems*. London: John Murray, 1979.

Bhabha, Homi. *The Location of Culture*. London: Routledge, 1994.

Birmingham Feminist History Group, 'Feminism as femininity in the nineteen-fifties?', *Feminist Review*, 3 (1979), 48–65.

Blair, Sara. 'Cultural Geography and the Place of the Literary', *American Literary History*, vol. 10, no. 3 (Fall 1998), 544–67.

Bloom, Harold. *The Anxiety of Influence: A Theory of Poetry*. Oxford: Oxford University Press, 1973.

Bogdanor, Vernon and Skidelsky, Robert eds. *The Age of Affluence 1951–1964*. London: Macmillan, 1970.

Bond, Edward. *Saved*, in *Bond Plays: One*. London: Methuen, 1977.

Bowers, Frederick. 'An Irrelevant Parochialism', *Granta*, 3 (1980), 150–4.

Bradbury, Malcolm. *The Modern British Novel*. London: Penguin, 1994.

Bradley, Jerry. *The Movement: British Poets of the 1950s*. New York: Twayne, 1993.

Brannigan, John. *Literature, Culture and Society in England, 1945–1965*. Lampeter: Edwin Mellen Press, 2002.

Brittain, Vera. *Lady into Woman*. London: Andrew Dakers, 1953.

Brivati, Brian and Jones, Harriet eds. *What Difference Did the War Make?* London: Leicester University Press, 1995.

Brown, Dennis. *John Betjeman*. Plymouth, U.K.: Northcote House, 1999.

Buford, Bill. *Among the Thugs* [1991]. London: Arrow, 1997.

Bunting, Basil. *Briggflatts*. London: Fulcrum Press, 1966.

Carter, Angela. *Nights at the Circus* [1984]. London: Picador, 1985.

—— . *Wise Children* [1991]. London: Vintage, 1992.

Caruth, Cathy ed. *Trauma: Explorations in Memory*. Baltimore: Johns Hopkins University Press, 1995.

—— . *Unclaimed Experience: Trauma, Narrative, and History*. Baltimore: Johns Hopkins University Press, 1996.

Castle, Terry. *The Apparitional Lesbian: Female Homosexuality and Modern Culture*. New York: Columbia University Press, 1993.

Chambers, Colin and Prior, Mike. *Playwrights' Progress: Patterns of Postwar British Drama*. Oxford: Amber Lane, 1987.

Chambers, Iain. *Border Dialogues: Journeys in Postmodernity*. London: Routledge, 1990.

—— . *Migrancy, Culture, Identity*. London: Routledge, 1994.

Choudhury, Romita. '"Is there a ghost, a zombie there?" Postcolonial intertextuality and Jean Rhys's *Wide Sargasso Sea*', *Textual Practice*, vol. 10, no. 2 (Summer 1996), 315–27.

Cixous, Hélène. 'The Laugh of the Medusa', trans. Keith Cohen and Paula Cohen, *New French Feminisms*, ed. Elaine Marks and Isabelle de Courtivon. Brighton: Harvester, 1981, 245–64.

Collins, Norman. *London Belongs to Me*. London: Collins, 1945.

Connor, Steven. *The English Novel in History, 1950–1995*. London: Routledge, 1996.

Corcoran, Neil. *English Poetry since 1940*. London: Longman, 1993.

Cranny-Francis, Anne. *Feminist Fiction: Feminist Uses of Generic Fiction.* Cambridge: Polity Press, 1990.

Crewe, Ivor. 'Values: The Crusade That Failed', *The Thatcher Effect: A Decade of Change*, ed. Denis Kavanagh and Anthony Selden. Oxford: Oxford University Press, 1989, 239–50.

Cunningham, Gail, 'Women and Children First: the novels of Margaret Drabble', *Twentieth-Century Women Novelists*, ed. Thomas F. Staley. Basingstoke: Macmillan, 1982, 130–52.

Curti, Lidia. *Female Stories, Female Bodies: Narrative, Identity and Representation.* Basingstoke: Macmillan, 1998.

D'Aguiar, Fred. *British Subjects*. Tarset, Northumberland: Bloodaxe, 1993.

Davies, Alastair and Saunders, Peter. 'Literature, Politics and Society', *Society and Literature: 1945–1970*, ed. Alan Sinfield. London: Methuen, 1983, 13–50.

—— and Sinfield, Alan eds. *British Culture of the Postwar*. London: Routledge, 2000.

Deleuze, Gilles and Guattari, Felix. *A Thousand Plateaus: Capitalism and Schizophrenia*, trans. Brian Massumi. Minneapolis: University of Minnesota Press, 1987.

Derrida, Jacques. 'The Theater of Cruelty and the Closure of Representation', *Writing and Difference*, trans. Alan Bass. London: Routledge, 1978, 232-50.

Drabble, Margaret. *The Millstone* [1965]. Harmondsworth: Penguin, 1968.

Draper, R.P. *An Introduction to Twentieth-Century Poetry in English*. Basingstoke: Macmillan, 1999.

Duncker, Patricia. *Sisters and Strangers: An Introduction to Contemporary Feminist Fiction*. Oxford: Blackwell, 1992.

Eagleton, Terry. 'Antagonisms: *v.*', *Tony Harrison*, ed. Neil Astley. Newcastle: Bloodaxe, 1991.

Easthope, Antony. 'Writing and English National Identity', *Contemporary Writing and National Identity*, ed. Tracey Hill and William Hughes. Bath: Sulis Press, 1995, 146–57.

Elsom, John. *Post-War British Theatre*. London: Routledge & Kegan Paul, 1976.

—— ed. *Post-War Theatre Criticism*. London: Routledge & Kegan Paul, 1981.

Empson, William. *Some Versions of Pastoral*. London: Chatto & Windus, 1950.

Felman, Shoshana and Laub, Dori. *Testimony: Crises of Witnessing in Literature, Psychoanalysis, and History*. London: Routledge, 1992.

Felski, Rita. *Beyond Feminist Aesthetics: Feminist Literature and Social Change.* London: Hutchinson Radius, 1989.

Fukuyama, Francis. *The End of History and the Last Man.* London: Penguin, 1992.

Fuller, Roy. *Collected Poems: 1936–1961.* London: Andre Deutsch, 1962.

Fussell, Paul. *The Great War and Modern Memory.* Oxford: Oxford University Press, 1975.

Fyrth, Jim ed. *Labour's Promised Land? Culture and Society in Labour Britain, 1945–51.* London: Lawrence & Wishart, 1995.

Galbraith, J.K. *The Affluent Society.* London: Hamish Hamilton, 1958.

Gąsiorek, Andrzej. *Post-War British Fiction: Realism and After.* London: Edward Arnold, 1995.

George, Rosemary Marangoly. *The Politics of Home: Postcolonial Relocations and Twentieth-Century Fiction.* Berkeley, Cal.: University of California Press, 1999.

Gervais, David. *Literary Englands: Versions of 'Englishness' in Modern Writing.* Cambridge: Cambridge University Press, 1993.

Gibson, Jeremy and Wolfreys, Julian. *Peter Ackroyd: The Ludic and Labyrinthine Text.* Basingstoke: Macmillan, 2000.

Gikandi, Simon. *Maps of Englishness: Writing Identity in the Culture of Colonialism.* New York: Columbia University Press, 1996.

Gilbert, Sandra M. and Gubar, Susan. *The Madwoman in the Attic: The Woman Writer and the Nineteenth-Century Literary Imagination.* New Haven: Yale University Press, 1979.

Gilroy, Paul. *There Ain't No Black in the Union Jack.* London: Routledge, 1987.

Goldthorpe, John H., Lockwood, David, Bechhofer, Frank and Platt, Jennifer. *The Affluent Worker: Cambridge Studies in Sociology Vols. 1–3.* Cambridge: Cambridge University Press, 1963–9.

Goodman, Richard. 'Return to England', *Penguin New Writing,* No. 23 (1945), 172–3.

Greene, Gayle. *Changing the Story: Feminist Fiction and the Tradition.* Indianapolis: Indiana University Press, 1991.

Hall, Catherine. 'Histories, Empires, and the Post-Colonial Moment', *The Post-Colonial Question: Common Skies, Divided Horizons,* ed. Iain Chambers and Lidia Curti. London: Routledge, 1996, 65–77.

Harrison, Tony. *v.* [1985]. Newcastle: Bloodaxe, 1989.

Harrisson, Tom. *Living Through the Blitz.* Harmondsworth: Penguin, 1978.

Hay, M. and Roberts, P. *Edward Bond: A Companion to the Plays.* London: Eyre Methuen, 1978.

Haywood, Ian. *Working-Class Fiction: from Chartism to Trainspotting.* Plymouth: Northcote House, 1997.

Hennessey, Peter. *Never Again: Britain, 1945–1951.* London: Jonathan Cape, 1992.

Hewison, Robert. *Under Siege: Literary Life in London 1939–45.* London: Weidenfeld & Nicolson, 1977.

——— . *In Anger: Culture in the Cold War 1945-60.* London: Weidenfeld and Nicolson, 1981.

——— . *Too Much: Art and Society in the Sixties 1960–75.* London: Methuen, 1986.

——— . *The Heritage Society: Britain in a Climate of Decline.* London: Methuen, 1987.

———— . *Culture and Consensus: England, Art and Politics since 1940*. London: Methuen, 1995.

Higdon, David Leon. *Shadows of the Past in Contemporary British Fiction*. Basingstoke: Macmillan, 1984.

Hill, Geoffrey. *Collected Poems*. Harmondsworth: Penguin, 1985.

Hobsbawm, Eric. *Age of Extremes: The Short Twentieth Century 1914–1991*. London: Michael Joseph, 1994.

Holmes, Frederick. *The Historical Imagination: Postmodernism and the Treatment of the Past in Contemporary British Fiction*. Victoria: English Literary Monographs, 1997.

Hopkins, H. *The New Look*. London: Secker & Warburg, 1963.

Hubback, Judith. *Wives who went to College*. London: Heinemann, 1957.

Ishiguro, Kazuo. *The Remains of the Day* [1989]. London: Faber & Faber, 1990.

Jack, Ian. 'Editorial: Whatever Happened to Us?', *Granta*, 56 (1996), 7–8.

James, Winston and Harris, Clive. *Inside Babylon: The Caribbean Diaspora in Britain*. London: Verso, 1993.

Jameson, Fredric. 'Ideology, Narrative Analysis, and Popular Culture', *Theory and Society*, No. 4 (1977).

———— . *The Political Unconscious: Narrative as a Socially Symbolic Act*. London: Routledge, 1983.

———— . 'Third World Literature in the Era of Multinational Capitalism', *Social Text*, 15 (Fall 1986), 65–88.

———— . *Postmodernism, or the Cultural Logic of Late Capitalism*. London: Verso, 1991.

Jefferys, Kevin. *Retreat from New Jerusalem: British Politics, 1951–64*. London and Basingstoke: Macmillan, 1997.

Jellicoe, Ann. *The Sport of My Mad Mother*. London: Faber & Faber, 1964.

Jephcott, Pearl *et al. Married Women Working*. London: Allen & Unwin, 1962.

Jhabvala, Ruth Prawer. *Heat and Dust* [1975]. London: Penguin, 1994.

Joannou, Maroula. *Contemporary women's writing: From* The Golden Notebook *to* The Color Purple. Manchester: Manchester University Press, 2000.

Kane, Sarah. *Blasted & Phaedra's Love*. London: Methuen, 1996.

Kenner, Hugh. *A Sinking Island: The Modern English Writers* [1987]. London: Barrie & Jenkins, 1988.

King, John. *England Away*. London: Jonathan Cape, 1998.

Lacey, Stephen. *British Realist Theatre: The New Wave in its Context, 1956–1965*. London: Routledge, 1995.

Laing, Stuart. *Representations of Working-Class Life, 1957–1964*. Basingstoke: Macmillan, 1986.

Lanone, Catherine. 'Scattering the Seed of Abraham: The Motif of Sacrifice in Pat Barker's *Regeneration* and *The Ghost Road*', *Literature and Theology*, vol. 13, no. 3 (September 1999), 259–68.

Larkin, Philip. 'Betjeman en Bloc', *Listen*, vol. 3, no. 2 (Spring 1959).

———— . *The North Ship*. London: Faber & Faber, 1966.

———— . *Required Writing*. London: Faber & Faber, 1983.

——. *Collected Poems*. London: Faber & Faber, 1988.

Lee, A. Robert ed. *Other Britain: Other British: Contemporary Multicultural Fiction*. London: Pluto, 1995.

Lefebvre, Henri. *The Production of Space*, trans. Donald Nicholson-Smith. Oxford: Blackwell, 1991.

——. *Writings on Cities: Henri Lefebvre*, ed. E. Kofman and E. Lebas. Oxford: Blackwell, 1996.

Lehan, Richard. *The City in Literature: An Intellectual and Cultural History*. Berkeley: University of California Press, 1998.

Lessing, Doris. *In Pursuit of the English* [1960]. London: Granada, 1980.

——. *The Golden Notebook* [1962]. London: Flamingo, 1993.

Lodge, David. 'Modernism, Anti-Modernism and Postmodernism'. Birmingham: University of Birmingham, 1977.

Lowenthal, David. *The Past is a Foreign Country*. Cambridge: Cambridge University Press, 1985.

Lucas, John. *England and Englishness: Ideas of Nationhood in English Poetry 1688–1900*. Iowa City: University of Iowa Press, 1990.

——. 'Discovering England: The View from the Train', *Literature and History*, vol. 6, no. 2 (Autumn 1997), 37–55.

Luckhurst, Roger and Marks, Peter eds. *Literature and the Contemporary: Fictions and Theories of the Present*. Harlow: Longman/Pearson Education, 1999.

Lyotard, Jean-François. *The Postmodern Condition: A Report on Knowledge*, trans. Geoff Bennington and Brian Massumi. Manchester: Manchester University Press, 1984.

——. 'Note on the meaning of "post"', *Postmodernism: A Reader*, ed. Thomas Docherty. Hemel Hempstead: Harvester Wheatsheaf, 1993, 47–50.

Macdonald, James. 'They never got her', *The Observer*, February 28 1999, 9.

Makin, Peter. *Bunting: The Shaping of his Verse*. Oxford: Clarendon Press, 1992.

—— ed. (2000). *Basil Bunting on Poetry*. Baltimore, Maryland: Johns Hopkins University Press, 2000.

Malkin, Jeanette. *Verbal Violence in Contemporary Drama: From Handke to Shepard*. Cambridge: Cambridge University Press, 1992.

Martin, Biddy and Mohanty, Chandra Talpade. 'Feminist Politics: What's Home Got to Do with It?', *Feminist Studies/Critical Studies*, ed. Theresa de Lauretis. Bloomington, Indiana: Indiana University Press, 1986, 191–212.

Marwick, Arthur. *British Society since 1945*. London: Penguin, 1990.

Maschler, Tom ed. *Declaration*. London: MacGibbon & Kee, 1957.

Matless, David. *Landscape and Englishness*. London: Reaktion Books, 1998.

Maynard, Jessica. '"Not the Sweet Home that it Looks": British Poetry, 1930–55', *Literature and Culture in Modern Britain: Volume Two, 1930–1955*, ed. Gary Day. London: Longman, 1997, 28–49.

Mazzoleni, Donatella. 'The City and the Imaginary', trans. John Koumantarakis, *Space and Place: Theories of Identity and Location*, ed. Erica Carter, James Donald and Judith Squires. London: Lawrence & Wishart, 1993, 285–302.

McEwan, Ian. *Amsterdam*. London: Jonathan Cape, 1998.

McGrath, John. *A Good Night Out – Popular Theatre: Audience, Class and Form.* London: Nick Hern, 1996, 7–15.

Meaney, Gerardine. *(Un)Like Subjects: Women, Theory, Fiction.* London: Routledge, 1993.

Mengham, Rod ed. *An Introduction to Contemporary Fiction.* Cambridge: Polity, 1999.

Middleton, Peter and Woods, Tim. *Literatures of Memory: History, time and space in postwar writing.* Manchester: Manchester University Press, 2000.

Miller, J. Hillis. *Topographies.* Stanford, Cal.: Stanford University Press, 1995.

Milne, W.S. *An Introduction to Geoffrey Hill.* London: Agenda/Bellew, 1998.

Mitford, Nancy. *The Pursuit of Love* [1945]. London: Penguin, 1949.

Montrose, Louis. '"Eliza, Queene of Shepheardes," and the Pastoral of Power', *ELR*, 10 (1980), 153–82.

Morgan, Kenneth. *Labour in Power, 1945–1951.* Oxford: Oxford University Press, 1984.

Morrison, Blake. *The Movement: English Poetry and Fiction of the 1950s.* Oxford: Oxford University Press, 1980.

Myrdal, Alva and Klein, Viola. *Women's Two Roles: Home and Work.* London: Routledge & Kegan Paul, 1956.

Nairn, Tom. *After Britain.* London: Verso, 2000.

Nancy, Jean-Luc. 'Finite History', *The States of 'Theory': History, Art, and Critical Discourse,* ed. David Carroll. Stanford: Stanford University Press, 1990, 149–72.

Nehring, Neil. *Flowers in the Dustbin: Culture, Anarchy and Postwar England.* Ann Arbor: University of Michigan, 1993.

Newland, Courttia and Sesay, Kadija eds. *IC3: The Penguin Book of New Black Writing in Britain.* London: Penguin, 2000.

North, Michael. 'Virtual Histories: The Year as Literary Period'. *Modern Language Quarterly,* 62:4 (December 2001), 407–24.

Orwell, George. 'England Your England' [1941], *Inside the Whale and Other Essays.* London: Penguin, 1957, 63-90.

—— . *Nineteen Eighty-Four.* [1949] London: Penguin, 1989.

—— (1998a). *The English People* [1944], reprinted in *George Orwell: The Complete Works,* vol. 16, ed. Peter Davison. London: Secker & Warburg, 1998, 199–228.

—— [Eric Blair] (1998b). 'Letter to Leonard Moore, 23 June 1945', *George Orwell: The Complete Works,* vol. 17, ed. Peter Davison. London: Secker & Warburg, 1998, 189.

—— (1998c). 'The Politics of the English Language' [1945], reprinted in *George Orwell: The Complete Works,* vol. 17, 421–32.

Osborne, John. *Look Back in Anger.* London: Faber & Faber, 1957.

—— . 'That Awful Museum', *Twentieth Century,* 169, 1961, 212–16.

Osborne, Peter. *The Politics of Time: Modernity and Avant-Garde.* London: Verso, 1995.

Parker, Peter ed. *The Reader's Companion to the Twentieth Century Novel.* London and Oxford: Fourth Estate/Helicon, 1994.

—— ed. *The Reader's Companion to Twentieth Century Writers*. London and Oxford: Fourth Estate/Helicon, 1995.

Paulin, Tom. 'A Visionary Nationalist: Geoffrey Hill', *Minotaur: Poetry and the Nation State*. London: Faber & Faber, 1993, 276–84.

Philips, Deborah and Haywood, Ian. *Brave New Causes: Women in Postwar British Fictions*. London: Leicester University Press, 1998.

Piette, Adam. *Imagination at War: British Fiction and Poetry 1939–1945*. London: Papermac, 1995.

Pike, Burton. *The Image of the City in Literature*. Princeton: Princeton University Press, 1981.

Priestley, J.B. *English Journey*. London: Heinemann & Gollancz, 1934.

Ravenhill, Mark. *Shopping and Fucking*. London: Methuen, 1997.

Read, Herbert. 'Art in an Electric Atmosphere', *Horizon*, vol. 3, no. 17 (May 1941), 310.

Regan, Stephen. '*In the Grip of Light*: Philip Larkin's Poetry of the 1940s', *New Larkins for Old: Critical Essays*, ed. James Booth. Basingstoke: Palgrave, 2000, 121–9.

Reiss, Timothy J. 'Perioddity: Considerations on the Geography of Histories', *Modern Language Quarterly*, 62:4 (December 2001), 425–52.

Rhys, Jean. *Wide Sargasso Sea* [1966]. Harmondsworth: Penguin, 1968.

Richardson, Brian. 'Remapping the Present: The Master Narrative of Modern Literary History and the Lost Forms of Twentieth-Century Fiction', *Twentieth Century Literature*, 43: 3 (Fall 1997), 291–309.

Ritchie, Harry. *Success Stories: Literature and the Media in England, 1950–1959*. London: Faber & Faber, 1988.

Riviere, Joan. 'Womanliness as a Masquerade' [1929], *Formations of Fantasy*, ed. Victor Burgin, James Donald, Cora Kaplan. London: Methuen, 1986, 35–44.

Robbins, Ruth. *Literary Feminisms*. Basingstoke: Macmillan, 2000.

Roberts, Neil. *Narrative and Voice in Postwar Poetry*. London: Longman, 1999.

Roberts, Philip. *The Royal Court Theatre, 1965–1972*. London: Routledge, 1986.

—— . *The Royal Court Theatre and the Modern Stage*. Cambridge: Cambridge University Press, 1999.

Rushdie, Salman. *Imaginary Homelands: Essays and Criticism, 1981–1991*. London: Penguin/*Granta*, 1992.

—— . *Midnight's Children* [1981]. London: Vintage, 1995.

—— . *The Satanic Verses* [1988]. London: Vintage, 1998.

Russo, Mary. *The Female Grotesque: Risk, Excess and Modernity*. London: Routledge, 1995.

Sage, Lorna. *Women in the House of Fiction: Post-War Women Novelists*. Basingstoke: Macmillan, 1992.

Scanlan, Margaret. *Traces of Another Time: History and Politics in Postwar British Fiction*. Princeton: Princeton University Press, 1990.

Schama, Simon. *Landscape and Memory*. London: HarperCollins, 1995.

Selvon, Sam. *The Lonely Londoners* [1956]. London: Longman, 1985.

Showalter, Elaine. *A Literature of Their Own: From Charlotte Brontë to Doris Lessing*. London: Virago, 1999.

Sierz, Aleks. 'John Osborne and the Myth of Anger', *New Theatre Quarterly*, vol. XII, no. 46 (May 1996), 136–46.

Sillitoe, Alan. *Saturday Night and Sunday Morning* [1958]. London: Grafton, 1985.

Sinclair, Iain. *Lud Heat and Suicide Bridge* [1975–79]. London: Vintage, 1995.

Sinfield, Alan ed. *Society and Literature, 1945–1970*. London: Methuen, 1983.

——. *Literature, Politics and Culture in Postwar Britain*. London: Athlone Press, 1997; revised edn.

Smithies, Bill and Fiddick, Peter. *Enoch Powell on Immigration: An Analysis*. London: Sphere, 1969.

Spivak, Gayatri Chakravorty. 'Can the Subaltern Speak?', in *Colonial Discourse and Postcolonial Theory*, ed. Patrick Williams and Laura Chrisman. Hemel Hempstead: Harvester Wheatsheaf, 1994, 66–111.

——. *A Critique of Postcolonial Reason: Toward a History of the Vanishing Present*. Cambridge, Mass.: Harvard University Press, 1999.

Spring Rice, Margery. *Working-Class Wives: Their Health and Conditions*. Harmondsworth: Penguin, 1939.

Sucher, Laurie. *The Fiction of Ruth Prawer Jhabvala: The Politics of Passion*. Basingstoke: Macmillan, 1989.

Swift, Graham. *Last Orders*. London: Picador, 1996.

——. *The Sweet Shop Owner* [1980]. London: Picador, 1997.

Taylor, D.J. *A Vain Conceit: British Fiction in the 1980s*. London: Bloomsbury, 1989.

——. *After the War: The Novel and England since 1945*. London: Flamingo, 1994.

Taylor, Elizabeth. *At Mrs Lippincote's* [1945]. London: Virago Press, 1995.

Taylor, John Russell ed. *John Osborne: Look Back in Anger*. Basingstoke: Macmillan, 1968.

Terdiman, Richard. *Present Past: Modernity and the Memory Crisis*. Ithaca, NY: Cornell University Press, 1993.

Theroux, Paul. *The Kingdom by the Sea* [1983]. London: Penguin, 1984.

Trout, Steven. 'Miniaturization and Anticlimax in Evelyn Waugh's *Sword of Honour*', *Twentieth Century Literature*, vol. 43, no. 2 (Summer 1997), 125–43.

Tuma, Keith. *Fishing by Obstinate Isles: Modern and Postmodern British Poetry and American Readers*. Evanston, Illinois: Northwestern University Press, 1998.

Tynan, Kenneth. 'The Voice of the Young', *The Observer*, May 13 1956, 11.

——. *Curtains*. Harlow: Longman, 1961.

Wandor, Michelene. *Look Back in Gender: Sexuality and the Family in Post-War British Drama*. London: Methuen, 1987.

Watkins, Susan. *Twentieth-Century Women Novelists: Feminist Theory into Practice*. Basingstoke: Palgrave, 2001.

Waugh, Evelyn. *Brideshead Revisited: The Sacred and Profane Memories of Captain Charles Ryder*. London: Chapman & Hall, 1945.

——. *Brideshead Revisited*. London: Chapman & Hall, 1960; revised end.

——. *The Diaries of Evelyn Waugh*, ed. Michael Davie. London: Book Club Associates, 1976.

——. *Evelyn Waugh: A Little Order – A Selection from his Journalism*, ed. Donat Gallagher. London: Eyre Methuen, 1977.

—— (1984). *Sword of Honour*. London: Penguin, 1984.

Waugh, Patricia. *Feminine Fictions: Revisiting the Postmodern*. London: Routledge, 1989.

——. *Harvest of the Sixties: English Literature and its Background 1960 to 1990*. Oxford: Oxford University Press, 1995.

Webster, Wendy. *Imagining Home: Gender, 'Race' and National Identity, 1945–64*. London: University College London Press, 1998.

Weldon, Fay. *The Life and Loves of a She Devil*. London: Hodder & Stoughton, 1983.

Wiegman, Robyn. 'Feminism's Apocalyptic Futures', *New Literary History*, vol. 31, no. 4 (Autumn 2000), 805–25.

Wilson, Angus. *Late Call* [1964]. London: Penguin, 1968.

Wilson, Elizabeth. *Women and the Welfare State*. London: Tavistock, 1977.

——. *Only Halfway to Paradise: Women in Postwar Britain, 1945–1968*. London: Tavistock, 1980.

Winterson, Jeanette. *Sexing the Cherry*. London: Vintage, 1989.

Wolfreys, Julian. *Being English: Narratives, Idioms, and Performances of National Identity from Coleridge to Trollope*. New York: SUNY, 1994.

Woolf, Virginia. *A Room of One's Own* [1929]. London: Grafton, 1977.

——. 'The Leaning Tower', *A Woman's Essays: Selected Essays, Volume 1*, ed. Rachel Bowlby. London: Penguin, 1992, 154–78.

Yeats, W.B. *Collected Poems*, ed. A. Norman Jeffares. Dublin: Gill & Macmillan, 1989.

Index